The Practical Theorist

Other books by Alfred J. Marrow

Living Without Hate

Making Management Human

Changing Patterns of Prejudice

Behind the Executive Mask

Management by Participation
(co-author)

Kurt Lewin

THE
PRACTICAL
THEORIST

The Life and Work of

KURT LEWIN

BY

Alfred J. Marrow

Basic Books, Inc., PUBLISHERS

NEW YORK   LONDON

There is nothing so practical as a good theory.

—KURT LEWIN

Preface

"Freud the clinician and Lewin the experimentalist—these are the two men whose names will stand out before all others in the history of our psychological era. For it is their contrasting but complementary insights which first made psychology a science applicable to real human beings and to real human society." Thus did Edward C. Tolman sum up the greatness of Kurt Lewin, in a memorial address delivered during the 1947 convention of the American Psychological Association shortly after Lewin's death at the age of fifty-six.

It may surprise some readers to know that Lewin was so highly regarded. His name has never been well known to the general public. But psychologists have known of the breathtaking sweep of his scientific endeavors. Many of his concepts have been so widely adopted that they figure as intrinsic to the science itself and their origin is not remembered. Often enough ideas and techniques Lewin originated are discussed without any reference to him. Among them are the concepts signified by such familiar terms as "group dynamics," "action research," "field theory," "sensitivity training." Even such of Lewin's observations as "There is nothing so practical as a good theory" are repeated without any idea of their source.

Different psychologists, of course, have different views on the meaning and worth of Lewin's original concepts. But most recognize the innovative thinking and pioneering experiments that led to his being described as the scientist whose originality, in Gordon Allport's phrase, "seemed to remove him from all comparison scales." In the years since Lewin's death, psychologists have kept finding in his work fresh support of what Allport termed "the revolution that Lewin created in the scientific study of men in society—a revolution due more to his work in social psychology than to the work of any other behavioral scientist."

It is not too soon, therefore, to evaluate what Lewin's place in contemporary psychology is; to inquire precisely what his role was; to measure what its significance has been. The available data on the course of Lewin's professional development are few and scattered; the complete summation and appraisal has yet to be made.

The reader of standard textbooks is apt to get a one-sided though impressive picture of Lewin's manifold role in the history of psychology. Some authors wrote of Lewin as the proponent of group dynamics; others describe him variously as the radical innovator in experimental psychology, the developer of field theory and topology in psychology, or perhaps as simply the pioneer in action research.

It may rightly be said that Lewin's psychology was concerned primarily with the actualities of men's daily lives with one another. He was singular in that he was one of the few psychologists who could transpose a life problem into controllable experimental form. The scientific method that Lewin provided has been used in studies in industry, education, and government. Lewinian ways have infiltrated the social sciences in fields that range from industry to anthropology, from child rearing to city planning, from clinical psychology to education. Both as a scholar and as a humanitarian, Lewin was concerned with the consequential import of scientific thinking and aware (as his phrase "group dynamics" indicates) of the teamwork upon which each individual depends for his own performance.

He has turned social psychology in all its aspects in new directions and given the psychological study of human relations more precise yet more humanely oriented methods. The variety of his concerns and the richness of his contributions joined to serve a single purpose: "to seek deeper explanations of why people behave as they do and to discover how they may learn to behave better."

Lewin's influence was in no small degree facilitated by his personal qualities, his intellectual power joined to his warmhearted concern for and rapport with other people. He extended a warm welcome to all who sought him out. He awakened in students an enthusiasm and a zest rare in teacher-pupil relations. Unlike the typical German professor, he was a natural, spontaneous democrat. Almost everyone called him by his first name, and he had time for everybody and everybody's problems. These he would consider with the same enthusiasm he brought to his own problems—even when he thought them to be insoluble.

He kept exchanging ideas with all sorts of men on all sorts of occasions—fellow professionals, students in his own and other fields, colleagues both sympathetic and unpersuaded by his theoretical position, research subjects, casual acquaintances. There was something charismatic in this, and it probably had a role in the Lewinian way of choosing and stating problems, of designing research in terms of action, and of applying its findings in programs of social change. He lived psychology—not only for his love of science but also for his devotion to mankind. Thus it is not surprising that Gardner Murphy should express the hope, in referring to Lewin, that "it would be possible for mankind in general . . . to sometime rear a shelter for men's minds and hearts where he will occupy a place fairer than any in which his imagination ever dwelt."

It was the late Douglas McGregor of M.I.T. who first suggested to me that it would be a good idea to seek out those who had worked and studied with Lewin, in the hope that their personal recollections would reveal the reasons for his great impact on them and would provide a clearer idea of what that impact was. McGregor felt that out of the experiences of these behavioral scientists a book could be made that would show Lewin in the full range of his extraordinary powers and genius, both as a man and as a teacher. I agreed to try.

The task has been rewarding, but more difficult than I had anticipated. Karl E. Zener, of Duke, who had worked with Lewin in Berlin, had died shortly before my talk with Douglas McGregor. Not long afterward, McGregor himself died unexpectedly. Other colleagues and former students were scattered around the world. Happily for me, however, almost all were eager to collaborate when I explained my purposes to them. Some responded by writing their reflections. Others preferred to hold expanded conversations. Most of them found it easy to reminisce. The time they had spent with Lewin was deeply etched in their memories, and they continued to feel his powerful influence on their own lives. This was true even though none of the many men and women whose reflections are included in this book were unquestioning disciples, precisely repeating the Lewinian discipline. They were students, colleagues, associates, and friends who, each in his own way, found in Lewin the most reliable guidelines for their own diverse endeavors.

Summarizing Lewin's important theoretical articles and the experimental reports was not easy. Some of the experiments reported in the *Psychologische Forschung* from 1924 to 1934 had never been fully translated into English. Most were doctoral dissertations, and a number were a hundred pages or more in length. Now all have been translated. A number of unpublished papers and letters were also made available to me, including some of the action-research projects of the Commission on Community Interrelations. These now appear for the first time.

I first met Kurt Lewin in November 1934, when he was at Cornell University. I had written to him late in October to say that I was working on a variation of the Zeigarnik experiment for my doctoral dissertation and that I would like to discuss with him some aspects of the investigation. I had originally hoped to explore this topic under him in Berlin, but the rise of Hitler had changed both our plans. Lewin wrote back at once, inviting me to Ithaca and promising me as much time as was needed to discuss the project. He offered to meet me at the railroad station if I came by train. If, on the other hand, I intended to drive, he suggested that I plan to stay overnight as a guest at his home. I was overawed and felt it would be inappropriate for a graduate student to accept this proffer of hospitality. I therefore arranged to drive to Ithaca, planning to return to New York immediately after our talk.

A date was set, and on a Saturday in November I drove to Cornell with my wife. We were greeted with great friendliness by the entire Lewin family. I was eager to get to work and take up as little of Lewin's time as possible, but he insisted that we visit the building in which the nursery school was located and see the one-way screens and other new equipment that had been installed for research purposes. We were introduced to his colleague Tamara Dembo and urged to sample a new variety of apple being developed at the Agricultural College (it has since become celebrated as the Golden Delicious). Eventually we began to discuss my projected study, and the talk continued for the rest of the afternoon.

After dinner, the conversation turned to political events in Germany and the flight of the Jews from there to Palestine and other lands. Lewin spoke of his own deep interest in Palestine, both as a permanent home for himself and as a place that offered a unique opportunity for research. He spoke of some preliminary plans for a Psychological Institute at the Hebrew University, and of his intention to raise the funds needed to establish such a research center. His enthusiasm was catching. When he asked me to lend a hand in this project I agreed at once.

We had retired to Lewin's study for our talk and were still at it after midnight when Mrs. Lewin came to remind him that it was not proper to keep guests up so late. By then all plans to return to New York that evening had been abandoned. Next morning we resumed our discussion of the proposed Psychological Institute at the Hebrew University in Jerusalem, and in our enthusiasm drew up a preliminary statement of how such an Institute should be organized. It was characteristic of Lewin that he could initiate a discussion of such length, on so serious a matter, with someone he had just met. An interested responsiveness in another person was all he needed to include that person in anything that was nearest to his heart and mind.

During the next twelve years our relationship grew increasingly close, and during the last five years of his life almost every aspect of it became involved with my own. Lewin, I discovered in those twelve years, accepted the unknown, not as a mystery, but as a frontier which scientists must strive to push back if they are to achieve a better understanding of the social world about which science still knows so little. His aim was to discover the determining conditions of human events; his approach was ideal for his kind of scientist—the kind who believes that his life as a scientist must be integrated with his life as a citizen.

At the time of his death in 1947, Lewin's conceptual formulations and the shaping of his concepts into a system patterned by this approach were far more highly developed than their experimental testing. Now this has been changed. Testing has been diversified and multiplied, and experimentation has amply confirmed his basic insights.

The range and scope of Lewin's undertakings were the product of a fertile and inquiring mind, joined with a confident reliance on the willing collaboration of colleagues and students. Through them, his influence has been kept alive and contemporary in many institutions of social research, in departments of psychology and sociology, in social agencies, and in the management of organizations. The Research Center for Group Dynamics, which Lewin founded at M.I.T., has moved to the University of Michigan, where it continues with many of the same people and remains one of the fountainheads of social research in the United States. The action-research studies, which he initiated, continue to illuminate and shape ongoing community experiments in integrated housing, equalization of opportunity for employment, the cause and cure of prejudice in children, the socialization of street gangs, and the better training of community leaders. Sensitivity training, which he helped to create, is considered by many people to be the most significant educational innovation of the century.

In the new science of organization development, too, Lewin's influence continues to be seminal. In the application of behavioral-science concepts to management methods, such authorities as McGregor, Likert, Argyris, and Bennis, among others, have built many of their formulations on Lewin's concepts and experiments.

Preface

It is in the light of Lewin's sustained influence on these diverse fields of social inquiry and of his impact on the work of friends and colleagues that I, as one of his very wide circle of co-workers, have assembled these remembrances of Lewin's life in psychology.

Alfred J. Marrow

New York
July 1969

Acknowledgments

It is my pleasure to make several acknowledgments and to express my thanks to a number of people. My personal indebtedness is greatest to the distinguished group of men and women who supplied personal reminiscences, points of view, ideas, information, and insights on Kurt Lewin and his life in psychology. All of them, by written replies or by personal interview, gave generously of their time to provide the commentary which will be found in the text. Their names appear in the list below.

To those colleagues whose work has been inadequately reported or bypassed completely, I ask forgiveness. The material I assembled was so vast that this book would have grown to several volumes if I did not omit much interesting material.

I wish especially to thank my friends who were kind enough to read the manuscript while it was in preparation. Their criticisms and comments helped make this a better book. They are Dorwin Cartwright, Jasper H. de Rivera, Leon Festinger, John R. P. French, Jr., Fritz and Grace Heider, Harry Levinson, Ronald Lippitt, Donald MacKinnon, and Beatrice Wright.

I benefited greatly from continuing criticism and discussion with my lifelong friend Horace Kallen. He deserves special gratitude for his helpful suggestions and constant encouragement.

I am indebted to Charlton Price, Richard Cohen, Robert Pearse, and Beatrice Pelzer, who provided invaluable assistance.

Finally, I am grateful to my wife, Monette, who patiently put up with the interferences in our daily life which were part of the cost of writing this book.

My grateful acknowledgments to:

Donald K. Adams	Duke University
Doris Twitchell Allen	University of Cincinnati
Gordon Allport	Harvard University
Chris Argyris	Yale University
Roger G. Barker	University of Kansas
Alex Bavelas	Stanford University
Warren Bennis	University of Buffalo
Leland P. Bradford	NTL Institute of Applied Behavioral Sciences
Dorwin Cartwright	University of Michigan
Stuart W. Cook	University of Colorado
Tamara Dembo	Clark University
Morton Deutsch	Columbia University
Herbert Feigl	University of Minnesota
Leon Festinger	New School for Social Research
Jerome D. Frank	Johns Hopkins University
Lawrence K. Frank	Spellman Fund
Carl Frankenstein	The Hebrew University of Jerusalem
John R. P. French, Jr.	University of Michigan
Maxwell Hahn	The Field Foundation
Mason Haire	Massachusetts Institute of Technology
Gordon Hearn	Portland State College
Fritz Heider	University of Kansas
Grace M. Heider	University of Kansas
Charles Hendry	University of Toronto
Simon Herman	The Hebrew University of Jerusalem
Horace Kallen	New School for Social Research

Acknowledgments

Harold H. Kelley	University of California, Los Angeles
Hedda Korsch	
Rensis Likert	University of Michigan
Ronald Lippitt	University of Michigan
Donald W. MacKinnon	University of California, Berkeley
Vera Mahler-Franck	Tel Aviv University, Israel
Norman R. F. Maier	University of Michigan
Margaret Mead	The Museum of Natural History
Gardner Murphy	The Menninger Foundation
Maria Richers-Ovsiankina	University of California, Berkeley
Kanae Sakuma	Toyo University, Tokyo
Robert R. Sears	Stanford University
John W. Thibaut	University of North Carolina
Eric Trist	University of California, Los Angeles
Ethel B. Waring	Cornell University
Beatrice A. Wright	University of Kansas
Erik Wright	University of Kansas
Herbert F. Wright	University of Kansas
Alvin F. Zander	University of Michigan

Contents

A group of photographs appears following page 140.

PART I

The German Years

CHAPTER

1

BEGINNINGS

*The psychologist finds himself in the midst of a rich
and vast land full of strange happenings: there are men
killing themselves; a child playing; a child forming his
lips trying to say his first word; a person who, having
fallen in love and being caught in an unhappy situation, is not willing or not able to find a way out; there
is the mystical state called hypnosis, where the will of
one person seems to govern another person; there is
the reaching out for higher and more difficult goals;
loyalty to a group; dreaming; planning; exploring the
world; and so on without end. It is an immense continent full of fascination and power and full of
stretches of land where no one ever has set foot.*

*Psychology is out to conquer this continent, to find
out where its treasures are hidden, to investigate its
danger spots, to master its vast forces, and to utilize
its energies.*

How can one reach this goal? [1]

Kurt Lewin, who wrote these challenging words, was born in the
tiny village of Mogilno in the Prussian province of Posen, now part
of Poland, on what he used to describe as "the ninth nine of ninety"
—September 9, 1890. His father, Leopold, owned and operated a
general store; the family lived above it. A few miles from Mogilno,
he also owned a small farm, which his son Kurt loved. As a small-

[1] Kurt Lewin, "Formalization and Progress in Psychology," *University of Iowa
Studies in Child Welfare,* 1940, *16*, No. 3.

town boy, free to wander in grassy fields and pine forests, Kurt developed a feeling for nature. He liked gardening, became handy with tools, and developed great skill in woodwork and mechanics.

The boy looked very much like his father, but in temperament seems to have been more like his mother, Recha. She was filled with energy and drive and nurtured high aspirations for her four children, whom she raised while she worked in the family store. Hertha was the eldest; then came three sons, Kurt, Egon, and Fritz. The mother, articulate and warmhearted, was always busy. Leopold ran the shop and took a hand in community affairs, serving for a time as president of the Mogilno synagogue. In this close and affectionate family, Fritz, who was tall, athletic, and high-spirited and excelled at sports, often came home late, but, no matter what the hour, his mother was always waiting for him. Her patience made a deep impression on Kurt, who also was frequently tardy. Kurt's wife, Gertrud, thinks that he measured the depth of a woman's love or a friend's affection by their willingness to accept his habitual tardiness.

The Lewins, a thrifty, middle-class family, were fairly comfortable. Their social life centered on family, relatives, and neighbors. Their circle also included the families of coreligionists from neighboring towns, for in the Germany of Kaiser Wilhelm II, all Jews were subjected to overt, publicly approved discrimination. In the small towns of eastern Prussia, the landed aristocracy and the army officers' corps constituted the top social level. Members of these groups shunned all social contact with Jews, though they were willing to do business with them. Few Jews, even though they might meet the educational requirements, could aspire to a responsible post in Germany's civil service or to a commission in the Kaiser's peacetime army. Thus, anti-Semitism was a fact of life with which Jewish children became familiar early, both at school and in the community. Since Prussian law required that every child receive religious instruction during the elementary-school years, Kurt and his brothers attended Jewish religious classes. At the age of thirteen, each went through the Hebrew Bar Mitzvah ritual. But this Jewish involvement did not inhibit the family's celebration of Christmas.

They exchanged gifts and looked upon the holiday as a festive occasion.

The Lewins wanted their children to have the best possible education, and they realized that Mogilno's limited facilities could not provide proper schooling. Hence, while he was still in elementary school, Kurt was sent to board with a family in Posen, the provincial capital. Then, in 1905, the family moved to Berlin, where fifteen-year-old Kurt was enrolled in the Kaiserin Augusta Gymnasium. In elementary school Kurt had not been an outstanding pupil. Though not a difficult child, he had displayed occasional temper tantrums and his family nicknamed him the "Furious Herring." His high intelligence was not even suspected until his last two years of high school. In 1907 he was introduced to Greek philosophy and fell in love with it. It was a love that lasted all his life. During this same period his scholastic record improved remarkably.

At this time in Germany there were three different types of gymnasia: the oldest (of which the Kaiserin Augusta was an example) was of the humanistic type and stressed the study of the classics—epecially Latin and Greek—with some mathematics, and very little science. The two other types, though they also laid less stress on the classics, offered more instruction in science. When Kurt entered the gymnasium in 1905, Berlin was not only an elegant imperial city but also the capital of German scholarship and a world center of scientific achievement. The universities were organized around the original "four faculties" of the medieval period—theology, jurisprudence, medicine, and philosophy—and any subject that could not be assigned to one of the first three was classified as philosophy. Thus all the natural sciences, the social sciences, the liberal arts, and the humanities came under the faculty of philosophy. It was therefore possible and customary for students to shift at will from the sciences to the arts and from the arts to the sciences. Psychology was still taught as a division of philosophy, as, indeed, it was in many American universities even years later.

In April 1909, Kurt, after completing his term at the gymnasium, entered the University of Freiburg, planning to study medicine and become a country doctor. Apparently he found the anatomy courses at Freiburg too distasteful, however, and he transferred his interest to biology—an interest that would endure throughout his life. But he stayed at Freiburg for only a single semester. In October 1909, he registered at the University of Munich, but he remained there too for only one semester, and, in April 1910, he registered at the University of Berlin, where he worked for his doctorate. He took courses, among others, in philosophy and was especially attracted to the theory of science. In one of his classes at Berlin, he wrote a paper on the question of concepts in the various sciences. His instructor challenged one of his statements and suggested he check to see whether it would hold true for psychology. It marked the beginning of Lewin's serious work in the Psychological Institute at the University of Berlin, whose director at the time was Carl Stumpf.

In 1910, the year in which he returned to Berlin, Lewin finally committed himself to a career as a university teacher. Neither of his parents seemed to object to his choice, although they knew that discrimination against Jews was strong in all German universities and that his chances of becoming a full professor with tenure were extremely slight. But they gave him their approval and furnished the needed financial support.

At the University of Berlin, Kurt found a lively group of students that included several girl graduates of the one school which did prepare girls for the university. "Kurt seemed to fit right in . . . a natural, good fellow," Dr. Hedda Korsch, one of them, recalls. "He was popular in whatever circle he joined. He was a person to laugh with. He enjoyed dancing, and was a genial companion to have along on weekend hikes, when we had long discussions about democratizing Germany and liberating women from the conventional restrictions on their freedom." The group, often as many as nine or ten, walked together to the University from their residences, noisily debating social problems as they went. Their talk soon led to action, and they organized a series of evening classes for working-class adults, which they staffed with members of their earnest group. "The public authorities," Dr. Korsch remembers, "were deeply suspicious of the project, which the students referred to as

6

'workingmen's courses' and which were for both men and women, though hardly any women came. The curriculum was severely restricted, and during the first year the instructors were allowed to teach only the 'three R's.' Courses in geography, history, or free composition were forbidden as likely to prompt subversive actions. But each year the group got more concessions for more subjects, and the pupil enrollment grew. The students serving as the faculty soon had two or three assistants. All who took part in this venture did so with intense enthusiasm."

The zeal and zest of this extramural activity did not extend to the students' own classrooms. There the professors lectured and the students took notes—but apathetically and without much real concern. During their third and fourth years, they attended seminars where one or another might ask a respectful question, offer an occasional objection, or raise an issue. (The privilege of speaking up was not, however, readily granted to the women students, whose presence was thought to inhibit such masculine academic freedoms as smoking and beer drinking.) When the time came for Lewin to choose a dissertation director (or "thesis-father"), he selected Carl Stumpf. A leader in redirecting the study of man's mind from the discipline of philosophy to that of science, Stumpf had been appointed professor of psychology and director of the Psychological Laboratory at the University of Berlin in 1894. He was a man of wide-ranging interests; both a philosopher and a psychologist, he was interested, too, in primitive music and created a psychology of sound. He also was the founder of the Berlin Association for Child Psychology and the developer of original theories of space perception and sensation.

Though he would preserve the traditional aloofness of the German professor in his relations with Lewin, Stumpf did not have the overbearing Prussian manner characteristic of Wilhelm Wundt, founder of the first laboratory of experimental psychology at the University of Leipzig in 1878. Wundt's work attracted distinguished students and brought him into contact with William James, but he managed to alienate almost everyone by his dictatorial approach.

For Stumpf, and for his contemporary Geheimrat G. E. Müller, Lewin never had anything but the highest regard. Both were members of the German Society for Experimental Psychology; they were decided empiricists; they had done a tremendous amount of exact experimental work in a variety of fields; and they had very definite ideas and were militant enough to put up, when necessary, a stiff fight in defense of their views. Lewin believed that Stumpf was an outstanding pioneer of the new epoch of experimental psychology in Germany.

Stumpf began to teach in Berlin at a time when, according to Lewin, it still took courage to approach questions of the soul experimentally, in an atmosphere in which philosophy was the accepted king and in which experimental procedures seemed to be hopelessly distant from any problems of real psychological importance. Lewin's high regard for his mentor was well merited, for, during Stumpf's tenure as director of the Psychological Laboratory (from 1894 until his retirement in 1921), he attracted a brilliant faculty —Wertheimer, Koffka, Köhler—and it was while he was director that a whole new school of psychology, Gestaltism, was founded.

Stumpf gave his students an unusual degree of freedom, though to some it might seem more accurate to say "lack of attention." The thesis topic Lewin had selected was presented to Stumpf by an assistant, while Lewin himself waited in another room to learn if it would be acceptable. Lewin could not remember having ever discussed the matter with Stumpf between the time the assistant relayed word that his subject was approved and the day of his final examination four years later.

As a student, Lewin himself generated excitement by his open criticism of conventional theories. His curiosity and unusual insights impressed his classmates. "Kurt was an exceptional person," reports Hedda Korsch, "and right from the beginning we felt that he was much more perceptive and active than the rest of us. He had a direct approach to the dynamic of people's minds. He would joke and say that he was like the boy in the fairy tale who saw that the emperor was wearing no clothes. 'That,' he said, 'was how *he* felt— that is what his approach to psychology should be.' "

Beginnings

In 1910, Lewin took a course in philosophy under Ernst Cassirer, toward whom Lewin always (as he put it) felt "the deep gratitude of a student toward his teacher." Thirty-six years after he listened to Cassirer lecture in Berlin, Lewin would write: "Scarcely a year passed when I did not have specific reason to acknowledge the help which Cassirer's views on the nature of science and research offered. . . . To proceed beyond the limitations of a given level of knowledge, the researcher, as a rule, has to break down methodological taboos which condemn as 'unscientific' or 'illogical' the very methods or concepts which later on prove to be basic for the next major progress." [2]

This was certainly true in Lewin's instance. He noted that, just as the infant science of psychology had to compete with the "grown-up sciences" of biology, chemistry, and physics, so did the experimental psychology of will and emotion have to fight for recognition "against a prevalent attitude which placed volition, emotion, and sentiments in the 'poetic realm' of beautiful words, a realm to which nothing corresponds which could be regarded as 'existing' in the sense in which the scientist uses the term. . . . Although every psychologist had to deal with these acts realistically in his private life, they were banned from the realm of 'facts' in the scientific sense." [3] Emotions were declared to be something too "fluid" and "intangible" to be pinned down by scientific analysis or by experimental procedures. "Such methodological argument," Lewin noted, "did not deny existence to the phenomenon, but it did have the effect of keeping it outside the realm of empirical science." Armed with Cassirer's vision and his own genius, Lewin assumed the task of breaking the taboo and of treating in the psychological laboratory topics which had been considered outside the realm of science.

[2] "Cassirer's Philosophy of Science and Social Science," in Paul Arthur Schilpp (ed.), *The Philosophy of Ernst Cassirer* (New York: Tudor, 1949).
[3] *Ibid.*

9

CHAPTER

2

FIRST CONCEPTS

After Lewin had completed the requirements for his degree in the early summer of 1914, he volunteered for army service. World War I broke out very soon after, and he served in the army for most of the bitter four years of fighting. (The degree was conferred on him in 1916.) He entered the army a private and left it a lieutenant with an Iron Cross. Despite his background as an intellectual, Lewin adapted very well to being a soldier. Forced to make long marches on foot, he learned the infantryman's trick of sleeping standing up— even when walking or marching. He spoke of this with amusement in later years and occasionally used this skill again.

The years 1914–1917 comprised the period of victorious advance for the Kaiser's army, but the great spring offensive of 1918, which was intended to be the final push, floundered by midsummer on the banks of the Marne. Lewin had, in the interval, been wounded and hospitalized. (His youngest brother, Fritz, had been killed in action.) On furlough as a convalescent, Lewin filled the time with considerable thinking and some writing. Although strongly antimilitarist and deeply opposed to German nationalism, he had not found the war experience entirely unbearable. Being the kind of person he was, Lewin developed an interest in some of his duties and occasionally even found a chance for fun or at least an escape from military boredom. What saved him from the monotony, horror, and despair of four years in the trenches of World War I was his unquenchable curiosity. He continually conceptualized his experiences—as may be noted in his article "The War Landscape," [1] which was published in 1917 during his furlough.

Professor Fritz Heider [2] points out that this article provides a preview of many of the concepts—such as "boundary," "direction," and "zone"—which Lewin later defined in a systematic way. Indeed, the article is the first preliminary statement of the concept of "life space" which was to become one of Lewin's lifelong themes. In it, he tells how the appearance of the landscape is transformed as a soldier approaches the front lines. The physical environment looks different because of the particular perceptual needs of the onlooker: a soldier at the front requires physical safety, food, a favorable position with respect to the enemy, and so on. It is a soldier's needs, Lewin wrote, that cause him to see the landscape in one way and not otherwise. When the soldier is still a long distance from the front the peace landscape—as Lewin termed it—seems to stretch endlessly on all sides and is without direction. But as he gets closer to the front, the landscape seems to take on boundaries. It has a direction and a front and a back. This transformation, Lewin wrote, cannot be described simply as an awareness of increasing danger. Rather, it is experienced as a feature of the objective landscape.

Lewin described the difference between "peace things" and "battle things"—how the same objects can be experienced differently when seen in the context of peace or of battle. "What lies within the battle zone belongs to the soldier as his legitimate property, not because he has gained it by force of arms, but because in the context of battle everything is seen as something to be used for military purposes. Even barbaric acts such as the burning of furniture in war cannot be compared with the same acts in peacetime." Lewin described the impression of incongruity when he had to get straw for bedding, or coal for fire to warm his dinner—in the battle zone. It seemed absurd, he declared, to suddenly use battle things as peace things.

[1] Kurt Lewin, "Kriegslandschaft," *Zeitschrift für angewandte Psychologie*, 1917.
[2] Fritz Heider, "On Lewin's Methods and Theory," *Journal of Social Issues*, 1959, No. 13.

In another paper[3] published the same year and based on his dissertation, Lewin expressed his growing belief that motives have much to do with association; indeed, he set motive over against the frequency and contiguity to which the force of association was attributed at that time. He wrote that his work in psychology "began before World War I with experiments on association" and then went on to explain that his "intention was not to criticize associationism but rather to refine the measurement of the 'strength of the will' "—as developed by Asch, whose work at that time was the most theoretically precise in the field. But after three years of experimenting with nonsense syllables and reaction times split to one thousandth of a second, Lewin came to a stop. He felt there was no point in trying further to improve the exactness of the measure. He was also convinced that "association" alone could not account for the phenomena under observation and that there was need for a new explanation and a major modification in theory.

For Lewin, the year 1917 was memorable for something other than the publication of the two papers. While on furlough, he married Maria Landsberg, a close friend of Hedda Korsch. Maria was a teacher of German and English in one of the new high schools for girls established in 1912. Considered outstanding in the classroom, she continued teaching, with brief interruptions, after her marriage. Lewin and his bride lived first in an apartment in the Berlin suburb of Charlottenburg. Around 1922, they bought a house in a development near Tempelhof Airport. The area was an oasis of small, moderately priced single homes, surrounded by the big city. Kurt's sister, Hertha, and her family, as well as Karl and Hedda Korsch, also bought homes in the same suburb. Their children—the Lewins' daughter, Agnes, was born in 1919 and a son, Fritz, in 1922—were all about the same age. This, and the circumstance that all three families lived within easy walking distance, made for close and frequent social contact.

The Lewins had begun their marriage in the period of civil and economic turmoil experienced throughout Germany after World

[3] Kurt Lewin, "Die psychische Tätigkeit bei der Hemmung von Willensorgängen und das Grundgesetz der Assoziation," *Zeitschrift für Psychologie*, 1917.

War I. The Kaiser abdicated, and, as the armistice went into effect, the German parliament met in Weimar to consider what to do. The stress and strain of political instability were in evidence everywhere. Inflation soon made German money worthless. But though life in Berlin, as elsewhere, was troubled and insecure in the early 1920's, the University tried to carry on. At the old Imperial Palace, which now housed a part of the University, a number of rooms had been assigned to the Psychological Institute, and it was here that Lewin came after being demobilized.

It was—despite the precarious political and economic situation—an exciting period for all intellectuals and especially so for Lewin, for whom the years at the Psychological Institute marked the beginning of his productivity and saw the laying of the foundations of his theoretical concepts and experimental methods. At the Institute, where Köhler and Wertheimer were breaking new ground in psychology in the formulation of their Gestalt theory, Lewin found an exciting setting for his own work. It seemed to him that Köhler and Wertheimer were opening doors too long held closed by the older revered figures of German psychology.

Against the traditional mosaic conception of phenomena as aggregates of distinct parts, the Gestaltists argued that perception could and should be considered in terms of "forms of organized wholes." The wholes, they maintained, are different from merely sums of their parts; they take on an added characteristic or quality; they are entities with distinctive structures—changeable, to be sure, by any change in any part, but, although changing, definitely recognizable wholes, or Gestalts. Thus, the "solidity" of a brick wall was something more than the sum of the bricks in it. All mental experiences are patterned in this way; they take on a new aspect which depends on how they are "organized." Such organization precedes and influences the experiences.

This Gestalt holism impressed Lewin. Though he was never a completely orthodox Gestaltist, he did become a vital force in the new movement and contributed to it his own special insights. To Lewin, Gestaltism seemed closer to actual experience than did piecemeal analysis, which had prevailed in psychology during his prewar student days. The broad implications of Gestalt principles for the process of perceiving and thinking held immense promise, particularly as they might be applied to men at work.

Early Views on Applied Psychology

Lewin's pioneer interest in the possible applications of psychology to the work environment was reflected in a paper he wrote in 1919 on the role of the laborer in agriculture,[4] and in a second, written in 1920, on the laborer in industry.[5] In the first essay, Lewin compared the organization of work on the farm with that in the factory. He pointed out that factory jobs are specialized and specific, whereas farming calls for much less division of labor. In the fields, more of the whole person is engaged and the farmer gets a certain satisfaction from working in the open air, caring for animals. The aptitudes involved are not as readily identified by aptitude tests as are the skills needed by a factory worker.

Furthermore, with the new machinery and advanced mechanization being employed in farming, more consideration should be given to their best use. This, obviously, turns on how the machines are designed and maintained and on their relation to the user's muscles, how he tires, recovers and so on. Doing a hard job standing up might be more "economical" physically than an easier job performed bent over; a more comfortable handle might be more essential to the effective use of a tool than the distribution of its weight according to the rules of physics. The relation of the tool to the material on which it is used is another factor. In sum, the most efficient tools are those which fit both the worker and the material with which he works.

Lewin proposed a series of studies aimed at finding the most efficient method of doing each job and the most effective handling of

[4] Kurt Lewin, in *Zeitschrift für angewandte Psychologie*, 1919.
[5] Kurt Lewin, "Die Sozialisierung des Taylorsystems," *Praktischer Socialismus*, 1920, No. 4.

each tool. The investigation of this complex psychophysical problem, Lewin suggested, might be restricted initially to a single tool—for example, the hoe—which could be examined systematically and experimentally. An investigator need only go where the work is, look, listen, and record. No apparatus is necessary. What is needed is a new angle of vision—and close cooperation between the research psychologist and the practical farmer. Such an inquiry, Lewin acknowledged, would be a scientific novelty. And, though practical results could not be guaranteed, the mere development of useful testing methods for farm work might be a vital contribution to a neglected area of psychology and life.

The second of Lewin's early papers discusses the "Taylor System." Frederick Winslow Taylor, an American industrial engineer often called the father of scientific management, aimed to achieve greater industrial efficiency by the elimination of superfluous effort. Taylor set up time-and-motion studies to establish a standard of production which combined the best skills of various workers rather than the movements of just the most proficient ones. The "Taylor System" was of intense interest to Lewin, who saw beyond it to new possibilities. Lewin was optimistic about scientific psychology as an aid in resolving problems of labor-management relations, and he felt that the industrial setting offered a rich field for exploring new facets of interpersonal relations.

He began his paper on Taylorism in industry with some observations on the central role of labor in life: work has a "life value"; a man's capacity to work gives meaning and substance to his whole existence. Accordingly, every job should sustain or enhance this "life value." Modern technology tends only to reduce the hours of labor, to raise output by making production more efficient. That it also creates overspecialization and monotony does not seem to matter to management so long as its goal of increasing productivity is met.

For the individual worker, however, it is important that new job methods also include ways of making his task richer and more satisfying. To discover how to do this, Lewin felt, is a task not alone for the efficiency expert but also for the research psychologist. Shortening the workday is not enough. The work itself must be made worth doing, no matter how long or short the task.

It is essential to recognize, Lewin declared, that the enriching and humanizing of work depends not only on the kind of work to be done but also on how far the job fulfills the laborer's psychological needs. From the point of view of production, it had been customary to measure work by an "objective" yardstick of cost and quantity turned out. For the worker, however, the more significant factors are the value he places on what he is doing and the satisfaction he derives from it. These in turn are major factors in determining how well the employee performs on the assembly line or at the workbench.

Production engineers' demand for the highest output at the lowest cost disregards the function of "job satisfaction." Few "efficiency experts" recognize that assigning people to the jobs they like best—and thus perform best—is also a great aid to increased skill. Recognition of a person's right to choose a job that he prefers, Lewin felt, can have a tremendously liberating effect on human effort.

Could psychology contribute to this liberation through its studies of work and the relation of individuals to the job they want most to do? Could psychological findings about people be used to balance the rival interests of employer and employee, foreman and worker, management and factory hand? Lewin believed that an affirmative answer to both questions was a possibility. If the psychologist can win the cooperation of both parties, workers and employers together might learn how to enhance the "life values" of work without hampering the smooth flow of production. For example, difficult jobs could be studied with a view either to making them less disagreeable, distributing them among a greater number of workers, or to offering those performing them some special compensation. Whatever the device ultimately found, its use could bring greater interest and enthusiasm on the part of the worker and, with it, higher output.

Lewin summed up his views by stressing that man does not live to produce but produces to live. Improving the psychological compo-

16

nents of man's work will thus accomplish far more for the worker's well-being than merely cutting down his hours on the job. What is important, what must always be sought, is an improvement in the *inner value* of the work as experienced by the man performing it.

In the Classroom

The psychologist Lewin continued to be intertwined with the philosopher Lewin throughout these years. "He never abandoned philosophy," says Gertrud Lewin. "In Berlin he lectured one year in psychology and had a seminar in philosophy; the next year he had a lecture in philosophy and a seminar in psychology." He taught these courses as a *privatdozent*, or lecturer (he was appointed in 1921)—a position which was the first stage in a university teacher's career and which carried neither salary nor tenure. To qualify for appointment as a full member of the faculty, it was (and still is) necessary for a candidate to submit a *Habilitationsschrift*—a report on a research project beyond the doctoral dissertation which must be presented before the faculty in a formal lecture—and he must also be approved by vote of the full professorship of the faculty. The *privatdozent* did not enjoy the status of *beamter*, or state civil servant. He was dependent for his income on his share of student fees. If his lectures were well attended, his income rose; but it was never large, no matter how popular he might be; and, in Prussia, Jewish *privatdozents* did not rise to the position of full professor.

To Horace Kallen, the American philosopher who first met Lewin at a meeting of the International Psychological Society in Holland in 1925, there seemed to be a fundamental difference in outlook between Lewin, who was a "psychologist first and coincidentally a philosopher of the mind," and Köhler, Koffka, and Wertheimer, who were "really philosophers first and psychologists afterwards." However, Fritz Heider feels there was no real difference between Lewin and the others in this respect. To him Lewin remained a philosopher at heart despite the turn his interests took later.

In 1922, Lewin published one of his most important theoretical papers, the title of which translates as "The Concept of Genesis (or Origin) in Physics, Biology and Evolutional History." [6] Donald Adams, who worked with Lewin in Berlin, considers it one of his most important theoretical works. The first paragraph of the preface with which Lewin began his genetic analysis of identity furnished, according to Adams, "a key to his productivity, the range of his inquiry and the depth and breadth of his impact on psychology. This study expressed his ultimate concern with the comparative 'science of the sciences.'" Lewin's whole career in psychology, observes Adams, actually was a single experiment in this historical-methodological field and he so regarded it. His broad and intensive pursuit of this inquiry, for example, arose from his conviction that psychology had reached a *Galileische Wendepunkt* (Galileian turning point) and needed only the push of some clearheaded conceptualizing and imaginative experimental work to achieve a breakthrough. With characteristic audacity, he himself set about giving it the nudge. *Begriff der Genese* will in time, Adams believes, be regarded as both Lewin's most original and comprehensive contribution and the source of the dazzling originality that characterized his experimental work in psychology.

Fritz Heider also considers *Begriff der Genese* most important because in it Lewin compares the various sciences in an entirely new way and tries to define the differences between them. He deals mostly with physics and biology, giving less attention to psychology. The concept on which his analysis centers he termed "genidentity," or the manner in which objects keep their identity over time. Even though an object takes on different appearances at different times, it is treated by us as identical, as the same object. For instance, physics considers its objects as extending over time; we speak of one and the same stone or star although it has been observed at different moments or epochs. Again, when we talk of the motion of an object, we imply "genidentity," that is, we imply that the *same* object is in different places at different times.

[6] Kurt Lewin, *Der Begriff der Genese in Physik, Biologie und Entwicklungsgeschichte* (Berlin: Julius Springer, 1922).

Lewin argued that "the concept of genidentity as used in physics is different from that used in biology." Let us consider an egg and the two-year-old chicken hatched from this egg. Egg and chicken are biologically genidentical; they represent different stages of development of the same biological matter. However, physically they are not genidentical, for the molecules composing them have changed. In the same way, a person at the age of forty is biologically identified with the same person at the age of twenty, though physically only a small number of molecules may be the same. He may have changed as a biological entity; but the fact that we can speak of a change means that we refer to the same organism.

Thus Lewin tried to show that physics and biology are essentially different in the basic units of description they use. This led him to assert that a fundamental incommensurability separates the sciences from one another: each science is a closed unit of systematically connected concepts. Paths of derivation lead along the lines of this network, but we cannot use the propositions or laws of one science for those of another. Going from one science to another means to change completely the way of dividing up reality into units.

Lewin expanded on this theme in his lectures and writings. He believed that development of the sciences only leads to a sharpening of the differences between them. Each science gradually purifies its concepts and segregates itself more and more from its neighbors. In line with these ideas, Lewin cautioned that our desire for meaning and unity of life must not lead us to look for an illusory satisfaction in the idea of a philosophical unity of science. The idea of an eventual unification of all sciences is wishful thinking. Of course, there are many bridges between the sciences, and we should be seeking more of them—for instance, in intermediate fields such as biochemistry and physiological psychology. But psychology should strive to build up a more or less autonomous realm of concepts and form a closely knit system. As psychology grows, it should become more aware of its own proper nature and should separate itself from other sciences such as physiology. Psychology should in this way purify itself.

CHAPTER

3

LEWIN
AS TEACHER

During the early 1920's Lewin established a reputation as a provocative lecturer and teacher and over the years attracted many of the students at the Psychological Institute. And while his own work took a new and independent course, veering away from the Gestaltist emphasis on perception, Lewin was anxious to hold the approval of his seniors. In a letter to Fritz Heider in June 1926, Lewin wrote about an article of his that had just been accepted for publication by the *Psychologische Forschung*: "It pleased me very much that Köhler and Koffka were quite impressed with it."

Several of his earliest students came from foreign countries, principally Russia and the Baltic states. Maria Ovsiankina, who—with Tamara Dembo, Bluma Zeigarnik, and Gita Birenbaum—was in the first group of Lewin's students, recalls that they soon divided themselves into "generations." She herself while still quite young was a "grandmother" because she was part of the first group.

These first four students had come to Berlin from Russia to study literature. In their gymnasia at home, they had become accustomed in their literature classes to psychological discussion and analyses of fictional characters, and they wanted to continue university work along those lines. But in Berlin they found no department of literature, only of philology. It was not at all what they had hoped for. One by one, however, all four discovered the Psychological Institute—the only place at the University to study human personality and motivation. The Institute—where Wolfgang Köhler had recently succeeded Stumpf—was housed in one of the annexes of the huge Kunstgewerke Museum, built originally as a residence for the Kaiser. Here the laboratories and offices were located, while the classes and large seminars were held in the University building.

Maria Ovsiankina attended her first class under Lewin in 1924. "He was discussing some research on memory," she recalls. "It was a seminar and there were only about fifteen of us in the room. What impressed me most was that Lewin was concerned not just with concepts but with behavior. He was young and tried to encourage classroom participation, although he was inexperienced and did not really know how to direct the discussion. We often came out of these classes stimulated but at the same time confused, and wondering, 'What am I taking home?' But he very quickly learned how to direct the discussion without depriving it of its democratic nature and stimulating quality. I remember going to one of his lectures about two years later. By then he was more skillful and rapidly becoming one of the more prominent members of a very eminent faculty."

Tamara Dembo, Lewin's third graduate student, came to him after hearing of his work from Bluma Zeigarnik and Maria Ovsiankina. She was drawn to industrial psychology, having resolved, after leaving gymnasium in her native Russia, to do "something about making machines more suitable to human beings, instead of human beings more suitable to machines." She had read the work of Taylor and considered studying engineering, but turned instead to industrial psychology and then to general theoretical psychology and thus came into Lewin's orbit. Like all of Lewin's students, Tamara Dembo was quickly impressed by his concentration on his subject: "He was already talking in terms of forces, goal-directed behavior, and the life situation, which later became the life space. For Lewin, psychology was his whole life. We also thought about it all the time, not as a profession but as our whole way of life too—

and a way of life that required precise answers, for Lewin would never accept an answer that was just good enough. So he always had time to talk about one's work and our answers were refined through the discussion."

In his classes, Lewin encouraged each member of the group to present a formulation of personal observations and theories for criticism in general discussion. Surprisingly—or perhaps not so surprisingly, since Lewin thought like a mathematician—the formulations which finally emerged had precision. Like a mathematician, too, Lewin liked to employ visual symbols; he was always at the blackboard. Some students disliked his strange drawings, contending that they were unscientific. Others regarded them as part of his effort to communicate entirely new approaches to new concepts.

"Time after time," says Dr. Vera Mahler, who also became one of Lewin's students in 1924, "he would interrupt his lecture about some aspect of child psychology, for example, and begin to draw funny little 'eggs' on the blackboard. These he called the 'total psychological field' or 'life space' of the child's world. These little ovals would in turn contain smaller circles representing the child himself, and containing plus and minus signs; arrows would appear to indicate the direction of the various field forces; thick lines represented the barriers. Quickly we were in the midst of a conflict in the child's life, or a situation representing reward and punishment. All this was graphic, all was made clear, in Lewin's little drawings on the blackboard."

Years later, in his *Principles of Topological Psychology* (1936), Lewin stated, "I remember the moment when—more than ten years ago—it occurred to me that the figures on the blackboard which were to illustrate some problems for a group in psychology might after all be not merely illustrations but representations of real concepts."

"Lewin was something new and refreshing after the conventional lectures on child psychology we were used to," Dr. Mahler remarks, "even though Lewin's concepts sometimes gave us the impression of too much novelty. But the longer we studied with him, the clearer it became that here was something not merely novel but a sound approach to the psychological development of the child that had to be taken quite seriously."

Dr. Mahler's first impression of Lewin, already in his thirties, was of a young man with apple-red cheeks who seemed more like a student than a professor: "At the start we were not greatly impressed with his lecturing, for Lewin was in no way a polished or outstanding speaker and we had been spoiled by the brilliant lectures of Köhler and others." But his indifferent skill with words was forgotten by the students once Lewin started to expound his ideas. "We would sit in our seats in the classroom completely absorbed, as Lewin began to develop his train of thought. I shouldn't say he lectured—he really didn't in a conventional, well-organized manner. He was often creating as he was speaking. Frequently he paused in mid-sentence and seemed to forget his audience. Thinking aloud, he vented the new ideas pouring quickly into his mind."

At times, Lewin seemed too ready with new ideas, as new ones followed earlier ones rapidly and were too abruptly displaced by yet newer ones. Dr. Mahler once complained to him, "How can we find our way when you keep coming up with new ideas that sometimes contradict the old ones we haven't yet thoroughly understood?" Lewin smiled, and replied, "That's what science is all about. Science means progress, and progress means change. True science doesn't admit to stagnation. Everlasting change—that's the essence of science."

To Carl Frankenstein, who—like the young women students from the Baltic states—studied at the Psychological Institute between 1923 and 1926, the seeds of Lewin's greatness as a thinker and teacher were not as evident. Lewin, he recalls, apparently made no effort to compete with the Institute's two stars, Köhler and Wertheimer. Nevertheless, according to Frankenstein, the students found him a highly stimulating scientific counselor when they were planning a piece of research, and, though he was known to make heavy demands on them, they felt he had more empathy with his students than did either Wertheimer or Köhler. Too independent in his thinking to become anyone else's disciple, Lewin still seemed to Frankenstein, and some of his friends, to be a "Wertheimer man"—

an analysis which Frankenstein now feels was inaccurate but which was probably based on Lewin's feeling of deference toward his senior and better-known colleagues.

The German university system did not set a rigid schedule of course requirements, examinations, and deadlines for papers and theses, so there was always plenty of time for discussion and—in a more or less continuous seminar—students reported on their current work-in-progress. From 1924 on, Lewin was looking after as many as twelve to fifteen doctoral candidates at different stages of progress toward their degrees. Also, those working with Wertheimer and Köhler often joined the Lewin group's dialogue. Everyone participated, talking about one another's projects and offering suggestions for change.

The students held regular meetings every Saturday morning. Before long this came to be the talk of the Institute, because of the novelty of Lewin's ideas, his highly charged way of presenting them, and his willingness to debate them in order to spark a formulation of still better ones. "The interaction between Lewin and this group of students was so free, and the disagreement so intense," said Norman Maier, "that I remember them as the most stimulating experiences I have ever had. Historical approaches to psychological problems were swept aside. It seemed as if all questions were being attacked from scratch. . . . These were creative discussions during which ideas and theories were generated, explored, and controverted. I'm sure that Lewin owes much to his students in working through the theories he himself finally reached."

Among Lewin's students were two young Japanese—Kanae Sakuma and U. Onoshima. He became especially friendly with Sakuma, with whom he published a paper in 1925 (in the *Psychologishe Forschung*) on the effect of moving goal objects toward and away from children. Sakuma and Onoshima had left Japan in 1923 to study psychology in Germany. With several other Japanese students they visited a number of German university centers for research in psychology—Gottingen, Halle, Wurzburg, Leipzig, Marburg, and Frankfurt—before settling at the Psychological Institute in Berlin. There the new director, Wolfgang Köhler, had agreed to let them attend lectures, take part in seminars, and carry out their own research projects. Sakuma and Onoshima had considerable difficulty in following the new material in a strange language and asked Köhler to have a member of his staff assigned to them as a kind of mentor and counselor. Lewin, who was assigned the task, entered into it with his customary enthusiasm, setting up ten special lectures to brief the young Japanese and demonstrating a number of experiments for them. "It was under Lewin's friendly guidance," Sakuma recalls, "that I was able to understand the brilliant insights of Gestalt psychology and appreciate the broad theoretical development of Gestalt theory." Lewin also took Sakuma rowing on the Wannsee, brought him along to Chaliapin concerts and Max Reinhardt theatrical productions, had him for dinner in his own house, and generally sought to make the young Oriental feel at home.

After about a year in Berlin, Sakuma felt sufficiently at home to start wondering what the rest of Europe looked like. He made a quick decision to leave the Institute and move to Paris. As a farewell souvenir, Lewin gave him an etching by Hodler showing a woodcutter chopping down a tree with an ax. The scene was symbolic of Sakuma's abrupt termination of his studies, Lewin told him with regret. In October 1925, Sakuma returned to Japan and at once busied himself with setting up a Psychological Institute at Kyushu University modeled after the one in Berlin. It was to this center of Gestalt psychology in Japan that Sakuma invited Lewin when Kurt stopped off in Japan on his way home to Berlin from California in 1933.

Never a clockwatcher, Lewin might inadvertently bring one or several students home with him in the afternoon, hold them over at dinner, and keep them occupied past midnight. Or, on occasion, he sat in his office with one or more students, analyzing some psychological phenomenon or planning an experiment; suddenly realizing that he was hungry, he would find, on looking at his watch, that it was nine o'clock and would invite whoever was with him to join him for dinner in a restaurant or at his home. Wherever it might be, though, the meal blended into conversations that went on long into the night.

Doris Twitchell (later Allen) was especially fortunate in that she was invited to live in Lewin's home so that she could tutor him in English in preparation for lectures he planned to deliver in the United States. She had come to Berlin after she had received her Ph.D. at the University of Michigan. She recalls, "I read an article by J. F. Brown regarding Lewin's work and I read of Kurt's differentiation between phenotypical and genotypical behavior. This had particular meaning to me as a person who had majored in chemistry and moved from there into biology, and from there into psychology. I began to realize that I was interested in the total behavior of a person in varied situations and that I undoubtedly would find laboratory work in regard to nerve impulses limiting. I therefore made a basic decision in regard to my future by going to Berlin to work with a person who I thought could probe with depth into the determinants of human behavior." She remembers that while she was in Lewin's home he was invited rather frequently to give talks before professional groups. "I particularly recall how impressed I was with the respect that the members of the Mathematical Society of Berlin extended to him on his presentation of hodological space. One or more of the students of the Institute usually went along for these talks, as an extension of studying with him in the regular psychology courses."

Within the Institute, Lewin's students formed a close-knit group which inevitably gave rise to another informal association. This one was called the *Quasselstrippe*. Maria Ovsiankina defines the word thus: "In German, *quassel* means to ramble on; *strippe* is a string. So the *Quasselstrippe* was a group with whom you could just get together and talk freely." The *Quasselstrippe* usually met at the Schwedische Cafe across the Schlossplatz from the Institute.

Donald Adams has recalled his part in these freewheeling groups: "On a particular day the group might range in number from four or five to as many—though rarely—as ten. It's literally true that at the end of one of these discussions, which might go on for two, three, or even more hours, often with shifting membership as people came and went, no one could say who was the source of a given idea, even of a very productive and ultimately influential one. The discussion might take off from a more or less casual question or notion, be changed over in this corner, qualified in that, reoriented in another, and catch fire in still another. Then someone might see a possibility of broader application or relevance to problems not under discussion so far—and after more tinkering and batting about, it might emerge as something only remotely related to the remark that had set off the whole *causerie* in the first place—but of real importance. Kurt was right in imputing creativity to the collective. . . . There was no doubt in anyone's mind that Lewin was the indispensable member. He neither dominated nor overwhelmed, but his willingness to grant an enthusiastic hearing to even the most adventurous speculation supplied the ferment that made each participant rise above himself."

The people who attended these sessions seem to agree that they were free and easy, with plenty of opportunity—indeed, encouragement—to express different (and differing) opinions. Lewin never imposed either discipline or loyalty on his students and colleagues—unlike Freud, who demanded fealty from all who sat with him in Vienna's Cafe Arkadan, and Adler, who held court in the Cafe Siller in Vienna and banished all who did not demonstrate their allegiance.

MacKinnon recalls that the students would sit around in the cafe and talk over their problems: "As is the custom in European cafes, you have a cup of coffee and talk and chat, then you order a piece of cake, more time goes by, some more cake, another cup of coffee, a process that may go on for two or three hours. On one such occasion, somebody called for the bill and the waiter knew just what everyone had ordered. Although he hadn't kept a written reckoning, he presented an exact tally to everyone when the bill was called for. About a half hour later Lewin called the waiter over and asked him to write the check again. The waiter was indignant. 'I don't know any longer what you people ordered,' he said. 'You paid your bill.' In psychological terms, this indicated that a tension system had been building up in the waiter as we were ordering and that upon payment of the bill the tension system was discharged. This approach intrigued me, because it was what I had been saying, that a lot of important problems had to be approached through observations of behavior of everyday life and that our task was to translate these into some kind of language and method that would bring them into the laboratory and permit some quantification of the phenomena in question."

This informal experiment led to Zeigarnik's famous study of the tension system, published in 1927 and completed under Lewin's supervision (see page 42). It was an obvious example of how sparks set off by Lewin in the cafe were often used in the laboratory by his students. The cafe, too, was part of Lewin's "life space." As in this instance, it was the scene of impromptu experiments based on the here and now of actual experience, of the posing and explorations of immediate and new questions.

CHAPTER

4

TENSION SYSTEMS
AND
FIELD THEORY

Lewin's evolving view of the human psyche was in sharp contrast to that held by most American and German psychologists of his time. The academically accepted psychology was still largely introspective; psychophysical methods were employed almost exclusively; problems of personality and motivation were largely ignored. Real-life problems were the exclusive concern of the psychoanalysts. However inadequate one might judge their methods to be, the Freudians at least dealt with vital, everyday issues that affected people. In his involvement with the dynamics of human motivation, Lewin demonstrated that problems which psychoanalysts had thought were outside the province of the experimental could be brought into the laboratory.

Prior to the 1920's, too, most psychologists busied themselves chiefly with laboratory experiments that were more or less unrelated to one another and consisted largely of collecting facts which were then further analyzed into their smaller components. As a result, experimenters often approached complex behavior problems with an oversimplified view of human conduct.

Lewin was highly critical of this approach. Psychologists, he insisted, should conduct their research within the framework of a theoretical system. Without *theory* it was impossible for any science to progress. The fruitfulness of theory lies in the unknown facts and relations it envisions, which can then be studied or observed under experimental conditions. Theory, Lewin held, should fulfill two main functions: first, it should account for what is known; second, it should point the way to new knowledge. Experiments should therefore be undertaken with the purpose of testing theoretical concepts, instead of merely collecting and analyzing elemental facts or classifying behavior statistically.

He ascribed this attitude toward science to Ernest Cassirer, who, Lewin felt, was the first to perceive that "the basic character of science is the eternal attempt to go beyond what is regarded as scientifically accessible at any specific time." For Lewin this meant a search for multidimensional theoretical concepts broad enough to encompass all the various psychological processes and all branches of psychology. He embarked on this quest for a theory that would permit the formulation of psychological laws in the fields of needs, will, and emotion. Some basic concepts had already been developed in the realm of perception and memory, but his fellow psychologists had made little progress in learning how to understand and predict such inner determinants of individual behavior as motivation, aspiration, or intention. Explaining human happenings, Lewin believed, called first of all for a more scientific knowledge of the source of their energies. The traditional explanations of their sources, such as "association," "instinct," or "libido," he found inadequate.

Slowly over the years Lewin evolved his conceptual system based on the "person" as a complex energy field in which all behavior could be conceived of as a change in some state of a field during a given unit of time. He postulated a theory of psychological tensions in which tensions function as a form of energetics. The term "tension" is popularly used to connote undesirable strain or stress, but this is not what Lewin meant by it. He referred rather to a highly desirable state, which is valuable for increasing a person's efforts toward the achievement of his goal. Lewin held that tensions arise when there is a need or want. It is their striving for discharge that supplies the energy for, and is consequently the cause of, all mental activity. The forces which Lewin postulated are in the psychic field, not the physical. Thus, to understand or predict behavior, one must deal with psychic tensions operating in a psychic field.

Again, the word "tension" as used by Lewin means a state of readiness or a preparation for action. For every mental event, the question arises, "Where do the causative energies originate?" Lewin suggested that the source of energy is not to be found in the stimulus or in the momentary perception. These may function to direct or control the energy resulting from the tension, but the energy which sustains a given psychic sequence does not derive from the perceptual process.

The stimulus, however, may cause any one of the following: (a) The development of a tension which did not previously exist. Psychologically, this manifests itself as an intention or desire which had not been present before. (b) The attachment of an already existing tension (due possibly to a need, purpose, or half-finished activity) to a specific object in such a way that this tension system gains control over the motor system. Such an object would then possess a "valence," which would function as a field force guiding and steering mental processes and behavior. The stimulus itself has no fixed valence. It may be positive on one occasion and negative on another, depending most directly on the momentary state of the needs of the person. (c) The reduction of tension to a lower level when satiation processes occur or the desired goals are achieved.

Lewin offered as an illustration the example of a child at play who suddenly discovers a ball at the bottom of a hole too deep for him to reach. The perception of the ball creates a tension with a positive valence. The behavior of the child becomes limited to such actions as may bring his attainment of the ball nearer. He makes numerous attempts to reach it. Unsuccessful, he obtains a long stick but still cannot get the ball out of the hole. Finally, he calls to an adult, who recovers it for him. The goal reached, the child's tension is released. He perceives some other toy, and the process starts over again. The totality of the field forces resulting from the positive and negative valences of the objects in the field, exerting influences of an attractive or repulsive nature, steer the child's behavior to particular goals. Some of the objects in the field may act as barriers; they compel a "detour" and cause a seeking for attainment in some other direction. But once a goal has been achieved, there is a lessening of the tension and a re-establishment of equilibrium.

Lewin's concept of "tension" was not consonant with the then popular association theory, which Lewin judged inadequate. It maintained that the performance of an act should strengthen the tendency to repeat it. When, however, on seeing a mailbox, one fulfills his intention to put a letter in it, there is no tendency to repeat the act of depositing the letter when another mailbox is encountered. The association theory simply does not apply in this illustration and in various other circumstances, and we must look for another explanation.

In Lewin's postulate, the existing tension, set up by the purpose of mailing the letter, was a causal factor that led to depositing the letter. The perception of the first mailbox set up an external field force and steered the individual to the posting of the letter. With the posting, the tension was released. In the absence of this necessary energetic factor, the passing of other mailboxes, or even the same one at a later time, evokes no impulse toward repetition. Or if, after writing the letter, one has given it to someone else to send off, there is again no impulse upon seeing the mailbox to drop the letter in it, since the tensions which are essential determinants of the action have already been discharged.

Thus Lewin developed a number of theoretical assumptions by equating the "release of tension" to a "satisfaction of a need," and the "setting up of tension" to an "intention." The sources of the energy of tension are to be found in a person's genuine needs and quasi-needs. The genuine needs are more fundamental and are due to an inner state, generally physiological, such as hunger or thirst. The quasi-needs are those involving a purpose or intention, such as completing a task, keeping an appointment, or wanting to eat in a particular restaurant. The quasi-needs occur much more frequently than the genuine and are much less stable. With them, *substitute* satisfactions may re-establish equilibrium more readily than when the tensions are genuine needs.

Whether or not there are physiological correlates was immaterial in Lewin's view. It was not necessary to delay psychological experimentation until science arrived at a better knowledge of the nervous system. The important dynamic concepts were *energy, tension, need, valence,* and *vector* (force).

Qualitatively, the tension back of the quasi-need is identical with that behind a genuine need. In the same way, the fulfillment of either need leads to the release of the tension and the restoration of equilibrium. There is relative isolation between tense psychical systems. Each such system tends as a whole toward regaining its own state of equilibrium, although partial processes may at the same time proceed in opposite directions.

Commonly, there exists a certain firmness or rigidity of boundaries in each system, so that it is possible for each to persist in its state of directed tension over long periods, relatively uninfluenced by other systems and influencing these other systems only slightly. This is especially true in adults, in whom many separate tension systems generally exist, each requiring its specific mode of discharge before equilibrium is reattained and each, at most, only incompletely affected by the discharge of other coexistent tension systems. It is these isolated tension systems, persisting for longer or shorter periods, that form a person's reservoir of total energy for action. A partially finished activity, for example, may remain as a relatively independent tension system for a protracted period of time though without apparent awareness of it. Yet if the appropriate situation should arise, the tension would strongly reassert itself.

Lewin was not concerned with describing the many kinds of needs that might exist in a person's psychological reality. To him a need existed only when it upset equilibrium. Being thirsty or hot becomes motivational only at the moment when it is disturbing a person's inner state. Relief from the disturbance comes with action which serves to bring the disturbed person within reach of an object that can satisfy his need.

33

Not until five or more years after his 1917 paper criticizing associationism did Lewin's "field theory" evolve further. With it came the highly unorthodox representation of psychological relations by means of topological and vector concepts. When asked what he hoped to accomplish by this theory, Lewin responded that he believed that only a field theory could adequately explain behavior in the realms of action, emotion, and personality.

Field theory had evolved in the physical sciences fifty years earlier. Physicists had led in developing it there, after many became suspicious of the method of analyzing phenomena into component parts and then into irreducible elements. In their view, a new concept was necessary to account for what occurs when a number of forces interact. This kind of explanation necessitated a change from thinking in terms of particles to thinking in terms of fields of energy in which forces are spread and which operate within a matrix. The Gestalt psychologists in the early 1920's had already begun to view perceptual responses as distributions of energy in which similar field principles were operative. Lewin broadened their concept to include all the psychological activity in which the person is confronted with psychological motion toward goals within defined regions of life space.

Field theory postulates that a person's behavior is derived from a totality of coexisting facts. The multitude of data from any event provides a dynamic "field" in which all facts are interdependent with all others.

Behavior, as Lewin emphasized so often, is a function of the person and his environment. Both person and environment are interdependent variables. Lewin, thinking in mathematical terms, converted his statement into the formula, $B = f(p, e)$—that is, behavior is the function of person and environment. This formula is now accepted everywhere.

According to Lewin, behavior of every kind—including wishing, thinking, achieving, striving—is the product of a field of interdependent variables, a result of change in some state of a field in a given unit of time. The field with which the psychologist must deal, Lewin terms "life space." For each individual, the life space consists of the needs of the person and his psychological environment. All psychological events occur within the life space; or, stated somewhat differently, the "life space is the total psychological environment which the person experiences subjectively."

Life space includes all facts which have existence for the person and excludes those which do not. It embraces needs, goals, unconscious influences, memories, beliefs, events of a political, economic, and social nature, and anything else that might have direct effect on behavior. The various factors in a given life space are to some degree interdependent, and Lewin strongly maintains that only the dynamic concepts of tension and force can deal with these sets of interdependent facts. This is what led him to define psychological needs as tension systems and their topological representation as vectors to denote motion.

According to Lewin's field-theory concepts, behavior depends neither on the past nor on the future, but on the present field in the "here and now." The present field has a certain time depth that includes both the reality and unreality level of the psychological past (as postulated by the associationists and the psychoanalysts), and the hopes for the psychological future that are defined by expectations, wishes, and dreams. Although these constitute part of the dimensions of the life space existing at a given time, it is on the psychological present that behavior chiefly depends. Lewin recognized that this theory varied widely from the historic belief of some psychologists that a future goal guides present behavior and from the claim of classic associationism that the past influences present behavior.

Lewin illustrates the need for mathematical representation by a reference to the novelist who, in telling his story, analyzes the personality and behavior of each of his characters. The author gives detailed information about relevant relationships with parents and friends, together with vital data about education, occupation, aspiration, and habits. He places all these data before the reader in their specific interrelations so that he may realize each person as part of a total situation. However, Lewin says, such descriptive terms are often vague and words are ambiguous and easily misunderstood. It is necessary for the psychologist, therefore, in his descriptions of conduct—as well as of the interdependent determinants of behavior —to express them by a mathematical system that represents the spatial relations of the psychological forces. If such everyday terms as "friendship," "moods," "goals," "will power" are to be used, they should be represented by geometric space concepts. He believed that the dynamic interplay of the multitude of coexisting parts of any social matrix, their positions relative to each other and to the surroundings which set off behavior, could be scientifically expressed only by some branch of mathematics that dealt with relations in space. A form of geometry, Lewin believed, offered possibilities. But what kind, he wondered, was best suited to express the spatial relations of psychological data?

In physics, Euclidian geometry had been replaced by Riemannian geometry. For psychology, Lewin found that another geometry would be suitable. This is known as "topology." Lewin felt sure that it could meet the need. "If one used the terms of everyday language, such as frustration, need, anger, learning, without being able to co-ordinate mathematical entities to them, one might as well use the normal form of reasoning," said Lewin. "But this could never be as valuable as a mathematical logical language." Topology, a nonquantitative geometry, he believed could be adapted to handling problems of structure and position in a psychological field. It could make possible a representation of the structural relations within the person's own psyche as well as in his psychological environment. It could be used to represent positions inside or outside a given region, to show the relations between a whole or its parts and a great number of other structural characteristics.

Topology now became a hallmark of Lewin's thinking. He made it his means of more precisely representing the total structure and the manifold dynamic factors existing in a psychological field. His later papers were filled with topological representations of psychological events. His diagrammatic method turned out to be well suited both to the description and analysis of events in sequence and to the representation of real-life activities such as goal-seeking and problem-solving.

36

Lewin was excited by the ideas that sprang from his observations of behavior of everyday life. Every psychologist's task, he thought, was somehow to state those observations of human conduct in a precise, mathematical language suitable to a method by which the observer could bring them into the laboratory and reliably measure them.

Because he was philosophically sophisticated, and had a strong sense of the history of his science, Lewin was little influenced by such trends of this period as operationalism, neo-positivism, and Hullian theory. To develop his divergent perspective was no small achievement, for it required a confidence in his ideas of the history of science which few other contemporary students of the subject possessed. Moreover, Lewin's grounding in the philosophy of science made it possible for him to recognize the fundamental role of phenomenology, or immediate perception, in all of science. This enabled him, as Donald Adams points out, to recognize clearly that the beginning of scientific inquiry and the ultimate test of its outcome was *somebody's experience*, and that this called for the conception of a dynamic quite independent of the physical one.

Various critics have commented that Lewin really did not use much more than some of topology's basic notions. Yet, in the view of many who worked with him, the use of these elementary concepts was highly productive. Indeed, Fritz Heider believes that Lewin's insistence that science creates a language in which everything can be precisely expressed is one of his most significant contributions to psychology. "If you want to express an idea clearly in topological terms," Heider has said, "you have to know what you are talking about. Otherwise you get into trouble. This sort of topology, then, is not just theory. It is a kind of language, something that helps represent psychological relationships."

Norman Maier, who worked with Lewin in Berlin, has commented: "I often felt that field theory was the product of communications by means of drawings, and it just so happened that each of the disciples seemed to think in terms of drawings. The drawings convinced me that Lewin and his students were trying to communicate concepts that were entirely new, and they suggested the need

37

to explore forces that went beyond psychological processes, as encompassed by the schools of functional psychology and behaviorism then in vogue. I believe that my own development of the concept of direction in problem solving may have originated in these graphic discussions with Lewin's group of students." Maier found that he could convey to others—as he never could to Köhler or Wertheimer—the validity of the notion that "problem solving, which involved the new combination of parts of isolated experience, required a dynamic selective mechanism (direction) which was set in motion by the problem situation."

Donald MacKinnon has written that "Lewin's topological and vector psychology, despite a common misunderstanding, has been developed, not as another school of psychology, but rather as a psychological language generally understandable and independent of schools, in terms of which the experimental and clinical findings of psychologists of quite different theoretical persuasions may be expressed. Lewin has explicitly stated that in developing topological and vector concepts in psychology he has sought to do no more than to describe 'a tool,' a set of concepts by means of which one can represent psychological reality. Whether all psychological problems will be illuminated if subjected to topological and vector analysis may well be questioned. But that a certain range of problems has already been fruitfully investigated by means of this conceptual tool is attested by the experimental work of Lewin and his co-workers."

Lewin maintained that applications of field theory were possible in all branches of psychology. He viewed the life space as the psychologist's universe. In it, person and environment are interrelated and individual behavior is always derived from the relation of the concrete individual to the concrete situation. Behavior, therefore, is a function of the life space: $B = f\ (LS)$, which in turn is a product of the interaction between the person, P, and his environment, E. Lewin proceeded to conceptualize through topology the life space or psychological field. To represent the separation of the person from the rest of the world, he used a "Jordan curve," an irregular closed curving line that the Berlin students called little "eggs." The size of the Jordan curve did not matter, nor did the exact shape. The principal characteristic was the spatial representation: everything inside the figure was the person and the totality of possible facts which are capable of determining the behavior of an individual.

Non-Psychological (*E (P) E*) Non-Psychological

(P + E = Life Space, *L)*

Thus the total space within the Jordan curve, including the ellipse, is the life space. It represents the person and the psychological environment. The space outside represents the non-psychological world —of either physical or social facts. The Jordan curve, Lewin pointed out, is a conceptual representation of reality which can serve as a map to guide the psychologist.

CHAPTER
5
THE EXPERIMENTS

Lewin's "major revolution in psychological research" consisted of a series of nearly twenty empirical studies done by his students, mostly as doctoral dissertations. They were theory-oriented and dealt with personality structure and the psychological environment. All were published as articles in the *Psychologische Forschung*, the journal of experimental psychology launched at the University of Berlin.

Lewin did not generally employ the apparatus that other psychologists were so fond of using in their experiments. Although he loved to tinker with complicated equipment and was considered one of the best laboratory technicians at the Institute, Lewin himself used a minimum of apparatus. For most of the *Forschung* experiments conducted by his students, pencil, paper, and a simple game or task were enough.

Lewin never told his students, that he had a system of this or that sort, Tamara Dembo reports. "Rather he would say, 'These are only the beginning concepts; we will have to find out more about them. We cannot do this yet; this is possible to do,' and so on. What he tried to do was conceptualize phenomena and connect them with other facts. He never produced a theory and then looked for facts to fit it. However, if you asked him, 'How can one do this topologically?' he would reply, 'What's the problem? Let's first look at the problem and see whether any of this is possible.' Those were the terms he thought in."

Lewin's fresh insights as a psychologist also stemmed from having the skills and competence of a clinician. MacKinnon feels that Lewin possessed "more critical insights, more depth psychologically than most psychoanalysts. You couldn't discuss any psychological problem with him without his immediately seeing it in some fresh perspective and putting it in a new light, which always included putting it down on paper, drawing circles, Jordan curves, vectors, and whatnots representing the life space of the individual. Putting it down on paper this way, topologically, was now one of Lewin's hallmarks. He recognized that psychology would extend to all sorts of human relations insofar as they could be dealt with experimentally. He believed that this would require the kind of language that could signify all manner of problems which earlier would have been deemed quite impossible to express. He was confident that it was not necessary to re-create the same intensities in the laboratory that obtain outside it, but what *was* necessary was to set up the same dynamic system. What he worked out, in following these insights, furthered the development of experimental psychodynamics."

Lewin hoped by means of these empirical studies to account for behavior as a function of the total psychological field. What he planned to do was to set up experiments in fields that had been believed psychologically unapproachable—experiments to investigate the meaning of success and failure, of reality and unreality, of the motivation of anger. These had, of course, to include studies of environment, its topology and dynamics, and its relation to psychological satiation, the levels of aspiration, substitution, and conflict. The conceptual tools were available, he believed, to measure the direction and strength of psychological forces.

It was Lewin's earliest pupils—Zeigarnik, Ovsiankina, Mahler, Dembo, and a handful of others—who in their pioneer studies charted what had been the no man's land of psychology. The series of studies, rated as among the most distinguished group of empirical inquiries in the history of psychology, can be grouped under the headings of (1) Recall of Unfinished Tasks, (2) Level of Aspiration, (3) Substitution, (4) Satiation, (5) Anger. In terms of Lewin's postulates they can be treated as coming under one heading and shaping into one design.

The Experiments—Theory and Purpose

The first published experiment [1]—and one of the most influential, in that a number of the subsequent studies were variations of the initial experiment—was done by Bluma Zeigarnik. A classic among Gestalt experiments, it was described by Lewin as "an attempt to break a first path through a forest of facts and assumptions using concepts that were still untested." The basis of Zeigarnik's study was an effort to test Lewin's theory that the desire or intention to carry out a specific task corresponds to the building of a system of psychological "tension" and that the need to release this tension serves to sustain goal-directed activity until the intended task is carried out. Dynamically, Lewin theorized, this means that the system created by the unfulfilled goal continues to make its influence felt in thought or action (or both) as long as the tension is not yet discharged by completion of the activity. Zeigarnik sought to discover whether the "quasi-need" (the impulse to release the tension) functions only to accomplish the intention or whether it influences other aspects of behavior, such as memory. She designed her study so that the expression of an intention would be found in the desire to finish interrupted tasks and the effect of the quasi-need would be seen in the tendency to remember unfinished activities more readily than completed ones.

Zeigarnik's findings offered the first laboratory confirmation of Lewin's theory of systems in tension, and particularly the idea that the decisive factor in the release of this tension is the reaching of a goal. The phenomenon revealed in this experiment—the preferential recall of uncompleted tasks—has become part of the language of psychology and is known as the "Zeigarnik effect." It is relevant not only to Lewin's assumptions about systems in tension but also to the Freudian thesis that wishes persist until they are satisfied and that slips of the tongue, dreams, and similar behavior are manifestations of the system in tension seeking discharge.

[1] A more complete summary of the procedures and results of the Berlin experiments will be found in Appendix B, pages 244 ff.

Bluma Zeigarnik carried out her experiment from 1924 to 1926. Her findings were published in the *Psychologische Forschung* in 1927. Several years later she returned to Moscow with her husband. She has continued teaching and doing research as a member of the faculty of the University of Moscow. (In 1966, at the International Congress of Psychology in Moscow, Bluma Zeigarnik held a re-union with Tamara Dembo and Maria Ovsiankina, her fellow students under Lewin four decades earlier.)

Following closely on Zeigarnik's work on the anatomy of goal tensions were the experiments of Maria Ovsiankina, another of Lewin's young woman students from Russia. Where Zeigarnik tested the recall of interrupted tasks, Ovsiankina sought to measure the spontaneous resumption of tasks after they had been interrupted. Her findings that interrupted tasks were almost always resumed offered further confirmation of Lewin's postulate that there is a direct correlation between the release of a tension and the satisfaction of a need.

Still another implication of the tension-system theory was explored by Vera Mahler. She sought to determine whether substitute actions might release the tensions arising from the interruption of assigned tasks, and if so, what the relative effectiveness was of various kinds of substitute actions, such as talking or thinking about the activity. The phenomenon of substitution (or "sublimation") had been used extensively by Freud to explain behavior. Under Lewin's direction, Mahler began to investigate the dynamics of such substitution. How did substitute actions originate? What did substitute satisfaction mean? Which substitute activities led to satisfaction, and under what conditions? Fräulein Mahler's conclusions on the substitute value of any particular action in terms of its relation to the inner goal of the original activity served to refine further Lewin's idea of tension systems and goal achievement.

Along the lines of Mahler's study of substitute value, Sarah Sliosberg gave herself the task of investigating the relationship between reality and need satisfaction in the life of a child. In an experiment on the dynamics of play, Fräulein Sliosberg asked the question: Does a child accept as a substitute an object which is functionally different from the original but which is suitable to represent it in play? Her conclusions shed new light on the differing psychological responses of younger versus older children and of the different effects of real-life versus play situations.

Yet another variation in the study of tension systems was worked out by Gita Birenbaum, who sought to identify the factors that determined whether an intention, once formed, is either carried out or forgotten. Birenbaum anticipated some of these influences, among them the nature and emotional tone of the person forming the intention, the nature of the intention itself, and the connection between the intention and other intentions in the subject's life. What she sought to measure was the strength of these influences in terms of the individual's overall psychic activity.

Lewin's theory of the role of goal achievements in the release of tensions raised a series of questions about goal setting. What are some of the factors that go into the decision to attempt a difficult goal or try for an easier success at a lower level? What are the reactions to success or failure in reaching the goal decided upon? The first experiments in this area were done by Ferdinand Hoppe and published in the *Psychologische Forschung* in 1930. Hoppe's subject was "level of aspiration," a phrase originally coined by Tamara Dembo to mean "the degree of difficulty of the goal toward which a person is striving." (Thus, the more difficult the goal, the higher the level of aspiration.) Hoppe aimed to investigate the factors which influence goal-setting behavior by measuring the effect of success or failure on the individual's decision to raise or lower his aspiration level.

Hoppe's pioneering work had major practical as well as experimental significance. Before this study little had been known about the everyday problems a person faces when trying to decide which goals to seek. More than any of the other areas explored by Lewin's students, Hoppe's experiment touched off a veritable chain reaction of additional studies.

One of the first was by another of Lewin's Berlin students, Sara Jucknat, who sought confirmation of Hoppe's findings with a larger group of subjects. (Hoppe had worked with only 10 subjects;

44

Jucknat studied 650 children and 52 adults.) Her conclusions bore
out Hoppe's findings on the factors that influence the choice of a
difficult or easy goal, with the further refinement that the *kind* of
success experienced also affected the aspiration level.

The work of Lewin's students in the uncharted area of level of
aspiration was an early indication of the implications of Lewinian
theory for social phenomena. Morton Deutsch has pointed out that
the factors that determine level of aspiration provide new insight
into the reasons for social apathy in the face of pressing political and
international problems. "People are not likely to attempt to seek
even highly valued objectives when they see no way of attaining
them," Deutsch has written. Similarly, he adds, level of aspiration
"sheds some light upon why social revolutions tend to occur only
after there has been a slight improvement in the situation of the
oppressed groups; the improvement raises their level of aspiration,
making goals which were once viewed as unattainable now perceived as realistic possibilities."

Another major area of pioneering psychological research launched
by Lewin's students at Berlin was that of emotion. Tamara
Dembo chose anger for her experiment. She began her *Forschung*
article by pointing out that the emotions—although one of the most
vital of all areas of human concern—had been relatively unexplored,
whereas perception had been exhaustively studied since the turn of
the century. Even Freudian theory—the most important movement
toward the psychology of affect with non-experimental methods—
was still dominated by the principles and practices of association
psychology.

Dembo devoted special attention to the genesis of anger and to
why it was that frustrations in achieving one's aim or purpose
caused anger in some instances but not in others. Her point of departure was Lewin's postulate that behavior is determined by the
structure and state of the person in his life space and by the psychological environment at that particular moment. In a series of experiments remarkable in their originality (and their ability to provoke
her subjects' anger), Dembo showed that the emotional effect of a
felt need depended on the intensity (as opposed to the importance)

45

of that need. Thus, a person engaged in a triviality could react violently to frustration because—in this field and at this moment—trivial objects had received special significance. She demonstrated that a barrier which frustrated a person's attempt to reach a goal led to anger only if the person was surrounded by an outer barrier that prevented him from leaving the field.

Another of Lewin's students, Anitra Karsten, studied still another emotional phenomenon: satiation. In an ingenious experiment, Karsten showed how repetitions of the same activity can cause the subject to reach the point of refusing to continue (psychic satiation) irrespective of fatigue or other physical factors. Karsten linked these findings to a lowering of the tension level after numerous repetitions, thus explaining why mere repetition, if carried on long enough, can have a harmful effect on learning. Practice, Karsten's study implied, does not necessarily make perfect.

A variation on Karsten's satiation study was undertaken by Alex Freund, who sought to measure the effect of menstruation on the speed of satiation. Freund's study, which found that during menstruation psychological satiation occurred 26 to 30 per cent faster than at other times, further confirmed Lewin's view that, in general, the speed with which any activity is satiated increases with the degree to which the activity is psychologically central. (During menstruation, Freund postulated, all activities tend to be central.) This theory would also provide the reason why satiation occurs sooner in younger children than in older ones. "Children are likely to be involved in activity with their whole person," said Lewin, "and the velocity of satiation is therefore much greater."

For several more years new studies came in succession, each seeking additional evidence of the theory of a system in tension. Sara Fajans examined the effect of the distance between a child and an attractive object (such as a rattle or a doll) and the strength of the attraction in determining the direction of the child's behavior in reaching the toy. Fajans recognized that the *strength* of a valence might depend on a number of things—the kind and quality of a particular object, the state of the individual's need (is he hungry? satiated? oversatiated?), the presence of other objects with a posi-

46

tive or negative valence, and the direction of the object in question from the person. But her study revealed that the distance from an attractive object was so important as to determine a change in the children's behavior.

Lewin was content to let his students who were preparing for the doctorate follow their own bent in the design and conduct of their experiments. They could range over all the aspects of psychic behavior rather than being limited to the traditional laboratory subjects of perception and memory. Lewin believed that the real significance of an experimental finding lay in the contribution it made toward defining a general principle of universal application. In determining the general validity of a law, he wrote in 1931, "reference to the totality of the whole concrete situation must replace our reference to the greatest possible historical collection of frequent repetitions."

CHAPTER

GROWING RENOWN

Lewin's study of human behavior was never separated from his philosophical consideration of method, especially the role of experience in method. What should authentic science do? he asked. Which way should it face, in the light of the past and the present? Dorwin Cartwright, in reviewing Lewin's thought, recently pointed out that, from the very beginning, Lewin sought to discern clearly what the formal properties of a developed human science must be. Lewin, Cartwright says, held to this aim all his life and thereby infused his work with a developmental continuity that, manifold and diverse as is its content, nonetheless achieves unity.

Lewin's ideas and performance became better known to psychologists in the English-speaking world through articles by J. F. Brown, one of the first Americans to study with him in Berlin. Brown's paper, "The Methods of Kurt Lewin—A Study of Action and Affect," was published in *The Psychological Review* in 1929, shortly before the meeting of the International Congress of Psychologists at Yale. It provided the first evaluation in English of Lewin's general contribution to psychology and brought him a number of new American students.

Brown set the work of Lewin and his group in a perspective that could not be gained alone from Lewin's own writings and the scattered reports of his group's experimental investigation then appear-

48

ing in the *Psychologische Forschung*. "Lewin has done something that will tend to clarify our heterogeneous science," Brown wrote. "Like all pioneers, his work, rather than to dictate finished laws, has been to indicate directions and open up new paths of experimentation from which the laws must eventually come. The experimental situations chosen make use of total acts. Rather than validity through repetition, Lewin stresses validity through careful control and variations."

Brown observed that American psychologists might at first be dubious. They might ask, "Where are the absolute psychological laws of which Lewin has made so much? " "Such a criticism would mean a complete misunderstanding of Lewin's attitude," Brown wrote. "He was not yet able to set up his laws, but was simply in a position to show the material from which they must eventually come. That is, he had shown that any law must be a genotypic description of behavior, that the associationists and the behaviorists had confused the genotypic and the phenotypic. He was able logically to prove the existence of tensions, to measure them roughly and to indicate that dynamic laws must be in terms of energy exchanges and field equations. His most important contribution was methodological rather than factual."

Brown's article served as a helpful background for Lewin's appearance at the Yale meeting of the International Congress of Psychology. Lewin had accepted the invitation to read a paper and had also brought along a short motion picture he had made of an eighteen-month-old child—his wife's niece Hannah—trying to sit on a stone. It was something she had never done before, and her attempts ably illustrated some of Lewin's novel concepts.

Hannah was not sure that if she took her eyes off the stone she would be able to hit the right spot when she sat down. In order to sit she was going to have to turn her back on the stone; but in trying to do this without taking her eyes off it, she circled it many times. Sometimes a distraction would occur, and she would deviate from her little orbit. Her difficulties on her way to her goal were many and varied, but finally, with obvious satisfaction, she reached it by putting her head between her legs and backing over to the stone.

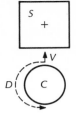

Lewin pointed out that, in order to achieve her goal, the young child had to turn around; but if she did, her movement had to take a direction opposite to the field force. The positive valence toward the stone was so strong that it was difficult for the child to move in a direction contrary to the field force. So she made energetic but unsuccessful movements toward the valence. As a child of only eighteen months, she could not yet restructure the field so that she could perceive a general movement *away* from the goal as merely the first phase of a general movement *toward* the goal.

"The direction of the field forces," Lewin said, "plays an important part in intelligent behavior that has to do with detour problems." Little Hannah's difficulties resulted not from the length of the detour but from confusion caused by the circumstance that the initial direction of the appropriate route did not agree with that of the vector of the valence. The more the barrier made it necessary for Hannah to detour by starting off in a direction opposite to the direction of the valence, the more difficult the detour would be.

By means of the film, Lewin also made clear what he meant by forces in a field. Little Hannah had passed the stone many times before without wanting to sit on it. When she finally did want to, it wasn't because of the stone but because she was tired. The audience was greatly impressed. "This ingenious film," said Gordon Allport, "was decisive in forcing some American psychologists to revise their own theories of the nature of intelligent behavior and of learning."

With his appearance at the Yale meeting, the impact of Brown's articles, and the early *Forschung* series of reports, Lewin became a world figure in psychology. Among those who read one of Brown's papers in 1929 was Donald MacKinnon, then at Harvard. Intrigued, he went to hear Lewin talk at Yale. They did not meet at that time, but, having heard Lewin speak and having seen his film, MacKinnon said later, "He was a genius at being able to follow children around with his camera and get bits of behavior to illustrate the principles he was already developing. And he came across as a terribly exciting man—excited about what he was doing and about the presentation."

Maria Ovsiankina could have attested to this, too. She had been responsible in Berlin for the processing of the film clips that Lewin was constantly making. On one occasion, at the end of a busy day, she finally cornered the tireless professor to show him the latest batch. "There's nothing much here," she told him, but Lewin's comments on the films brought forth a wealth of new material. Maria Ovsiankina and her fellow students in the projection room were astonished at how much he had perceived that was new.

To many other American workers in the field whom he met at Yale in 1929, Lewin was also impressive because he was propounding a new psychology. Most psychologists had accepted the traditional notion of the hierarchy of the sciences—the idea that you could *describe* psychological phenomena with psychological concepts but that, if you wanted to *explain* them, you had to go down the hierarchy of the sciences to something more basic. Thus, psychological phenomena such as perception and behavior were to be explained in terms of physiological and neurological concepts, although this seemed to diminish, if not nullify, psychology itself as a science. What Lewin proposed to do—and indeed was doing—was to assert that psychological concepts could be scientifically accounted for, as well as described, in purely psychological terms.

He was extraordinarily expressive: this was part of his charm, the reason he stirred people so much. MacKinnon was "not sure how much of his talk the Yale audience understood, for Lewin spoke in German and few of his hearers had much fluency in that language; but if you just took the man and his behavior—the way in which he was acting—it was quite clear that he was an original—an exciting psychologist and a dynamic person to work with."

MacKinnon recalls that "as an undergraduate at Bowdoin I thought I wanted to be a psychologist and took first-year psychology. I was so disgusted with it that I said, 'If this is psychology, I want nothing to do with it.' It didn't tell me anything about human nature, motivation, character, or personality. I majored in history; it turned out later that Harry Murray had done so too. He also had wanted to be a psychologist but majored in history. We both finally ended up in psychology. When I was approaching graduation, I found that if I went to the library I could find some very exciting things in psychology which I hadn't gotten in the course at all —MacDougall, Freud, Jung, and others—and at the last minute decided to be a psychologist. At Harvard, where I began my graduate work, the really acceptable psychology was still largely introspective, using psychophysical methods and again having very little to do with human nature or problems of personality and motivation. Then Harry Murray arrived on the scene and he was someone that I could talk to about the problems and who in turn would stimulate me.

"My feeling at the time was exactly the same as that of J. F. Brown, namely, that in the late 1920's psychology seemed to have experimental methods but they used these methods on absolutely unimportant, insignificant problems. Psychoanalysts were dealing with real problems—a very large number of them the most important psychological problems—but their methods were highly defective or not adequate. And so very early I got the idea that what I would like to do would be to bring these two together and try to develop some bridge between experimental psychology as the thing existed and psychoanalysis—the different schools of psychoanalysis. And when I first heard about Lewin I was very excited because it seemed to me that he was already doing it, although he was not at this time concerned with psychoanalysis but he *was* concerned with dynamic problems of human motivation."

In 1930, MacKinnon was offered a traveling fellowship by Harvard. "I had no question as to where I would go," he says. When he arrived in Berlin, he discovered that Lewin had not learned any more English than had been at his command in New Haven. Because MacKinnon's German was limited, he arranged for Maria Ovsiankina to serve as interpreter and intermediary.

But the language barrier was only one stumbling block. Lewin's idiosyncratic way of working was another. MacKinnon remembers having arranged to meet him at a *Konditorei* near the Institute at five o'clock one autumn afternoon: "Finally, Lewin showed up three hours late, breathless and full of apologies. He had just come from working up a new experiment in a local prison, where he had gotten so absorbed that he simply forgot about the appointment. When he did finally remember our date he couldn't leave his experiment, until he had worked it out. I learned during the year I worked with him that this was nothing unusual; he would sometimes never show up at all for appointments he had made with some of his students. At all events, when he and I finally settled down at our table in the *Konditorei* and I told him what I wanted to do, everything was fine.

"What I hoped to demonstrate in the laboratory with some kind of quantification was that experiences which stir guilt presumably activate early associations and impulses that had been associated with the guilt and had undergone repression. When I got to Berlin this was what I proposed to work on with Kurt. I found at once an openmindedness and a reaction of great excitement that his methods could be used to effect some kind of a bridge between experimental psychology and psychoanalysis. Moreover, he was tremendously generous of his time, busy as he always was."

MacKinnon was the first American who had come to Berlin saying, "I want to work with *you*, Kurt Lewin," but of course several other Americans had preceded him. Besides J. F. Brown, who had been at Berlin two years when he wrote his article, both Karl Zener and Donald Adams had come earlier, originally to study with others. Like Brown, they had stayed on and grown deeply interested in Lewin's work.

The appearance of Brown's articles also stimulated Jerome Frank to come from Harvard, where he had just finished his undergraduate work in psychology. Frank was particularly attracted by Lewin's ability to pinpoint important problems of human functioning and reduce them to an experimental level. "I was rapidly welcomed into Lewin's inner circle," he relates, "even though I was only a graduate student." He was especially grateful for Lewin's democratic informality, which was unlike that of most other German teachers: "Each new idea or problem seemed to arouse him, and he was able to share his feeling with colleagues and juniors. He had the energy to think at a high level continuously for many hours, or struggle with a difficult problem even while he had a bad headache. Seminars were held in his home, and it was hard to distinguish the influence of his ideas from the influence of his personality.

"Because Lewin could be critical without hurting, he stimulated creativity in all those about him. You could get into tremendous battles with him over ideas, and he would never hesitate to show you where he believed you were wrong. But neither was there ever the slightest hint of any personal feeling about it, and if you came up with a good idea a minute later, he'd be as pleased over it as you were. He seemed to enjoy all kinds of human beings and, open and free as he was, shared his ideas immediately—even if they were half formed—eager for comments and reactions while the original idea was still being developed."

During his years at the Psychological Institute in Berlin, Lewin had founded a whole new way of studying human beings—in his demonstration of the extent to which perception and memory depended on motivation, by his stress on seeking the causes for behavior, by using the past as a way of understanding some of the factors present in current interactions rather than as the primary causes of behavior, and by his insistence that complex problems of human interactions could be put in some kind of experimental framework.

In 1927, he was appointed *Ausserordentlicher nicht beamteter Professor* (associate professor without civil service rank), essentially an honorary promotion. This rank, which did not carry tenure, was as high as most Jews could go in the Prussian academic hierarchy, though it is possible that, had the Nazis not risen to power, Lewin might have been offered a "chair" of psychology at a university in one of the other more liberal German states. The promotion to *Ausserordentlicher Professor* was, however, a meaningful acknowledgement to Lewin of the value of his work.

Though he was not one to dwell on the barriers to attaining a higher rank, it did bother him, nevertheless. Doris Twitchell Allen, who was living at the Lewin home at the time, remembers that he

54

occasionally expressed unhappiness at his lack of a permanent appointment, and she feels that he enjoyed a sort of wry satisfaction when, on being invited to teach for a semester at Stanford University, he was designated as "Visiting Professor." That at least coincided with the estimate of many of his prominent colleagues who hailed him as a "rare intellectual leader."

Meanwhile there were problems in Lewin's home life that were becoming increasingly difficult to resolve. His son, Fritz, had developed very slowly during his first year. When he seemed unable to walk at the expected time, the physician discovered that both hipbones were dislocated. He had evidently been born with this handicap. Walking would therefore be impossible until the disability was remedied. When the child was strong enough, major surgery was performed on the hipbone on one side, and after a long convalescence a similar surgical procedure was done on the other hipbone.

The bones mended very slowly and the sick child required constant care. To help the youngster move around, Lewin designed and built a special wagon in which the child could push himself in the house and garden. But raising an ailing youngster created stresses in the little daughter as well as the parents. The atmosphere in the home was tense and troubled. While both Kurt and Maria were deeply devoted to the children, they could not agree on the best ways to cope with the special difficulties that had developed. Maria was especially upset by Kurt's frequent absences from home and his erratic schedules. This made the situation worse even though he apparently spent considerable time with the children. As domestic strains became more pressing, Lewin felt that divorce was the only solution. He moved out of the home and Maria and the children continued to live there. He visited them frequently until the family moved to Palestine when Nazism took over Germany. In 1929 Kurt remarried. His new wife was the former Gertrud Weiss, a friend whom he and Maria had known since 1921. He later arranged to build a new home in Schlachtensee, a Berlin suburb.

Not long after he returned from the International Congress at Yale, Lewin read a paper before the Kant Gesellschaft in Berlin on the transition from an Aristotelian to a Galileian concept formation

55

in psychology. He was anxious to have it translated into English for publication in Murchison's *Psychologies of 1930* [1] and asked Köhler to speak to Donald Adams, who was fairly familiar with German, about translating it into English.

Adams had first heard of Lewin from Karl Zener and Junius Brown when they had dined at Adams' home in New Haven in 1927. They were both excited about him and his work. Adams was able to see and hear Lewin for the first time at the Ninth International Congress at New Haven in September 1929. A few weeks later, Adams met Lewin in Berlin, where he had gone on a National Research Council fellowship to work with Köhler.

"Lewin would like to ask a favor of you, but is too shy," Köhler told Adams.

"I had heard the paper and had been interested in it," says Adams. "After expressing misgivings appropriate to the primitive state of my mastery of German, I undertook the job with the understanding that Kurt Koffka, then at Smith, would review my translation before it was sent to Murchison."

It was already 1930, late for Murchison's deadline, and the translation went slowly. "Anyone who has read much of Lewin's earlier writings in German will be aware of his tendency to coin neologisms, much as Edward Tolman did in English, and some of these gave me great difficulty. *Anspruchsniveau* was not one; it translated simply and literately as 'level of aspiration,' but others were not so simple. Of the tough ones, I remember particularly *Aufforderungscharakter*. This had been translated by J. F. Brown in his 1929 article as 'invitational character.' That is literal enough but hardly seemed appropriate to a feature of the psychological environment that could be either positive or negative and that varied with the tension in the 'psychical system' related to the object concerned.

"I'd been struggling with this problem for a month or so without perceptible progress when Wolfgang Metzger and his wife gave a party for the Institute one Sunday evening at their home on the

[1] The article, entitled "The Transition of the Aristotelian Mode of Thought to the Galileian Mode of Thought in Psychology and Biology," did not appear in the Murchison volume; it was published instead, under a slightly different title, in the *Journal of Genetic Psychology* in 1931.

Muggelsee, one of the Havel lakes southeast of Berlin. On the way back that night, while strap-hanging on the crowded Stadtbahn, it suddenly occurred to me, as in what Lewin called an 'A-ha! experience,' that there was once a meaning of the English word 'valence,' long before its appropriation by chemistry, that might do the job. So the first thing next morning I went to the Prussian State Library on the Unter den Linden Strasse, not far from the Institute, and looked it up in the Oxford English Dictionary. I was wrong about 'valence,' but 'valent' (1765) as a substantive was defined as 'value or worth.' And the first meaning of 'valency,' dating from 1623, was given as 'might, power, strength'; the fourth meaning (1897) was given as 'importance, significance.' Out of an old aversion to excess syllables, I dropped the 'y' and translated *Aufforderungs-charakter* as 'valence.'

"Unfortunately, between my tardiness in completing the job and my correspondence with Koffka, we missed the deadline for *Psychologies of 1930*. It may have been Koffka who noted the near identity of 'valence' with Tolman's concept of 'demand value' and arranged with him to join in using 'valence.' At all events, it has been generally adopted and now appears in Webster III, where it is defined (2b)—although only in the positive sense—as 'the degree of attractiveness an individual, activity, or object possesses as a behavioral goal.' It has also displaced *Aufforderungscharakter* in German, which now uses the word *Valenz*."

In his article on the transition from the Aristotelian mode of thought to the Galileian, Lewin proposed answers to such questions as: Is it possible to determine general laws in psychology and undertake precise experiments to reveal emotional life? Doesn't psychology deal with individuals who differ so much from one another that it is impossible to find laws of general validity applicable to each individual? Is it possible to study and explain inner emotional processes in the same kind of quantitative and objective way that physics has done?

Lewin answered again that, for one thing, a great many similar cases were *not* needed in order to find general laws. On the contrary, a psychologist should instead study the single concrete case and determine its nature according to both its external appearance (phenotype) and its genetic-conditional nature (genotype). Lewin based this conclusion on what he considered to be the fundamental change that had taken place in scientific thinking and conceptualizing ever since Galileo had made his crucial break from Aristotle.

Instead of Aristotle's static concept of contrasting pairs of phenomena—good-bad, black-white—in which each member of the pair is in an area of value alien to that of the other member, Galileo had introduced the dynamic concept of sequence, in which the two contrasting parts of a pair belong to a unified area or continuum within which they form two extreme ends. In Aristotelian terms, black and white belong to one pair of concepts, but each color exists in its own area only, separate from and alien to the area of the opposite color. In Galileian terms, black and white belong to the same sequence as parts of the same continuum—extreme ends of an uninterrupted sequence in a continuous transition without boundaries between its various separate components.

Psychology, too, Lewin wrote, must use the dynamic concept of sequence instead of the static concept of pairs. The transition from the Aristotelian mode of thought to the Galileian also changed the criteria which determined whether a given phenomenon represented a scientific law or was only accidental. Aristotle's criterion of scientific law was the predictable and orderly repetition of the same phenomenon: only a great number of cases established laws. It was necessary, then, for a scientific investigation to study as many similar cases as possible in order to establish laws of general validity.

But Galileo's criteria for validity were altogether different. For him, the single case was just as valid as the law of the free fall in a vacuum, a scientifically acceptable phenomenon which does not exist at all in real life. It was not important in modern physics whether a given process occurred once or twice, frequently or permanently: historic frequency was not at all decisive in determining the "lawfulness" of a phenomenon.

Psychology could and must adopt the Galileian mode, Lewin wrote. It must move from the average of many cases to the single case. But, he pointed out, the single case was valid only if it were grasped in its totality; that is, only if both the total concrete situation and its specific properties were understood. The concrete single case had to be described, then, in its phenotypical and its genotypical aspects. It was not the frequency of a case's occurrence that was decisive, but the exact description of *all* the forces operating in and upon it at a given moment, including the inner forces (needs) as well as the external ones (environment).

This assumption led Lewin to another: That the behavior of a person can be predicted—but only if his *total* psychological field or life space at a given moment is known. And it is more useful to know a single concrete case in its totality than to know many cases in only one or a few of their aspects. For, in the latter instance, both the wholeness of the person and the potential wholeness of the psychological field are overlooked.

This original article on Aristotelian versus Galileian mode of thought captured the imagination of psychologists in all parts of the world and contributed greatly to Lewin's growing reputation. Many of his innumerable friends of later years first became aware of his work through this essay. Claude Faucheux, an eminent psychologist at the Sorbonne in Paris, recently commented that this article continues to this day to be a major influence in French psychology.

Environmental Forces in Child Behavior and Development

In addition to the Galileo article, Lewin had requested Donald Adams to translate another paper he had written, "Environmental Forces in Child Behavior and Development." It was published in 1931 in the *Handbook of Child Psychology*, edited by Carl Murchison. In this theoretical paper Lewin analyzed the shortcomings of the conventional method of measuring child behavior and suggested a dramatically new approach, based on the findings of his students' experimental work.

He began by challenging some of the statistical approaches then widely used to define the psychological environment of the child. He questioned the value of such approaches as, for example, that in which the school records of the oldest, middle, and youngest child in a family of three children are compared and conclusions drawn about the "average oldest" and the like. He argued that defining behavior on the basis of such extrinsic characteristics as the number of siblings, their position in the family, or the age of the parents—rather than the actual situation in which the child finds himself—was an error, since specific individuals have quite different psychological characteristics. Thus the calculation of an "average" one-year-old child was designed to eliminate such accidents of the environment as being an only child. Such "facts," Lewin said, rarely offer more than hints about the *forces* of the environment. Not to consider the really significant factors in a situation was, he felt, wrong. "For the very relation that is most decisive for the investigation of the individual child in the individual situation is thereby abstracted." The "average" child and the "average" situation were, to Lewin, mere formulations, of no use in the investigation of social dynamics.

In Lewin's view, the study of environmental factors had to start from a consideration of what he called "the total situation." He denied the possibility of an "average" environment, for the same environment may assume a different quality depending on a number of characteristics, all of which affect the immediate circumstances surrounding the child.

Lewin then stated his own theoretical position. The life space of an infant, for example, is extremely small and undifferentiated, in both the perceptual and the effective sense. As the child grows older, however, his life space is gradually extended. The environment becomes differentiated, and facts that formerly were unnoted acquire psychological existence. More and more, as the child becomes aware of things around him, he seeks to control them; at the same time, he learns that he is becoming increasingly dependent upon a growing circle of environmental events. If a doll is broken a few feet away from a six-month-old baby, Lewin pointed out by way of illustration, there is not likely to be any reaction. Doing the same thing in front of a three-year-old, however, will usually evoke a violent response.

"Such social facts as friendship with another child, dependence upon an adult, and so on, must also be regarded from the dynamic point of view as no less real than this or that physical fact," Lewin continued. He called attention to the frequency with which identical physical objects assume very different meanings for children of the same age—or even for the same child in different situations. Thus a wooden cube might at one time be a missile and at another a building block or a locomotive. The significance of any physical object at any time would depend both upon the total situation and upon the momentary condition of the child involved; and this would be equally true for the social factors.

Lewin drew a distinction between "quasi-physical" objects (a table, a bed, a knife or fork) and objects of a "quasi-social" nature—dogs, friends, "grownups," neighbors. "All of these are defined for the child partly by their appearance, but above all by their functional possibilities. A flight of steps, for example, is something that one could (or could not yet) go up and down, or something that one climbed yesterday for the first time. Thus history, as the child experiences it, is also a psychologically essential constituent of the things of the environment."

Despite this, he added, certain critical properties of the psychical environment remain undescribed. "To the child, objects and events are not neutral; rather, they have an immediate psychological effect on behavior. Some might attract the child to eating; others to climbing, to grasping, to manipulation, to sucking, to raging at them, and so on." This "imperative environmental fact" which, Lewin held, determined the "direction" of behavior, he called the *Auforderungscharakter*—the term which Adams translated as "valence." "In the context of dynamics," Lewin wrote, "these valences, their kind, strength, and distribution, must be regarded as among the most important properties of the environment." Furthermore, he noted, these valences change—not only with the varied needs of increasing age but also with the momentary state of the child. When a child's need for nourishment, for playing with a doll, or for reading a story is in a "hungry" or unsatisfied condition, a cookie, a doll, or a picture book will attract him—that is, the object will have a positive valence. On the other hand, when this need has been satisfied, the child will be indifferent to the objects. Indeed, they could acquire a negative valence and be regarded as disagreeable if the child is in a state of "oversatiation."

Lewin suggested that distance or direction is not the same in the psychological field as in the physical. This is more apparent in older than in younger children. Thus, when a child fetches a tool or appeals to the experimenter for help, it does not mean—even when it involves physical movement in a direction opposite to the goal—a turning away from it, but is, rather, an approach to it. Such indirect approaches, particularly of movement in a direction opposite to the goal, are, however, exceedingly rare among very young children. As the child grows older, temporally distant events also become more significant. To the psychological situation now belong not only those facts that are "objectively" present but also many past and future events. This explains why "a censure or a commendation might remain a present physical fact for the child over a long period, and an expected event could acquire psychological reality long before it happens."

Lewin then discussed the behavior of a child in three basic "conflict" situations. He defined conflict psychologically as the opposition of approximately equally strong field forces. In the first conflict situation, the child stands between two positive valences—for example, staying home to play with a friend or going to the zoo to see the animals. The decision is a relatively easy one to make.

In the second conflict situation, the decision becomes more difficult because the conflict is between a positive and a negative valence of equal strength. He may want to go into the ocean but is afraid of the waves. In this situation the decision depends on the increasing strength of the negative vectors. The child may turn away and withdraw or choose what seems like the less unpleasant alternative.

In the third conflict situation, the child stands between two negative valences, as when he must perform a task—for example, practice the piano (which he wants to avoid)—or face punishment for failing to do it (which he doesn't want). In this type of situation an "escape" from the conflicting valences is sometimes possible by going out of the field. The child will always try this maneuver if he is not prevented from doing so. Thus, the behavior can be limited only if escape is not possible and the choice is restricted to performing the unattractive task or accepting the punishment. It is therefore necessary, says Lewin, to limit the child's freedom of movement, thus creating (by physical or social means) a more or less constrained situation.

Lewin next put forward his view that a change of environment may have great significance for a child's development. He pointed out that the operation of the environment always produces a change in the individual himself and thus changes his basis of reaction to all later situations.

Finally, Lewin discussed what he terms the circular causal relation between self and environment. A feebleminded child, for exampel, is at a disadvantage among other children in two ways. In the first place he finds it difficult to perform the tasks that they are capable of—for example, adding numbers, keeping score, etc. There is a second difficulty that creates even more problems. When the intelligent child is given a task, he is likely to look for the least difficult solution. The child of below normal intelligence is less likely to discover the easiest solution. Thus, not only is the intellectually subnormal child less able, but the actual demands made upon him by problems are frequently greater than those made upon the intelligent child faced with the same problems.

The publication of Lewin's paper on environmental forces in child behavior brought him increased attention among psychologists. It dramatized the fact that his influence was no longer limited to those students who came to Berlin to study at the Institute, and pointed up his growing reputation as a brilliant thinker and original experimenter.

CHAPTER

7

LAST DAYS AT THE BERLIN INSTITUTE

During this period the work of the Psychological Institute was at its crest. Then danger signals appeared. As the 1930's opened, Europe's economic prosperity began to fade. The Wall Street crash of 1929 dried up American investment. Amid the bitter grumblers and scapegoat-seekers, reinforced by the economic distress of the country, Hitler and his party gained the political strength to take over the German government.

On the day in 1930 when the new Reichstag met, a Nazi delegation of 107 marched to the meeting in their brown uniforms, shouting in chorus, "Germany awake! Jews get out!" They smashed the shopwindows of Jewish-owned department stores on the Leipzigerstrasse. Three Nazi-inspired riots broke out at the University. The rioters demanded: *"Juden heraus!"* and one Jewish student was murdered. The University was closed three times; but most of the faculty, though troubled by what they saw and heard, continued to feel that the situation was temporary, that Nazism was a passing madness and that "it couldn't happen here." Still, it was unsettling, and the Lewins, who saw more clearly than some of their friends what might happen, were apprehensive. And then, of course, it did happen.

64

About this time, and by happy coincidence, Kurt received an invitation to spend six months as a visiting professor at Stanford University in Palo Alto, California. The bid came from Lewis M. Terman, Chairman of the Psychology Department at Stanford, who had asked Edwin G. Boring, Director of the Psychological Laboratory at Harvard, to recommend a distinguished visiting scholar with a broad background. Boring had heard Lewin at the International Meeting at Yale in 1929 and suggested that Lewin was the best man. Lewin welcomed the invitation and decided to accept.

In May 1932, Kurt arrived in New York, where he stopped for a few days en route to California. Gerti and their year-old daughter, Miriam, went ahead by boat through the Panama Canal. As a guest at the Columbia University Faculty Club, Lewin was introduced to a young assistant professor of psychology, Gardner Murphy, who subsequently became a good friend. Murphy remembers being introduced to a "slender, rosy-cheeked, eager, thoughtful young man," who, in his rather broken English, spoke earnestly of the political happenings in the Germany he had just left. Then Lewin went on to describe experiments he had been conducting at the Psychological Institute. He projected an interest in his subject that was warm and intense. Murphy was fascinated; he hurried home to look up Lewin's recently published article on the environmental forces in child behavior and development.

Shortly after reaching Stanford, Kurt was asked to deliver a paper before a meeting of the Western Psychological Association. According to Roger Barker, Terman was considerably worried for fear Lewin couldn't speak English. "And, as I soon learned, rightly so. He couldn't. I know *now* what the paper was about," says Barker, who, as a doctoral student in psychology at Stanford, attended the meeting. "But at the time I hadn't the faintest idea—partly because of his language, and partly because his ideas were so entirely foreign." Lewin discussed the subject of "substitute play"—that is, activities that serve as substitutes for uncompleted tasks. But since none of his hearers was familiar with his experiments with uncompleted tasks, nobody understood what he was saying.

In his classes, however, Lewin was able to get across to his stu-

65

dents, some of whom began to get an inkling of his theme. "He was a great communicator," observes Barker's wife, Louise. "He could gesture and he was so eager to tell you what he was trying to say that you just had to understand, and so you did."

One of Lewin's students that summer was Pauline Sears (Mrs. Robert Sears), who enrolled in Lewin's class at Terman's suggestion. She does not recall having too much trouble with Lewin's English, but she did have difficulty in understanding his ideas about topology and in following his diagrams—a new experience for her. "His English wasn't terribly good," she remembers, "but he was a stimulating personality, vital in his gestures, and he had brought with him marvelous motion pictures." Years later, in 1938, Lewin invited Robert Sears—who had done work in level of aspiration at Illinois—to a meeting of the Topological Society at Cornell. Sears and Neil Miller, who went with him, were the only non-Lewinians there. Both Robert Sears and Roger Barker recall one phrase from Lewin's then limited stock of English which delighted his classes and stayed in his students' memories. Someone challenged Lewin on a point, and he retorted, "Can be, but I sink absolute ozzer." The remark became a kind of slogan among Lewin's increasingly numerous friends and supporters.

For one thing, the German professor was a natural democrat, something his students were quick to appreciate. Barker remembers Lewin's lying down on a table in a classroom one afternoon. "I guess it was a long day, so he just lay down but kept the class going—certainly an un-German thing to do. Yet, despite his popularity, his ideas were so new—so startling, really, and so far beyond any of us at the time—that he really didn't have much impact on his students or even his fellow faculty members. Lewin had a background in philosophy and he had his own theory of science. None of us were equipped to follow him because we lacked his background. So we listened but did not fully understand or appreciate the originality of his ideas and the scope of his theory."

Lewin's appointment at Stanford ended with the beginning of the spring semester. Early in January 1933, Gertrud, who was expecting a second child, had set out across the United States with Miriam to return to Germany by ship. Kurt had decided to return by way of the Pacific, so that he could make stops in Japan and Russia, where he had been invited to lecture. Leaving Japan, he would proceed by way of the Trans-Siberian Railroad across the U.S.S.R. to Moscow and continue later by train to Berlin.

At Yokohama, Lewin was met by his student of a decade earlier, Professor Kanae Sakuma, who had modeled the Psychological Institute at Kyushu University upon the Institute in Berlin. Lewin's reputation had preceded him to Japan, and there was a lively discussion following his lectures and the showing of his famous movie of Hannah learning how to sit on a stone. Lewin was delighted to discover that a number of young scholars in Tokyo had formed a group to study his work, which they called the "Lewin-Klasse"—a group largely responsible for Lewin's influence on Japanese psychology.

He had an intense discussion with Professor Koreshige Masuda of Tokyo University, who expressed some serious doubt about the merits of Lewin's topological psychology. It was typical of Lewin's approach to a problem that, several days later while on a train from Tokyo to Kansar, he worked out a diagram that he felt would dispel Professor Masuda's reservations and asked Professor Sakuma to show it to him.

Meantime, little Miriam became ill en route to New York, and Gertrud had to delay their sailing. They were house guests of Fritz and Grace Heider in Northampton, Massachusetts, on January 30, when word came that Hitler had become Chancellor of Germany. Kurt heard the news just before he began his long train journey across Siberia, but, as he could not read the Japanese newspapers, he did not grasp the full impact of the event. Only after he reached Moscow, where his friends Bluma Zeigarnik and the distinguished Russian psychologist A. R. Luria were able to discuss it with him in German, did he fully realize what had happened.

By this time Lewin had concluded that he could not remain in Berlin. He foresaw then that no Jew and no man concerned with the spirit of free inquiry could live in Nazi Germany. He cabled

Fritz Heider at Smith College and Donald MacKinnon at Harvard: GERTILAND IMPOSSIBLE. DO YOU KNOW OF A JOB?

Gertrud and Miriam had arrived back in Germany in April, about a month before Kurt himself returned. The Nazi grip was already tightening. She and the little girl went to Gertrud's mother in her home town of Sagan, and Gertrud sought to engage the non-Jewish obstetrician in Berlin who had delivered Miriam. The doctor was disturbed that she had come to him—German medical men were no longer supposed to treat Jewish women—but he did deliver the Lewins' newest child, Daniel. Gertrud saw more of what was happening in Germany. A Jewish physician in Sagan had the temerity to contradict a Nazi bully in the street. He was beaten so terribly that he died of heart failure a few days later.

Gertrud was at the railroad station in Sagan to meet Kurt on his return in May 1933. There he told her of his decision not to stay in Germany any longer. He said he would not teach at any university where his own child could not be a student. Shortly thereafter, he formally resigned from the University of Berlin and was proud ever after that he had not waited to be ousted.

Gertrud gave birth to Daniel in July and slowly recovered her full strength. One Sunday morning as she and Kurt talked of their hopes of getting to America and how difficult the life of a mere immigrant might be as compared with that of a visiting professor, the maid brought them a cable from Dean Robert Ogden of Cornell University: CORNELL INVITES YOU TO JOIN THE FACULTY. Lewin was elated, but there was so little time and so much to be done before the arrangements for the family exodus could be completed that it was decided that Kurt should go ahead without Gertrud and the children. He left Germany in August 1933, never to return.

The great days of the Berlin Institute had come to an obscene end; its "extension," the Lewin home, would no longer belong to them. The cafes, so often the scenes of brilliant intellectual debate, had become the hangouts of the toughs of the Nazi *Schutzstaffel*—the so-called Elite Corps. The Nazis took over the Institute in 1935. Though Köhler could have kept his professorship, he resigned in the summer of 1935 and accepted an appointment at Swarthmore

College. He was the last of the big four to leave. Max Wertheimer was at the New School for Social Research, Koffka at Smith College, and Lewin by then was moving to Iowa.

En route to the United States, Lewin stopped at the University of Cambridge in England, as the guest of Sir Frederick Bartlett, the distinguished British psychologist. The visit remains particularly vivid in the memory of Eric Trist, later of London's Tavistock Institute, who was then a student of Bartlett's at Cambridge. Trist had come across Lewin's article on Aristotelian and Galileian modes of thought in 1932 while studying psychology at Cambridge. "I read it almost by accident," he says, "while browsing through some psychological journals in the Cambridge library. It was a revelation. When I returned to the department, Professor Bartlett asked me, 'What happened to you?' My eyes were evidently sparkling. I told him about this extraordinary paper. My interest in and debt to Lewin began from that moment."

A year later, when Lewin visited Professor Bartlett at Cambridge, Eric Trist was one of those whom Bartlett invited to tea.

Trist vividly remembers Lewin gesticulating and talking excitedly about topological psychology. Trist got the feeling then that Lewin "had a sense of musical delight in ideas." He was reminded of Coleridge and thought that Lewin was like him in that he too was a poet with a brilliant imagination. Trist added, "I always look at books like *Topological Psychology* and the ideas of vectors and hodological space as the first drawings for a Michelangelo picture—the sketches being the design of a theory."

The conversation at tea and during the visit to the centuries-old college was so vigorous that Lewin barely made his train to London for the connection with the boat-train to Southampton. Trist recalls pushing Lewin into the compartment as the train was moving.

Lewin's ideas had a powerful effect on British psychology and resulted in considerable Lewinian influence during World War II and in the decade that followed.

PART II

The American Years

CHAPTER

THE BEGINNINGS
OF A NEW LIFE

In the fall of 1933, Kurt Lewin began a new life in a strange land—not as a visiting professor, but as a refugee scholar with a temporary appointment supported by Foundation funds. His new country was experiencing the worst economic depression of its history, its people struggling with an economy of scarcity that suffused all of American life. Some fifteen million men, more than a quarter of the work force, were without jobs. Soup kitchens, bread lines, men selling apples on street corners—these characterized the scene in 1933. There were fewer students in the nation's colleges, faculties were reduced, salaries slashed. Scholars fortunate enough to hold faculty appointments—and Americans who were seeking them—were not enthusiastic about the competition for jobs by foreign refugee scholars. Lewin had sensed this when he was visiting professor at Stanford in 1932; he was very much more aware of it when he came back to the United States.

Rensis Likert remembers meeting Lewin for the first time in 1933 at a luncheon in New York City with Douglas Fryer of New York University. Lewin had stopped in New York for a few days on his way to Cornell. "His forecast of developments in Nazi Germany was depressing—but accurate," Likert recalls. Among other things, Lewin expressed the view that the German people would neither overthrow nor replace Hitler. Only a major war and a German defeat, Lewin said in 1933, could result in Hitler's removal as dictator of Germany.

The invitation to Cornell was in good part the work of Dr. Ethel Waring of the School of Home Economics there. A specialist in child development, she had first met Lewin in 1929 at the Psychological Institute in Berlin, where she had been particularly impressed by his motion-picture studies of children. On her return to Ithaca, she became a missionary for Lewin's experimental techniques and theoretical concepts. On many occasions she urged Dean Robert Ogden to find a way to invite Lewin to Cornell. The critical political situation in Germany caused her to redouble her efforts. She pressed Ogden to find a place for him in Ithaca—and then find the money for it.

The Cornell appointment was for two years only. It was made possible by a grant from the Emergency Committee on Displaced Scholars, then under the chairmanship of Lawrence K. Frank. It carried an annual salary of about $3,000 and could not be renewed. Nor was the appointment to the Cornell Psychology Department; it was, rather, in the School of Home Economics.

Once established at Cornell, Lewin set to work on a systematic series of studies of the effect of social pressure on the eating habits of children in the Cornell Nursery School. Tamara Dembo and Jerome Frank, pupils of his in Berlin, soon joined him in Ithaca and began research on related projects.

Of the years at Cornell, Tamara Dembo has observed that, "while the atmosphere at Iowa in later years was in many ways as exciting as Berlin, Cornell wasn't." Perhaps the difference was due to their unfamiliar location in the School of Home Economics, a radical change from the Faculty of Philosophy at Berlin. Nevertheless, Dembo believed, the groundwork was laid here for some of Lewin's later consequential experiments. "At the nursery school there were problems created by children who were poor eaters, and the question came up of how the teacher could change their eating habits. This was a problem involving social pressure from the teacher. Although the area of social relationships wasn't yet central to Lewin's work, it was at least already peripheral at Cornell."

Lewin's two years in Ithaca were busy ones. He concentrated on the work at the Nursery School; he drafted plans for the Psychological Institute he hoped to get established at the Hebrew University in Jerusalem; he worked doggedly at readying for publication some of the records of the research he had conducted in Berlin. Aware of the academic "publish or perish" atmosphere of America, he decided that he must get his earlier work into print as soon as practicable. Of the numerous papers he had written in Germany, few had appeared in English, and his mastery of the language of his new country was too imperfect for him to attempt the translation on his own. But he had devoted friends and students who quickly rallied to help him.

A few of his most important articles were assembled and translated by Donald K. Adams and Karl E. Zener, both members of the psychology faculty of Duke University. These were published by McGraw-Hill in 1935 under the title *A Dynamic Theory of Personality*. When Fritz and Grace Heider undertook to translate into English Lewin's book-length manuscript *Principles of Topological Psychology* (eventually published by McGraw-Hill in 1936), the Heiders and the Lewins arranged to spend the summers of 1934 and 1935 together. They boarded with a farm family in Milford, New York, about midway between Ithaca and Northampton, Massachusetts, where the Heiders had been living. For a study, they set up a tent in the back yard.

Lewin dedicated the book to the Hebrew University in Jerusalem but prefaced it with a letter to Wolfgang Köhler, his colleague and friend at Berlin, who had shown himself a courageous opponent to Hitler and vigorously resisted Nazi efforts to impose restrictions against Jewish students and faculty members at the Institute. The families were friendly, even close at times. When Köhler had visited America in 1932 to deliver a series of lectures, Gerti Lewin had taken the Köhlers' daughter Karen into her own home for three months while Frau Köhler accompanied her husband. At that time Köhler had spoken with Dean Ogden of Cornell about Lewin, thus playing a key role in Lewin's invitation to Cornell.

Köhler was one of the Christian academicians and scientists who left Hitler's Germany. But in the United States he and Lewin grew apart, though Lewin always retained enormous respect and admiration for Köhler. The physical distance between them—Lewin at Cornell, Köhler at Swarthmore—ended the close association of Berlin. There were other changes as well. In America, Lewin was no longer Köhler's junior, either in prestige or importance. Indeed, Lewin was gathering a following of his own as he developed his own concepts and methods and opened up new areas of study and research. His work challenged the Gestalt school in some areas and went beyond it in others.

A year earlier, in his first book, *A Dynamic Theory of Personality*, Lewin had expressed his appreciation of the teaching of Wertheimer and the collaboration of Köhler. "I need not emphasize my debts to these outstanding personalities," he had written. "The fundamental ideas of Gestalt theory are the foundation of all our investigations in the field of the will, of affect, and of the personality."

Lewin's open letter to Köhler in his preface to his second book, *Principles of Topological Psychology*, thus marked both a farewell to the past and a forward look to the future. The letter is a reasoned and reasonable statement in which Lewin strikes out on his own, charting his own path in psychology while acknowledging his debt to his former colleague. He recalls the "collective of friends" who worked together during the "happy and lively" days in Berlin, and he closes with a statement of affection and respect for the friend from whom he must now take leave, voicing the hope that the book might "prove to be somewhat worthy of the spirit of this collective and of the leading influence you have had on each of its steps. For the friends scattered throughout the world, this feeling of cooperation seems to continue and the circle steadily to widen. I would enjoy nothing more than to have contributed to this broad cooperation." Turning then from past to future, Lewin dedicated his book "to a young scientific center at the meeting of the East and West (the Hebrew University in Jerusalem), where I hope new productive collectives will arise."

But if the letter to Köhler was a reasonable statement, it may also have been, Grace Heider believes, a little self-conscious. Lewin may have been aware that his decision to deal entirely with the psychological life space and to disregard the physiological level could be seen as a heresy and could therefore be a source of tension between him and Köhler. To others, the publication of *Principles of Topological Psychology* somehow formalized Lewin's action in leaving the "present" group of Gestaltists behind and setting boldly out on his own path. And so, even while striking out on his own, Lewin expressed his continuing identification with the Berlin "collective," acknowledging that he had "always found myself unable to think productively as a single person."

That Lewin hoped to remain in personal and professional touch with Köhler was made clear in the very next sentence: "Those who are acquainted with you know that you are not interested in 'psychological schools,' and one of the main incentives of this book is to help develop a psychological language generally understandable and independent of schools." That this turned out to be true was pleasing to Lewin. His personal and professional friendship with Köhler remained warm during the remaining years of his life.

The manuscript of *Principles of Topological Psychology*, written in German, was never published in that language. But the Heiders completed their labors in time for the book to be published in English in 1936. It was a comprehensive and systematic statement of Lewin's psychology. In it Lewin comments that too little experimental work had been done on the psychology of will, of needs, and of personality. The few experiments that had been reported he found artificial and abstract. He challenged the view held by many psychologists that these processes were too elusive and complex for scientific experiments. He explained his admiration for the pioneering work of Freud, but he criticized the findings of psychoanalysts as unscientific since they were based entirely on case studies and therapeutic work. Such derivations he considered methodologically unsound.

Lewin stressed again his conviction that "psychology" must develop concepts that are equally applicable to the facts of child psychology, animal psychology, or psychopathology; to problems of the infant, the adolescent, or the aged; to personality and environment. "We cannot unify the different fields of psychology," he argued, "until we can include will, needs, and personality. We can do this. There are already a number of studies that have shown that an experimental attack of these fundamental problems is quite possible." He pointed out that these investigations dealt with the whole person and took into account the characteristics of the person, his momentary state, and his psychological environment. This was in contrast to the conventional experiments on sensations in which the individual's ideals, ambitions, and social relationships play no role at all or only a subordinate one.

Lewin devoted most of the text to the task of psychology and the foundations of topological and vector psychology. "Topologically the person is represented as a connected region which is separated from the environment by a Jordan curve and within this region there are part regions, such as the 'inner-personal' region and the motor-perceptual region. The latter has the position of a boundary zone between the inner-personal region and the environment." This scheme is shown in Figure 8–1.

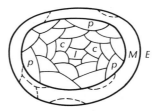

FIGURE 8–1. Topology of the person. M, motor-perceptual region; I, inner-personal region; p, peripheral parts of I; c, central parts of I; E, environment. (From *Principles of Topological Psychology*, p. 177.)

The drawings in Figure 8–2 are Lewin's conceptual representations of the person in three situations—calm, stress, and very high tension.

Lewin's mathematical representations of empirical phenomena can be viewed as one would a road map. Markings indicate direction and distance, and other symbols represent the relations between rivers, cities, and mountains. The Jordan curve conceptually represents the person, the psychological environment and the life space. The Jordan curve (or elliptical ring), Lewin maintained, is not an illustration but a representtaion of reality. Lewin cautioned that these representations correspond primarily to momentary situations and that these are constantly being altered. Psychological reality, he reminded psychologists, is forever changing because of the dynamic forces in the person and the environment.

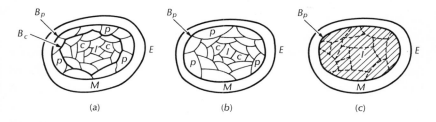

FIGURE 8–2. Relations between various strata of the person under different circumstances. (*a*) The person in an easy situation: the peripheral parts *p* of the inner-personal region *I*, are easily accessible from outside *E*; the more central parts *c* are less accessible; the inner-personal region *I* influences the motor region *M* relatively freely. (*b*) The person under stress, in state of self-control: the peripheral parts *p* of the inner-personal region *I* are less accessible than in (*a*); peripheral and central parts (*c* and *p*) are more closely connected; communication between *I* and *M* is less free. (*c*) The person under very high tension: unification (primitivation, "regression") of the inner-personal region *I*. *M*, motor-perceptual region; *I*, inner-personal region; *p*, peripheral parts of *I*; *c*, central parts of *I*; *E*, environment; B_c, dynamic wall between *c* and *p*; B_p, dynamic wall between *I* and *M*. (From *Principles of Topological Psychology*, p. 181.)

Lewin's book did not get the attention many of his colleagues felt it deserved—perhaps because its concepts were so unfamilar or because the terminology (in spite of all the Heiders' efforts) was so difficult. American psychologists were not used to the idea of mathematical models and none of them knew topology. Moreover, as few were willing to learn it, most of them never really understood the book. Many interpreted the topological representations as mere pictures or illustrations, rather than as mathematics. Besides, the mathematics was not very powerful in that early form; so a psychologist had to have faith that it could be developed further and that such development would be a gradual process.

There were unfavorable reviews by Brolyer in 1936–1937, Heidbreder in 1937, and Garrett in 1939. Additional reviews—some favorable, others unfavorable—appeared more frequently in the 1940's. But during the same period many of Lewin's concepts—such as vector, valence, life space, field theory, and tension system—became indispensable parts of psychology. Morton Deutsch, in commenting on Lewin's topological concepts, says, "It would be foolish to neglect the suggestive value of his imaginative attempt to develop a geometry suitable for psychology. Lewin pointed out the need for a new mathematics based on axioms different from those of the mathematics developed for the physical sciences. He indicated some of the properties that would be required of a geometry adequate to handle psychological space and he stimulated a more widespread interest in the development of such a geometry."

Dorwin Cartwright recently observed, "Lewin's attitude toward mathematics displayed a strong ambivalence; he was attracted by its rigor but fearful of what he called 'premature formalization.' He was unwilling to allow the requirements of mathematical convenience to dictate the content of psychological theory. As a result, his own use of mathematics was essentially programmatic, setting a style of thought and indicating prospects for greater rigor in the field of psychology (and perhaps that of mathematics, too). He was fully aware that his use of topology was quite primitive from a mathematical point of view, but he was undaunted by the critics. He was convinced that someday the potentialities he saw would become actualized."

At the time Lewin was so completely absorbed in his other outside interest, the founding of a Psychological Institute at the Hebrew University, that the reception of his book did not trouble him as much as it might have. His concern over the future of Palestine led him to anticipate challenges to its Jewish population which could be met only by a Research Institute specially tailored to the needs of a small state that would be peopled largely by immigrants. In November 1934, he produced a preliminary statement of what such an Institute would need to do. The statement forecast many of the difficulties that would face prospective newcomers to the ancient

Jewish homeland and how the Institute could serve in helping to overcome them.

"The problems of Jews emigrating from European countries to Palestine will be tremendous," he wrote. Their integration into Palestinian life would involve hardships and conflicts. The Palestinian economy would be basically agricultural, and most of the immigrants would be coming from cities and small towns; so they would have to be taught farming and would need special training in human relations for living and working together on cooperative farms. Although he admired the kibbutz form of agricultural development, Lewin clearly recognized that all the newcomers would not adjust readily to this communal living.

Moreover, the Jewish immigrants were bound to have varied backgrounds. They would come from many parts of Europe and from different occupational and economic levels, with differences in personal habits, manners, speech, even folkways and worship. The differences could occasion serious social friction. Lewin was especially concerned about those escaping from Nazi control who would bring tragic, terrifying memories. These would present a double problem, one of maintaining their morale and hopes while they waited tensely for entrance visas, and one of somehow enabling their new country to meet their hopes. "The relation of people's expectations and the reality they experience," Lewin wrote, "profoundly affect their behavior."

Lewin proposed an international study project to find ways of easing these hardships. Quantitative and experimental research should seek out the wisest solutions and strive for a set of practical administrative alternatives. The application of the kind of scientific methods he had in mind would generate data that could materially lessen human suffering, develop better communities, and reduce costs by millions of dollars.

Among the problems for which experimental solutions might be sought were: the rate at which immigrants adjusted to Palestinian conditions; the forces at work on them; the range and degree of adjustment of the immigrants in terms of their countries of origin; the varieties and roles of preparatory training; the influences in Palestine most favorable to the assimilation of newcomers; the problems of human relations generated by change of habitat; the means and methods by which these problems could best be met; steps which could develop the immigrants' commitment to an economy of survival and growth in a desert land; the means of developing such changes of attitude in the radical adjustments required to balance their past experience with their new conditions of life; and the best means of coping with an inevitable atmosphere of suspicion, distrust, and fear. Working on these problems, Lewin expressed for the first time his new interest in what became known as action research. It marked a radical departure from the type of research he had been conducting up to that time.

All through 1934–1935, Lewin devoted his energies to winning American support for the Institute. Within a few months, thanks in no small measure to the help of Horace M. Kallen of the New School for Social Research, he had gathered a distinguished group of sponsors for the project. Lewin traveled back and forth between Ithaca and New York City. He went personally to see prospective sponsors, many whom he had never met before, and won their support. He gave considerable time to insignificant details, such as ordering stationery and answering correspondence, since the sponsors produced neither clerical help nor office space. A letter he sent me in July 1935 reveals Lewin's meticulous attention to detail, much as he was averse to it and usually inept at it.

But he never succeeded in getting the project for the Institute financed. It was too remote from the more immediate endeavor to rescue Jews from the Nazi inferno. Jewish and other philanthropy from 1935 to 1939 was largely concentrated on that task. To Lewin this singleness of purpose by the Jewish leaders was a mistake. He believed that what happened after a Jew had been rescued could be almost as vital as the rescue itself, and he was convinced that an Institute in Palestine would produce insights that would later be of use the world over. He had in mind making this service the goal of his own career. Then, too, his appointment at Cornell was approaching the end of its term, and no other American opening was yet in sight. Horace Kallen and some other friends and admirers,

PSYCHOLOGICAL INSTITUTE OF THE HEBREW UNIVERSITY
JERUSALEM, PALESTINE

AMERICAN COMMITTEE
45 EAST 9TH STREET
NEW YORK, N.Y.

DR. A. S. W. ROSENBACH
Chairman
ALFRED J. MARROW
Secretary
GRAMERCY 5-2308

SPONSORS COMMITTEE

FRANK BOAS
    Professor of Anthropology
    Columbia University

EDWIN G. BORING
    Professor of Psychology
    Harvard University

MORRIS R. COHEN
    Professor of Philosophy
    College of the City of New York

JOHN DEWEY
    Professor Emeritus of Philosophy
    Columbia University

LIVINGSTON FARRAND
    President of Cornell University

FELIX FRANKFURTER
    Byrne Professor of Administrative Law
    Harvard Law School

SIGISMUND S. GOLDWATER
    Commissioner of Hospitals
    New York City

HORACE M. KALLEN
    Professor of Philosophy
    and Psychology
    New School for Social Research

WILLIAM H. KILPATRICK
    Professor of Education
    Teachers College
    Columbia University

PAUL KLAPPER
    Dean of the School of Education
    College of the City of New York

WILLIAM MCDOUGALL
    Professor of Psychology
    Duke University

ADOLF MEYER
    Henry Phipps Professor of
    Psychiatry
    Johns Hopkins University

MRS. HENRY MORGENTHAU, JR.
    Washington, D. C.

WILLIAM A. NEILSON
    President of Smith College

WILLIAM F. OGBURN
    Professor of Sociology
    University of Chicago

MRS. FRANKLIN D. ROOSEVELT
    Washington, D. C.

EDWARD SAPIR
    Professor of Anthropology
    Yale University

EDWARD L. THORNDIKE
    Professor of Education
    Teachers College
    Columbia University

LEWIS M. TERMAN
    Professor of Psychology
    Stanford University

Milford, New York
July 13, 1935
c/o Mrs. Stanley Martin

Mr. Alfred Marrow
45 East Ninth Street
New York, New York

Dear Alfred:

Please find enclosed a copy of a letter to Rosenbach and the draft for a letter which should be sent to the sponsors, with the exception of Mrs. Roosevelt.

The letter to Rosenbach tells you the situation. I am afraid of two things: A delay in the sending of the letters, and that the letters may not be properly copied. I outlined these letters with some of the professors in Cornell and I don't like to have them changed.

I fear that if the friends handle the business something will go wrong. Would it be possible that you could supervise it or even let the copies be made in your office and let Rosenbach just sign them? It is very important that no copy is sent to Mrs. Roosevelt.

I sent under separate cover, fifty of our letterheads. I hope you will like them. May I ask you or Monette to telephone to Rosenbach to find out whether he agrees to send the letter and then to make out a definite procedure?

I have a second favor to ask from Monette. I would like to get in touch with this Dr. David Levy, whom I mentioned in the letter to Rosenbach. Would it be possible to find out his address and whether he is now in New York. He has worked or is working with the Child Welfare Organization, the chairman of which is Mrs. Sidney Gruenberg.

Should I order envelopes and what should be printed on them?

Cordially yours,

Kurt Lewin

83

even though they were strong sponsors of the Palestine project, strongly preferred to keep Lewin and his innovative insights and techniques in the United States.

Lawrence D. Frank, who, as a staff member of the Laura Spelman Rockefeller Fund, had been instrumental in securing the funds for Lewin's appointment at Cornell, wrote that he found the prospect of Lewin's leaving the United States appalling. He felt that the studies begun at Berlin and Cornell had to continue. But where could Lewin go?

Among others, Frank contacted the Iowa Child Welfare Research Station (now the Institute of Child Behavior and Research), whose director was George Stoddard, about a place for Lewin there. Iowa had no funds for new staff members, but Frank succeeded in getting an appropriation from the Rockefeller Fund's General Education Board to cover Lewin's appointment to the faculty of the University of Iowa for a three-year period, with the understanding that Stoddard would make every effort to continue the appointment at the termination of the grant. Stoddard, as it turned out, managed to keep Lewin on at Iowa when the grant ran out.

The University of Iowa was an important center for psychological research and education. George Stoddard and Beth Wellman were doing important work on environmental influences on intelligence. Carl Seashore had done much to attract the interest of psychologists everywhere. Kenneth Spence later joined the faculty because of its fine reputation. The General Education Board provided a number of fellowships so that Lewin could organize a research team. One went to Tamara Dembo; two others to Roger Barker, who had just completed his doctoral studies at Stanford, and Herbert Wright, who had just finished his at Duke University.

Lewin never gave up his interest in the Jewish state, nor did the move to Iowa diminish his dedication to the idea of setting up a Psychological Institute at the Hebrew University. But at Iowa he entered a new field of fresh problems—problems relevant to the American scene. He was to pioneer in a double sense and give a new turn to the theory and practice of the behavioral sciences.

Lewin was now forty-five. He had lived through the developments and crises of the years between Bismarck and Hitler. He had been an officer in an army that had been deemed the greatest military machine of its time yet had gone down to harsh defeat. He had been deeply affected by the political turmoil and economic catastrophe of the Weimar Republic. He had encountered the violent and increasingly barbaric anti-Semitism of Hitler Germany. This, combined with an intense commitment to the problems and values of science, sharpened his awareness of the relationships between knowledge and policy, of the need for attention to political issues if human life and culture were to grow and be renewed. He had a view of what kind of human community the democratic society should be, having seen at first hand the enemies of such a society.

Thus, like Tocqueville a hundred years earlier, Lewin looked at American life using his European experience as a continual and inescapable point of reference. In his speculation and research, this led in the ensuing years to a deepening interest in problems of democratic leadership and of the conditions for effective individual and group growth; it gave rise to a widening concern about ways in which greater knowledge of human behavior could be used to deal with social problems.

Donald MacKinnon believes that "in some ways it was a good thing that he did emigrate and find himself in an entirely new environment. This was the stimulus which directed his energies to problems that he might never have dealt with if there hadn't been an upheaval in the world at that particular time. All these terrible events deepened his commitment to mankind and the betterment of man's lot."

CHAPTER

SETTING
NEW FORCES
IN ACTION

Though the Iowa appointment was primarily for research, rather than for teaching, Lewin, being Lewin, was surrounded by students throughout his nine years at the university from 1935 to 1944. They gathered around him as they had in Berlin—from many parts of the country, from a variety of educational backgrounds, for many different reasons. He, in turn, considered the appointment at Iowa a piece of timely good luck. A full-time academic post, with a possibility of continuity, meant greater security for his growing family, the chance to work with students over a long enough period to develop and test ideas, and freedom to look to the future. None of these had been possible during the preceding several years.

The Lewin family moved to Iowa in 1935 after the summer they had spent in Milford with the Heiders. They found Iowa City different in many ways from both Cornell and Berlin. But it was not completely different, for he continued to explore the same ideas and to carry on experiments as he had in Berlin during the late 1920's. Very soon new vistas opened. "Iowa was exciting," recalls Tamara Dembo. "I felt that here we had Kurt Lewin himself, and a constant feeling of something fresh and very worthwhile. For some of us it was a very deep experience, even more than Berlin."

Lewin first attracted a few students who were already on the Iowa campus; then others came from elsewhere, as more and more were increasingly eager to study with him. His distinctive approach soon stirred controversy and helped maintain the Iowa Research Station's reputation as one of the leading centers of American psychology. The interests of the Lewin circle were broad. Although his academic title was Professor of Child Psychology and most of the studies in the years that followed were of children, Lewin's concern continued to be general psychological theory and experiment.

Roger Barker, who had first encountered Lewin at Stanford, was the first to arrive at Iowa. Lewis Terman had recommended him and when a fellowship was offered he accepted it as a great opportunity. Although he had found Lewin's English difficult to understand, he appreciated the potential challenge of working with someone who was unlike the professors he had known before. Barker did not feel that he had the background to work with Lewin. "But I believed he had something that I needed and wanted. Working with Lewin was like waking up from sleep for the first time and realizing that there is this whole world of ideas about science. I hadn't known anything about this."

Many students who joined Lewin, at least after 1938, came with a practical interest in the social uses of psychological research. They found that in an era when life problems rarely received consideration from psychologists, and then only when they had reached the stage of abnormality and malfunction, Lewin's thinking was strongly life-connected. His theories were tools to attack everyday human problems. They led Lewin, in chicken-and-egg fashion, to place increasing emphasis on experimental studies of the how and what-for of individual and social change—studies which later were consummated as "action research" and "group dynamics." These students provide us with an invaluable account of his working and teaching methods, as well as another personal picture of Kurt Lewin the man.

Those who worked with Lewin at Iowa cannot always remember precisely how their basic research interests and those which followed them came into focus; but, as his group of students grew, the informal relationship of the *conditorei consortium* that had been a part of life at the Berlin Psychological Institute was re-created. There was, of course, nothing quite like the Berlin Schwedisch Cafe in Iowa City, but an acceptable substitute was found in the Round Window Restaurant. There, in a top-floor room where the proprietor allowed students to bring their own lunches if they purchased coffee or tea, Lewin's Midwestern *Quasselstrippe* (the Iowa students translated it as the "Hot-Air Club") met informally each Tuesday noon.

At lunch, animated conversation, bad puns, and much laughter prevailed, with Lewin joining in the fun as much as anyone. Frequently his humor was unintended and sometimes traceable to students who had fun teaching him malaprop American colloquialisms. His unintentional gaffes often convulsed his volunteer English teachers. Ron Lippitt remembers the occasion when Lewin was to comment on a paper at the Midwestern Psychological Meeting. Alex Bavelas and Harold Sheels told him that "slobbered a bibful" meant "said a lot." When Lewin wanted to say something nice about Dr. Wheeler's having a lot to say, he ad-libbed, "As you Americans would say, Dr. Wheeler has certainly slobbered a bibful."

Lewin was "warm and fun-loving," recalls Alvin Zander, a member of the Hot-Air Club. "He liked and told good jokes—poorly." But that did not matter to the meetings of the Iowa *Quasselstrippe*, where one or another of the dozen students present would either report on his current research or propose a project he wanted to take up. One contribution would build upon another and group-formed ideas emerged for a testable hypothesis or an enthusiastic consensus on how a new area of investigation should be explored.

Erik Wright recollects that "none of the group ever felt that he was on stage when he spoke. He was among his peers, sharpening his ideas on their criticisms of his experimental procedures or recruiting assistants for some phase of a project. How Lewin kept the talk moving constructively without seeming to direct it at all has stuck in the minds of many of us. It was one of the things I have tried to carry over among my own students and I have learned how very difficult it is to establish that kind of atmosphere."

The group never became large. The membership merely altered as new students arrived, presented their work, wrote their theses, and departed. There were neither bars to nor requirements for membership; no one was "screened" either formally or informally. It was not thought to be especially "fashionable" or "unfashionable" to eat one's lunch with the Club on Tuesdays. If one was a graduate student in one of Lewin's seminars and had a problem to discuss, he—or she—would probably bring it to the next meeting of the Club.

Robert Leeper, who was teaching at a college some twenty-odd miles from Iowa City, wrote that he made weekly trips "to participate in a seminar in which Lewin was presenting his interpretation of a monograph on psychological forces." Leeper ranks his encounter with Lewin as "among the pleasantest memories of my life. It was a privilege both emotionally and intellectually to share in the discussions with Lewin and his eager students and associates. The seminars often met at Lewin's home, in a room with brown-stained wooden walls and a floor littered with sheets of brown wrapping paper on which Lewin and the students drew their diagrams in colored chalk. The 'full-fledged topologists' came to these sessions equipped with four-color pencils, to squat on their hands and knees and draw on wrapping paper."

Donald MacKinnon has remarked that the group around Kurt Lewin was "as loyal as the early group around Freud." But, where Freud required a kind of fealty and conformity to his views, Lewin never made any such demands on his students or colleagues. "As a result, for sound psychological reasons, the inevitable apostasies against Freud were very messy, whereas people could move out of Lewin's immediate circle even during his lifetime and still maintain ties with him and others in his circle. If you drifted away, you wouldn't feel guilty about it, and you weren't accused of disloyalty. I think Kurt was quite right in saying that he didn't want to develop a school of psychology; he was merely trying to develop a language for the representation of psychological phenomena."

Nevertheless, at Iowa Lewin did tend to build warmer relationships with his students than had most other eminent men in American psychology. Alex Bavelas says, "It was a very close group. We were at his home frequently. The offices were all adjoining, and we ate lunch together even when not at the *Quasselstrippe*. Someone was always reporting on something."

Lewin never saw himself as the proponent of a set doctrine. "He did not care for power or for prestige as an expert," says John R. P. French, Jr., "so he was just as open to influence from his students as they were to him. Thus his relationships with his students could be intimate without becoming crippling; they retained their independence of mind while realizing their fullest potential."

Dorwin Cartwright recalls that his first exposure to Lewin's thinking came in 1938 when he was a college senior at Swarthmore and read *A Dynamic Theory of Personality*. "It was so stimulating that following my first year of graduate study I enrolled in a summer session at Iowa in order to learn more about him. I found a whole group of people whose waking hours were devoted fully to working on ideas generated by Lewin. Almost immediately they made me a part of the group and I was engaged in their endless discussions. In less than a month's time Lewin got me interested in the problem of 'decision time' and started me on work which subsequently constituted my doctoral dissertation."

Cartwright, who went to Iowa in 1940 as one of the General Education Fellows, says, further, "In retrospect, it is clear that Lewin was the ultimate source of all this stimulation, but his influence was exerted in large measure through the interacting social system that had grown up around him. His ideas dominated this microculture, but he was never domineering. In seminars and informal bull sessions, the talk was invariably animated, often heated, and everyone participated. Lewin always kept control of a corner of the blackboard, but everyone was encouraged to use the rest of it to display competing ideas. In such a setting, it was hard not to become committed to a life of research."

Lewin loved seminars and loved the group. As he was going to a seminar, he'd happily tell his secretary, "Nobody is to disturb me except my wife and the President of the University."

Margaret Mead attended some of the later sessions held during the early years of World War II. "I was financing my travel by lecturing," she recalls, "but I managed to get to Iowa City very often to spend long intensive weekends discussing hypotheses and experiments, raising new questions about involvement of different kinds of participants—all conducted with the Lewin household as the center, the Lewin children interested listeners, the students intensely related to the work they were doing together. In it all, Kurt was like the fire around which other people gathered for warmth and for light by which to read their own thoughts more clearly."

Beatrice Wright chose to study with Lewin for her doctorate at the urging of her professors, Abraham Maslow and Solomon Asch. "I was attracted to Lewin," she said, "by his idea of explaining behavior by taking into account both the person and the environment in the conceptual formulation of intervening variables. My present interest in psychological problems of rehabilitation was furthered by my association with Lewinians Barker and Dembo and involves the person-environment system with special emphasis on social-emotional relationships."

It was through Harold Seashore, his first psychology teacher at Springfield College in Massachusetts, that Alex Bavelas met Lewin. Lewin had visited Springfield College and had given a talk in one of the dormitories on topological psychology and related matters. "I understood very little of it," Bavelas confessed, "but I was interested and enthusiastic." Very much influenced by Lewin's lecture, which treated of the problems of satiation, Bavelas conceived a related problem and designed an experiment, which he carried out with Seashore. Bavelas and Seashore published the study. "I was proud of being in print, in *General and Experimental Psychology*, and Seashore encouraged me to try to get admission to Iowa." Seashore and Bavelas sent Lewin the article and Bavelas arranged to go and talk with him about it. "He very gently explained to me that my study really wasn't of satiation," Bavelas recalls. "I still did not understand him very well, but as a result of that visit I was offered a research-assistantship at Iowa. I think Lewin may have been swayed by his growing interest in group processes and my background in group work. When I got there, I met Leon Festinger and all the other students in Lewin's circle."

Leon Festinger also sought out Lewin at Iowa: "When I received my degree at C.C.N.Y., I was already interested in studies of the level of aspiration and went out to Iowa in 1939 specifically because Kurt Lewin was there. My introduction to this problem had been through Max Hertzman, who was lecturing on it at C.C.N.Y. His wife, Rosalind Gould, was working on the same topic for her doctorate at Columbia. Hertzman and I did a study together on group variables involved in the level of aspiration. That was my first published study, done in 1938–1939; it appeared about 1941. I was attracted to Lewin, and the areas in which he worked, by his ability to bring a rigorous experimental approach to problems such as the Zeigarnik effect and the level of aspiration. It is a rare ability in psychology. These problems became more interesting than others to me because of the precise experimental approach, together with the effort to pull out the general theoretical importance of the finding."

Erik Wright came to Iowa in 1937 "because Al Hicks had completed his Ph.D. during Lewin's first year here. I had taken my Master's degree under Hicks and was enthusiastic about going there for my doctorate. I was able to get an appointment as a fellow in the Child Welfare Research Station, where Lewin worked. After one semester with Lewin, I determined to take every course I could with him—and I did."

Alvin Zander visited Lewin at Iowa during Christmas vacation in 1941 while still a student at the University of Michigan, and in February Lewin offered him a job. Zander worked with him on food habits, leadership training, and observations of Boy Scout troops. Zander left Iowa in 1942 to move to the national headquarters of the Boy Scouts, where Ronald Lippitt had already brought in Lewin as an adviser on field research. Zander recounts how Lewin involved almost everyone with whom he came into contact. "A student came to ask him a question one day while I was in his office. Lewin replied to the student that he could best learn what he wanted to know by joining us in our current research endeavor.

"We will help you by exploiting you," Lewin told him, and the student cheerfully chipped in.

Lewin was also concerned about the personal growth of his fellow workers. He often talked to Zander and others about the students who were studying with him at the Child Welfare Research Station, telling of his hopes for their improvement and what he was doing to help them excel. His was the attitude of a parent asking himself what he must do for a gifted child. He often paid calls on his co-workers, students, and their families. "He treated his students in a fatherly way," Zander said, "and his research assistants could expect visits from him in their homes with no advance notice of his coming. On such an occasion he chatted about personal matters and in many ways acted as though he were part of the family." Lewin frequently invited his students and colleagues to accompany him and his family on picnics and drives. Sometimes the rides were hair-raising experiences. Lewin, his mind absorbed, would pay more attention to his talk than to his driving, and he would often take his hands off the wheel to make excited gestures.

"One of the many things that the Lewins did for us," said Louise Barker of the early days at Iowa, "was to help us to see lots of things about our own country—and life in general—in a new perspective, since they came from such a different background and were so easy to communicate with. You see things more clearly when you have something else to sight against. Kurt and Gert gave us that."

John R. P. French, Jr., who came from Harvard to study with Lewin, says, "Lewin had a basic respect for the ideas of others, no matter who they were. He never hesitated to examine a suggestion and usually found in it interesting things that ought to be talked about. He greeted new ideas with glee and would get so excited about them that he sparkled."

Lewin never ceased to be as interested in the ideas of his juniors as in those of his equals. To many of his students he brought a rare sense of recognition and Roger Barker remarked on this gratefully. "It was the first time that anyone had taken my ideas seriously."

Sometimes, however, Lewin seemed insensitive. If, on occasion, a member of the class would try to get a point explained, he might say, with a sigh, "Oh, do we have to go into *that* now?"—with an expression of annoyance that he himself would have been the first to criticize had he seen it on someone else.

Lewin could also be sharp with those who could not, or would not, understand what he was trying to accomplish. Roger Barker says, "A classmate of mine was doing a thesis with a well-known member of the faculty on balance in painting. This professor had developed photographic techniques for mapping out visual fixation points, in order to observe what a person looks at in a picture. This was to be related to artistic principles of balance; for example, unbalanced pictures might cause the viewer to fixate on one side. There would be a relationship between balance and these fixation points. The student explained this to Lewin, and Lewin replied, 'Ach, nonsense! Just nonsense!' To a student struggling with a thesis based on a new idea such as this, it's not very encouraging to hear your ideas called nonsense. Well, it turned out to be nonsense."

Another of Lewin's minor shortcomings, as a teacher and supervisor of research for academic dissertations (requiring demonstration of the relevance of the reported studies to previous or related work), was his apparent inability to guide the student to investigations or theories that lay outside his own immediate fields of interest. Therefore, students had to develop considerable ingenuity in seeking out other faculty members or more advanced graduate students who could provide this kind of background and guidance.

But in their own research Lewin constantly stressed the importance of going beyond a mere piling up of facts which can only lead to a chaotic and unproductive situation. The simple collecting of facts is indispensable at certain stages of a science, he maintained, and is a wholesome reaction against a philosophical and speculative building of theories. But it cannot give a satisfactory answer to questions about causes and conditions of events. Only with the help of theories can one determine causal interrelationships. A science without theory is blind because it lacks that element which alone is able to organize facts and give direction to research. Even from a practical point of view the mere gathering of facts has very limited value. It cannot give an answer to the question that is most important for practical purposes—namely, what must one do to obtain a desired effect in given concrete cases? "To answer this question it is necessary to have a theory, but a theory which is empirical and not speculative. This means that theory and facts must be closely related to each other." Guided by these beliefs Lewin addressed himself to a number of research projects, which have since become among his major contributions. These are discussed briefly in Chapter 21.

CHAPTER

10

EARLY
IOWA YEARS—
SOCIAL THEORY
AND
SOCIAL PROBLEMS

The Iowa to which the Lewin family had moved in 1935 was located in the most typically American region on the continent, the Midwest. Its residents felt secure in the belief that the Atlantic and Pacific oceans constituted a broad and watery barrier against any possible attack on the United States. Midwesterners saw no reason to look outward at all.

Lewin chafed at this isolationist attitude toward events abroad during this period. On both the East and West coasts of the United States, thinking Americans received with grave foreboding the news of Mussolini's attack on Ethiopia in October 1935 and of renewed Japanese attacks on Manchuria two years later. But in America's great heartland these tidings were either disregarded or used to buttress arguments in opposition to any further American involvement in foreign wars.

By contrast, Lewin was devoting more and more time to social issues. The direction of his thinking was changing. His emphasis was now on social psychological problems. And though many Americans refused to look at the outside world, their own country became the target for increasing anti-Jewish propaganda—particularly from the Nazi regime in Germany. The field was a fertile one. As early as 1933 John J. Smertenko wrote in *Harper's Magazine*, "Today it is no secret that Jews have great difficulty in gaining admission to the institutions of higher learning and that their opportunities for legal and medical training are limited to a minimum. It is equally well known that the professions of banking, engineering and teaching are closed to all but a few, and the quasi-public service corporations vigorously exclude them."

This growing anti-Semitism, Lewin realized, was part of the American reaction to World War I and the Russian Communist Revolution. After the Depression hit, this prejudice became more pronounced as the less-informed among the millions of unemployed sought an answer to, and a scapegoat for, their miseries. In the Midwest, with its relatively small Jewish population, it was easy to accept the notion that unseen hordes of East Coast Jews were selfishly holding on to all the money that should be spread throughout the country. In Detroit, Father Charles E. Coughlin, the "radio priest" who had converted his children's catechism hour to a weekly tirade aimed at their parents, provided further identification of the profiteers: they had been *Jewish*.

Busy as he was with his work, Lewin nevertheless paid sharp heed to the expression of these ominous political and social sentiments. It did not make him critical of his new homeland—indeed, Lewin's whole approach was so exuberant and democratic as to suggest that spiritually he was born an American—but the evils that grew out of Midwestern isolationism disturbed him. During the period from 1936 to 1940, he wrote several articles dealing with his reaction to this situation.

One of the first articles,[1] considered by Gordon Allport to be one of the most brilliant of Lewin's papers, appeared in 1936. It was concerned with the problem of comparative national psychology. In it he demonstrated how psychological differences between Germany and the United States had developed and how these differences could be measured in terms of his concepts of life space and field theory. Though he admitted that to some extent human nature was the same everywhere, and that certain social characteristics were alike in all the so-called "Western" cultures, he found major distinctions between the cultures of Germany and the United States.

Having worked with German children in Berlin, and then with American youngsters in the nursery schools at both Cornell and Iowa, Lewin was first struck by the differences between the two cultures at the child's level. The contrasting social background, reflected in the two educational systems, was a mirror of the true cleavage between the two societies. He measured this fundamental difference in terms of what he called the "space of free movement" available to the members of a society.

Indeed, for Lewin—chronically late all his life—the American emphasis on punctuality for meals was a source of amazement, as well as the most striking evidence of how the two cultures were unlike. "That a dozen guests who have been invited to an informal dinner party at seven should all arrive between 7:00 and 7:08 is as unheard of in Germany as it is common in the United States."

The degree of independence among children in the United States, especially the "lack of servility of the young child toward adults or of the student toward his professor," was pointed up as another dissimilarity between the two countries. He found it remarkable that American adults tended to deal with children more as equals than as superiors dealing with their inferiors, as was true in Germany. This too was a reflection of a national political philosophy which, in America, stressed independence of opinion. He recalled an instance in Germany, soon after the inception of the Nazi regime, when the staff of a leading training school for nursery-school teach-

[1] "Some Social Psychological Differences between the United States and Germany," *Character and Personality*, 1936, *4*, 265–293.

ers was instructed to advise its students never to explain an order to a child, who should acquire the habit of blind obedience. Though he conceded that this was an extreme example, Lewin felt that it expressed the philosophy underlying the relationship between persons in Germany.

Just as American education was characterized by rather well-delineated areas of activity with varying degrees of freedom, so, too, it seemed to him, the various realms of social activity in the United States were more sharply separated than in Germany. In America, two scientists or two political candidates might engage in a furious theoretical or political fight and yet be on cordial terms with each other; this was in sharp contrast to how it would be in Germany. There, he said, political or even scientific disagreement implied moral disapproval.

Lewin had been in the United States in 1932 when Franklin D. Roosevelt had been elected to the presidency, and he could not imagine a German candidate congratulating his successful opponent as Herbert Hoover did. It would be "inconceivable" in Germany, he said. That it happened all the time over here was another aspect of the same separation of areas of activity which permitted certain groups to regard one another as equals in politics and business, though they had almost no connection in social life.

He observed, too, that the democratic idea of equal rights sometimes seemed to be extended so far as to "ascribe even the same abilities to every person and to consider lack of success as a proof of moral inferiority."

Theoretically, Lewin felt that the examples he used pointed up the dissimilarity of Germans and Americans as groups when it came to measuring the "social distance" between persons in the group. Citing the measurements used on the Bogardus test for social distance (in which A is asked whether or not he would share certain situations with B—such as traveling in the same car, playing games, dancing, or marrying), Lewin concluded that the central core of the American personality is surrounded by more easily penetrable peripheral layers than is the German, as shown graphically in Figure 10–1.

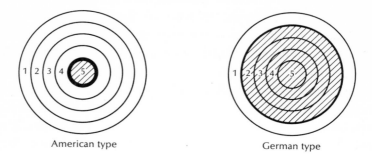

American type   German type

FIGURE 10-1. Personality Structure. The thickness of the boundary lines between the personality layers represents the difference in accessibility. The
hatched area corresponds to the "private" region of the person.

This would also account, he felt, for a difference in the American
and German responses to what might be termed annoying situations.
The American tends to ask first what should be done to remedy
the situation, whereas the German first asks who is to blame for it.
All this meant that it would be possible to have relatively close
relationships with Americans on a number of levels without deep
personal friendship, but, consequently, there also was less danger of
friction in these relationships because so little of the central core of
each person was involved.

Though Lewin cautioned at the conclusion that his analysis dealt
"only with the present situation without statement as to its duration
or history," and that he intended his definition of the different characteristics to be regarded only as tentative, he nevertheless was persuaded of a fundamental opposition in the German and the American attitude toward rights and duties.

Though he found Americans so unlike Germans in most of their
social attitudes because of a basic difference in the American personality structure, Lewin was sadly surprised to find that, on the question of anti-Semitism, Americans displayed many of the prejudices
directed against him while he was growing up in Germany. That it
was a matter of concern for him is reflected in the number of pieces
he wrote during the late 1930's on aspects of Jewish life.

When Lewin was at Cornell, and when he came to Iowa, he

found himself in a situation repeated on campuses throughout the United States at that period. In every institution there were a few Jewish students, but their percentage in proportion to the total number of the student body was small—and was kept so deliberately. The concept of the "Jewish quota" was so common in American higher education as to be taken for granted. It was simply another expression of the attitude conveyed by the insulting sign one occasionally saw outside resort hotels, "Restricted." These hostile attitudes had a long history and had produced the Immigration Act of 1924, which had sharply reduced immigration from East European countries and thus cut off the major escape route for European Jews facing the horrors of mounting anti-Semitism. Lewin was keenly aware of the discrimination practiced against racial and religious minority groups which characterized much of American life.

It was President Abbott Lawrence Lowell of Harvard who, in his graduation address in June 1922, had first publicly proposed a quota system to limit the number of Jewish university students. The trustees of Harvard rejected Lowell's proposal, but there could be no doubt that during the next ten years the idea took root in American higher education. Nor was there any doubt that anti-Semitism was growing in other spheres as well. Though a comparative newcomer to this country, Lewin reacted with unusual vigor and wrote a number of theoretical articles on group prejudice and tension and on the psychological problems confronting minority groups whose space of free movement was restricted by discrimination.

His zeal for research never flagged, and he prodded his helpers ceaselessly. Often after a heated discussion on method, the group would adjourn to his office with the idea of working out specific plans for an experiment. Tamara Dembo, Herbert Wright, and Roger Barker would be there, and sometimes others. Lewin would discuss the research and make notes. Then he would say, "I'd better dictate this" (because nobody could read his handwriting), and dictate rapidly, while those present furiously wrote it down for their own notes.

Barker recalls "being so tired I ached. Lewin would go on and on.

After two hours I would be bleary-eyed, but he apparently was just getting warmed up. I can remember going until six or six-thirty, hoping that someone would phone in and break it up. If I hadn't had the excuse of a wife waiting at home, he would really have worn me out. He never had any idea of when to stop." Working with Lewin might have been physically draining, but Barker also felt himself grow. Lacking Lewin's extensive background in philosophy and biology, he kept getting new insights in psychology, the subject he thought he knew.

"Lewin was so strongly involved in what he was doing that he couldn't help being evangelical," says Barker. "He was not always objective, except that he was determined to search for truth. He would have vigorous discussions with a man like Clark Hull. I am sure Lewin knew what Hull was trying to do—and disagreed with him; but to the students and people around him, Lewin could not present an objective picture when stating what he thought of Hull's beliefs, or what everyone else thought. He believed he himself had the truth and was following the path. One was not educated under him in the sense that education gives a broad view. He did not give a nonpartisan view of the scientific world; he gave the 'true' view, the one he believed in. He did recognize that others disagreed. He could talk to a man like Hull. Once or twice he wrote an article in which he specifically disagreed with Hull, but he would not enter into controversy. In Germany, a lot of science involved hot public disputation, and he said, 'I didn't do it in Germany and I won't do it here. That does not help science go ahead; science progresses through research, not through defending your viewpoint.' "

Yet to some extent the academic disputations of Germany followed him even to the cornfields of Iowa. Wolfgang Köhler had taught at the University of Iowa during the summer preceding Lewin's arrival. Apparently he spoke fairly often of Lewin and his ideas, in conversations with Herbert Feigl, who had been a member of the Philosophy Department there since 1931. Feigl notes that Köhler expressed appreciation of the "fruitfulness" of Lewin's topological-dynamic theories, though he disagreed with some aspects. The conversations were sufficiently detailed for Feigl to feel that he was "well prepared for Kurt Lewin's arrival on the Iowa campus a month or two later."

To Barker it seemed that Feigl's orientation had put him in an argumentative mood. Feigl himself, as a member of the "Vienna Circle" of philosophers, held views Lewin opposed. Today Feigl recalls very little of the controversy and feels that "there was practically complete agreement between us in matters of the general philosophy of science." Lewin's outlook helped Feigl to overcome "some remnants of an all too narrow logical positivism"; and in Feigl's view the leading members of the Vienna Circle who had come to America were moving in the same direction. Lewin, on the other hand, was quite willing, Feigl felt, to continue to place a high value on the role of postulates (implicit definitions) when specifying the meaning of theoretical concepts.

The "only sharp disagreement" between himself and Lewin which Feigl now recalls concerned Lewin's active espousal of Zionism. Feigl was convinced that creating "a homeland for the Jews in the midst of radically hostile Arab countries" was not a good idea. Lewin was impatient with this attitude and, during a vacation of several weeks at a lake in northern Minnesota in the summer of 1938, convincingly expounded his own point of view. Lewin's "more penetrating socio-psychological insight" convinced me, says Feigl, "that Israel was the only practical solution."

If Lewin's relations with his colleagues were subject to different interpretations, so were his relations with his students. Inevitably some students felt that Lewin had favorites. At times a big push would be on in certain areas, and then one inquiry received preferred attention and help. Also there were students who had worked with Lewin longer and on problems in which he was more deeply involved. Still others were working on problems Lewin had just begun thinking about. So the notion that he had favorites may have conveyed an "inner circle, outer circle" feeling. "Yet," says Erik Wright, "the circle was a flexible one with varying levels within a congenial frame of reference. If there were inner-outer rings, they were very subtly distinguished. A group such as the *Quasselstrippe* would be unusual today; but if Lewin were alive now he would probably function that way. He had enough drive and vision to encourage people to work with him after they received their doctorate."

Other colleagues felt that Lewin allowed, or ignored, or could not handle, strained relations among his subordinates. He was not always tactful in concealing that he had favorites. There often swirled around him a certain amount of competition for his attention, if only because a student's work was immensely brightened and heightened by his interest. He added to this dissension, perhaps unwittingly, when he lectured, for then the audience usually heard about the work of his young colleagues. He would outline the research of some student, speak enthusiastically, even extravagantly, about that person's performance. Naturally everyone wanted to win this distinction.

Bavelas states that Lewin reacted mildly to controversy. "If one disagreed with him, even emotionally or violently, he treated it as another interesting point of view rather than a personal attack. Lewin probably felt fundamentally secure. I was convinced that most of his students by the time they got their degrees felt they were much brighter than he, because he was so generally unassuming. If he had an idea and a student had a different one, Lewin would talk about his and the student could talk about his own. We felt that we were operating as equals."

Bavelas remarks, "Kurt did not really try to make disciples. No one ever felt committed to work topologically because he worked with Kurt. Everyone got different ideas, and there was no feeling that out of loyalty one had to use his system. For example, Ron Lippitt and Leon Festinger both were Lewin's students; but they worked downstairs with Spence's rats, and it made no difference to Kurt. It might have bothered Spence, though, if some of his students had done topological work with Lewin."

Lewin was always soaking up stimuli from his environment, including the verbalized ideas of others, but he was also almost simultaneously acting on those ideas with his own creative imagination. Therefore, he often did not really hear everything the other person said; yet he had been greatly influenced by his exchanges with the other person. When involved in clarifying a theoretical point, as in a dialogue with Clark Hull, or in conceptualization with Barker or Leeper or Adams or White, he certainly did listen carefully and had a large share in the creative process of modifying old ideas and forging new ones.

"One of his tremendous skills," Lippitt comments, "was to derive or generate high-level abstractions about the most concrete situations. He would spend many seminar sessions or personal work periods on very abstract issues of hodological space or issues of historical causality, but one always felt that the empirical world was just around the corner providing internal feedback and guidance. He might be immersed in the most minute concrete details of a child's feeding behavior or behavior with toys, but one always knew that high-level abstractions were in the back of his mind, guiding his perception of the concrete realities."

To Erik Wright, Lewin had a kind of personal style which made it possible to begin working even though one did not have all the exact operations to translate into. He frequently brought forth the idea that it was good to begin with first approximations. This was not new or original, but if one were not satisfied with the first results, one could consider them a first approximation. Lewin would advise not trying to go beyond what you were able to do until you had done that much and had seen what happened.

Barker points out that Lewin was always getting ideas from common observations. He recalls that Herbert Wright did his thesis with Adams on the effect of a barrier upon a valence—that is, grass on the other side of the fence is greener. Lewin had proposed this idea, which he had derived from observing people in the cafeteria as they reached over the pies that were near for the ones in back. Herbert Wright used this for one of the sources of data. He had the staff in the cafeteria at Duke place the pies in order. Wright kept track of which ones the customers chose. And it's true, says Barker —people tend to choose the ones which are more distant. Lewin could observe an ordinary situation and see it as a problem in a context which makes it significant.

To Kallen, Lewin had a kind of objectivity about himself, a lack of self-consciousness, which enabled him, for instance, to telephone prominent people whom he had never met and discuss his problem with them. It was not himself he was concerned with, but rather the problem and how to solve it. He was like an inventor trying to sell an invention, no matter what the cost to himself; or like a poet trying to get a hearing, not for himself, but for his poetry. "Lewin had what is known today as great cool. I remember Wertheimer at some of our New School seminars—a man of passionate convictions, who was extremely intolerant of all differences and who would shout against anyone who took issue with him. Kurt, on the other hand, I never heard to shout against opposition. He reasoned and demonstrated, and if he did not convince you, he would not go away angry. He had the rare ability to get along with people with whom he disagreed, because he respected the opinions of others, because he was no fanatic, and because he was sure of his own views."

When Cartwright worked with Lewin at M.I.T., they would meet regularly to discuss topology and hodology while Lewin was having his afternoon tea. Cartwright remembers that Lewin was eager to get the help of the mathematicians, and Cartwright believes "it is a major tragedy that he was never able to find one able to tolerate the ambiguities and imprecision of the psychological data with which he was concerned." Lewin's faith in the "mathematics of space" was somehow transmitted to Cartwright. When the opportunity came, a decade later, Cartwright established a program for mathematical work in the Research Center for Group Dynamics at the University of Michigan.

But Lewin had little use for statistics, according to Festinger, who "never saw him do mathematics" and never knew if he was "much of a mathematician." "But," says Festinger, "we started very early to argue about statistics. I think his dislike for them was a misconception on his part about what statistics could do for him. He seemed to identify statistics with data that could be collected without systematic theories, and to feel that an individual case would get lost in statistical analysis. Things that don't belong together would be put together, and their meaning obscured. A technique I learned from Kurt is that it is good to put together things that belong dynamically together, and very bad to put things together that do not dynamically belong together. He frequently used this with great cleverness and insight."

Bavelas suggests that Lewin was wisely practical in his approach to a complex problem. Lewin would say that his slogan was "Start strong, and the trick is to go through the doors you can open—not to kill yourself trying to go through where you can't open the doors."

Lippitt recalls, "When I went to Iowa as a graduate student, I was not aware of Kurt Lewin and did not go to Iowa in order to study with him. I had planned to go to the graduate school at Columbia University, but Professor Harold Seashore, with whom I studied, met George Stoddard of Iowa at a meeting of the American Psychological Association and persuaded him to offer me an assistantship which had opened up at the last minute because of a change in plans of another student. Professor Seashore urged me to accept the offer, so I found myself leaving New Jersey on a Greyhound bus headed for the University of Iowa. When I arrived at Iowa, I met Dr. Beth Wellman, who was assigner of graduate assistant jobs. The first assignment she gave me was to help Barker and Dembo code the material of the frustration-regression experiments. I met Lewin while on this assignment. At first he struck me as a funny, interesting, relatively inarticulate man whose ideas always seemed to be changing the coding categories. I soon discovered that Lewin was influenced by reflective collaborative dialogue and by the organized presentation of ideas and units of material for reaction by colleagues and students. I was greatly influenced in daily interaction with Kurt for the next four years as a graduate student, another two years as a colleague in the war effort (designing training activities), and a final two years as a staff member at the Research Center for Group Dynamics at M.I.T. During all this period, I felt I was the object of his interest, respect, and, during the later years, affection. These were certainly the bases of his influence."

French remembers Kurt saying that many scientists waste years struggling with difficult problems on the assumption that they are soluble when in fact these problems really are insoluble! So one should more readily reformulate the whole problem—if a problem can't be solved, maybe it is wrongly stated. "This policy of his prevents getting in a rut and forces new ideas." French remembers several discussions with Kurt that illustrate one aspect of his thinking. It was early in World War II, during the German attack on France. At that time, everyone in America was saying that the Maginot Line was impregnable, that Germany would be stopped. I argued in the same way with Kurt, but he was absolutely certain that Germany would crack the Maginot Line. I presented some of the tactical arguments about how impossible it would be and asked Kurt how he thought the German army would do it. He replied that he had no idea *how*, but that that was not the way to think about it. One should forget about the tactics of *how* and make a correct prediction just on the basis of the relative power of the two countries. There might be hundreds of ways to defend the line, but eventually the Germans would break through because they had overwhelmingly superior power."

Lewin's interest in the psychological study of social issues resulted in his writing a number of significant articles that aimed to build a bridge between social theory and social action. The problems they treated are of undiminished importance today. In the face of the vigorous action demanded by black militants and the complex social problems created by these demands, we have something to learn from Lewin's system of thought. In the first of this series of important papers,[2] Lewin describes the challenge confronting minority groups everywhere, and then specifically analyzes the Jewish minority and the nature of the dilemmas it faced.

Every individual, Lewin pointed out in this article, has a base for his life—a "life space"—and one of its most important components is the group to which he belongs. Though he may eventually belong to many groups, the family group usually presents the first and most lasting part of the ground on which he will stand as an individual. It

[2] "Psycho-Sociological Problems of a Minority Group," *Character and Personality*, 1935, 3, 175–187.

is rare, Lewin suggested, for a child to be uncertain about his belonging or not belonging to the family group. In those cases where such uncertainty exists, it is almost always both the result of conflict (between parents) and the source of further conflict for the child.

During most of his life, the adult, too, acts not simply as an individual, but as a member of a social group or groups. The various groups to which he belongs may not all be equally important at a given time—sometimes his membership in one will be dominant, sometimes another—but at each stage he seems to know to which he belongs at that moment and to which he does not. This knowledge of his proper place and allegiance determines his behavior.

Nevertheless, there may be transitional periods when belonging to a group may be doubtful or unclear to him. As a newcomer to a club, for instance, he may feel uncertain for a while as to whether or not he has been accepted. Such doubt generally leads to uncertainty in behavior. Hence the person who does not feel at home is apt to exhibit certain marked personality traits: he may be more or less self-conscious, inhibited, or inclined to overact.

There are, Lewin further observed, persons whose whole life is obsessed by doubt about their "belonging" as a result of being near the margins of groups. The *nouveaux riches*, for example, or others who cross the borders of social classes, as well as members of religious or ethnic minorities, may all exhibit these symptoms of uncertainty as they try to enter the dominant culture. Individuals who cross the border of social groups are not only uncertain about their belonging to the group they are ready to enter, but also uneasy about their membership in one they are leaving. It is, for example, "a principal facet of the Jewish problem," Lewin states, "that Jews are often—and to a high degree—confused about their relation to others who call themselves Jews." They are uncertain about whether they are actually in the Jewish community, in what sense they belong to it, and to what extent.

Basic to the problem, of course, is the question: What does it mean to a man to belong to a group and how does that affect his behavior? Lewin held that the group to which a man belongs is all-important—the source of his social status and of his feeling of security. His reliance on the firmness of this ground might not be consciously perceived—just as one tends to take for granted the physical ground on which one walks—but dynamically the assurance provided by the firmness of this ground determines what a person wants to do, what he can do, and how he will do it. A person and his psychological environment, Lewin insisted, are dynamically one field and should never be treated as separate entities. From early childhood, social facts—especially the sense of belonging to particular groups—are among the most fundamental determinants of the child's growing world, for they shape his wishes and goals and what he considers right and wrong.

All this being so, should the minority-group child—or, particularly, the Jewish child—be made more or less conscious of his membership in a despised group? Would there be any danger that in stressing his membership in it he might be made to feel so isolated from his non-Jewish fellows that this would impair all his relationships with them? Lewin felt it would not. Indeed, he argued to the contrary. To attempt to dissociate the child from his group might plunge him into unnecessarily grave conflicts, weaken his ability to cope with them, and develop in him behavior patterns more likely to increase than to decrease antagonism toward him on the part of the majority group.

CHAPTER

11

TOPOLOGY AND THE REPRESENTATION OF PSYCHOLOGICAL FORCES

The Topology Meetings

If the *Quasselstrippe*—in Berlin or Iowa—was a forum for an exchange of ideas among Lewin's current students, the loose-knit organization that came to be known as the Topology Group performed the same function on a more extended basis for former students, associates, and those who simply counted themselves as Lewin's professional friends. It started spontaneously when some of those who had been with Lewin in Berlin decided they would like to get together with him to discuss theory on an informal basis. The group had no formal membership, no officers, and no by-laws—indeed, even the decision to meet annually was taken casually as a result of the success of the first gathering. Over the years the core group was augmented by friends or new members, but the number at any one meeting generally was limited to thirty-five or forty so that size would not hinder free interaction. With the exception of the World War II years, when travel was restricted, and two years in the early 1960's, the meetings continued annually through 1965.

The first get-together was held during the Christmas holiday at Smith College in Northampton in 1933. Kurt Koffka was on the faculty of Smith, and the group's informal meetings were held in his laboratory there. In attendance was the small circle of colleagues who had known Lewin in Berlin—among them, MacKinnon, Adams, Zener, Heider, Dembo, and several others. A few local people also joined in. There was no plan of continuing yearly meetings. The idea of other meetings developed as the group enjoyed and felt the value of these days that they spent together.

The second meeting, a year later, was held at Duke University, where Adams and Zener were faculty members; and the third gathering, held at Bryn Mawr, was one of the most memorable, for the eminence of its participants and for the spirited discussions which lasted over the three-day period. Adams and Zener came from Duke; Tolman and Krech, from California. Among the others present were Dembo, Erik Erikson, L. K. Frank, Fritz and Grace Heider, Koffka, Köhler, Gerti Lewin, MacKinnon, Margaret Mead, William Stern, and others. In part, the number of those able to be present was increased by the generosity of Lewin's benefactor Lawrence Frank, who obtained a grant from the Laura Spelman Rockefeller Fund to help underwrite expenses.

Despite its informality, with few prepared papers, it was an exciting meeting. As was true of the other topology meetings, everyone said something about what he was working on or what currently interested him. When Margaret Mead, Edward Tolman, Kurt Koffka, and Erik Erikson, with their quite different approaches, joined in, everything that was said and each response to it would stimulate a new idea. There was no atmosphere of attacking and rejecting, and there was none of the painful conflict often present in discussions of theoretical differences.

Typical of the format was the meeting at Harvard the following year, 1936. It opened with a paper by Henry A. Murray on factors within the personality and how they might be approximately estimated, giving details on specific experiments at the Harvard Psychological Clinic. Donald MacKinnon followed with a paper entitled "The Recall Value of Satiated and Non-Satiated Activities." David Shakow reported on the level of aspiration of schizophrenics, and David Krech ended the first day with a paper entitled "Measurement of Negative Valences Induced by Frustration." While the papers were being delivered, Lewin sat quietly in the back of the room, sometimes appearing to be only half listening. But once the discussion began, he was his usual animated self, bursting with ideas, comments, criticism, and encouragement.

The second day was as strenuous as the first, with a report by Barker on his experiments with frustrations and regression in children; one by Ruth Benedict on "Groups of Differentiation Type, Structure, and Degree of Differentiation"; and a paper by Tamara Dembo on "The Conceptual Representation of Certain Facts Important for Psychology and Sociology." By the third day the Topological Society members were down to only two papers—one by Harold Lasswell, on "The Effect of Political Circumstances on Changes in the State of Groups," and one by Gordon Allport, on "The Effect of the Group on the Individual."

Gardner Murphy, who had first met Lewin at the Columbia Faculty Club when he was en route to Stanford in 1932, became much better acquainted with him during the meeting of the Topology group at Cornell during Christmas of 1938. "Edward Tolman was there, and it was a gay, grand party—an intellectual feast—a personal glimpse of intense intellectual companionship," Murphy comments. "Lewin sat characteristically to one side, in an inconspicuous place, while various speakers presented ideas, methods, results. He was always in good humor; he particularly enjoyed having people disagree with him."

Margaret Mead, too, first got to know Lewin at one of the Christmas meetings—an earlier one held at Bryn Mawr in 1935. "Already the shape of later conferences was foreshadowed," she relates, "in that contributors each spoke from their special inspiration, referring to—but not using—Kurt's own complex diagrams and formulations."

One memorable year, 1940—when the group was again at Smith

College—Lewin himself opened the meeting on New Year's Eve with a talk entitled "Bringing the Life Space Up to Date." That evening, under the agenda heading marked "New Year Ceremonies," Margaret Mead led the group in a folk-dancing session that lasted past midnight. By 9:30 in the morning, however, the whole group was up and listening raptly to a lecture by Dan Adler on "The Nature of Repression," followed by Margaret Mead's paper, "Family Organization and the Superego." Brown, whose 1929 paper on Lewin in the *Psychological Review* first brought him to the attention of American psychologists, led the discussion of Miss Mead's paper in the light of psychopathological data.

Fritz Heider, who had known Lewin in Berlin from 1921 to 1924, attended most of the meetings with his wife, Grace. At the 1945 meeting at Smith, Heider gave his first presentation of balance or consistency theory and at the 1948 gathering gave a second talk on this important contribution to social psychological theory.

Jerome Frank, who attended many meetings of the Topology Group, states that these gatherings offered a particularly effective way for Lewin to develop his ideas. There was a quality of freedom and non-defensiveness in the discussion, and—one realized later—a good deal of planning of the sessions which was not apparent to the participants. "It seemed to me," says Frank, "that Lewin exerted influence through innumerable casual contacts of all sorts—perhaps at a meal or in a small group meeting or individually. Because he valued everyone's contribution and could be critical without hurting, he stimulated creativity in all those about him. He indulged in none of the power struggles waged by many of his contemporaries in experimental and clinical psychology or the other social sciences. Yet he was intensely ambitious. Confident of the importance of his own ideas, he accepted the contributions of others but had a way of melting them into his point of view. This self-confidence often made him indifferent to the question of how his work might relate to the theories, research techniques, or results reported by colleagues in the literature or at professional meetings."

MacKinnon, the host at the 1935 Bryn Mawr meeting, has remarked that "in every group of psychologists I was ever part of, it was Kurt's reactions and Kurt's ideas that stimulated the group more than anyone else's. I think the reason why Kurt had such a following was that he loved the ideas people brought with them. Kurt's rewards were the rewards of intrinsic motivation as opposed to extrinsic motivation. Lewin didn't do anything for the pay or other external rewards; he did it because he was vitally interested—in psychoanalytic terms we would say that he invested his own libido—and *loved* the problems we were talking about and he was working with. It was this love that existed and drew the group together—not a personal love of one person for another, but a love that was generated because of Kurt's interest in, and real devotion to, everyone's problems and the time he spent with us on them. Lewin enjoyed what he was doing."

The Topology Group continued to meet annually except, as previously noted, for several years during World War II. In 1964, by informal vote, the Group decided to cease further meetings except for a final dinner meeting in connection with the A.P.A. convention in 1965. Thus, after thirty-two years, as Roger Barker reports, "we put a period to an important sentence in the history of psychology." The meetings had continued to attract outstanding younger psychologists, as well as to retain many of the original participants.

The Representation of Psychological Forces

During his years in Berlin and continuing through Iowa, Lewin continued to be a vigorous advocate of the use of mathematical models in psychology and devoted a major effort to developing formal systems suitable for representing psychological phenomena. In 1938, two years after the publication of *Principles of Topological Psychology*, he completed a monograph entitled "The Conceptual Representation and Measurement of Psychological Forces," which was published that year in *Contributions to Psychological Theory*. In this he actually worked out a formal definition of "valence" in terms of fields of force, divorcing it somewhat from its original phenomenological flavor. The monograph was difficult reading, as was the earlier work on topology, and too few psychologists were willing to devote the time to careful study of his complex system of concepts.

Leeper[1] undertook the task of digesting and restating Lewin's concepts in a monograph published in 1943. This work is an indispensable guide to psychologists who want to understand what Lewin's concepts are all about.

In a 1940 paper [2] Lewin commented favorably on the new interest in theory among American psychologists. While enthusiastic about this trend, he thought it necessary to point to certain dangers. He wrote, "We will produce but an empty formalism if we forget that mathematization and formalization should be done only to the degree that the maturity of the material under investigation permits at a given time."

Lewin's basic aspiration for psychology was that it become a true science. He was convinced that in order to do so it must develop a formal system of concepts, coordinating definitions, and laws which, taken as a whole, would adequately deal with the empirical facts of psychology. He believed that mathematics, especially those branches dealing with the abstract concept of "space," provided an indispensable tool for the psychological theorist. It was this belief that led him to spend so much time on efforts to construct formal systems. Despite this fundamental commitment, he recognized the dangers of what he called "premature formalization," and he was quite prepared to deal with research problems not amenable to rigorous treatment.

Lewin expanded on his own basic position on a number of later occasions. He explained that to him the guiding principle of psychology was to find new knowledge about, and deeper insight into, psychological processes. For this purpose, theory, mathematization, and formalization are the tools. They are of value only insofar as they serve as a means to fruitful progress in subject matter. They

[1] R. W. Leeper, *Lewin's Topological and Vector Psychology: A Digest and a Critique* (Eugene: University of Oregon, 1943).

[2] "Formalization and Progress in Psychology," *University of Iowa Studies in Child Welfare*, 1940, *16*, No. 3, 7–42.

should be applied, as complex tools always should, only when and where they help and do not hinder progress.

Lewin was optimistic that quantitative measurement of psychological forces would soon be accomplished. "This," he added, "will provide the answers for the laws of the composition of forces and aid in the measurement of tensions." When such progress had been made, he believed, it would be realistic to expect that phenomena such as hope or friendship could be presented by mathematical concepts.

At Iowa and later at M.I.T., empirical studies made use of formal derivations from Lewin's theory. Among them were Kounin's work on satiation, Cartwright's thesis on decision time, Festinger's on the same topic, and Bavelas' thesis and subsequent work on the mathematics of group structure.

Lewin wrote a paper with Karl Korsch in 1939 [3] in which he again strongly expressed his commitment to the idea that the dynamic interdependence of psychological processes could be mathematically represented. He attributed the progress of psychology to three developments: (1) strict experimental procedures, (2) progressive formalization and mathematization, and (3) the dynamic constructs of field theory. "But," he concluded, "all methodologial problems today are overshadowed by the problem of how to find a mathematization which adequately represents this dynamic interdependence between psychological processes." Lewin did not claim that topological psychology had arrived at the answer. He offered it as a highly promising approach.

In another article, written for the *American Journal of Sociology* in 1939, Lewin described more fully the need for a unifying approach which a mathematical model could provide. He said, in part, that the variety of facts which social psychology has to treat might really seem frightening to even a bold scientific mind. They include "values"; "ideologies"; "the style of living and thinking" and other aspects of culture; "sociological problems," of group and group structure; "psychological" facts, such as the intelligence of a

[3] "Mathematical Constructs in Psychology and Sociology," *Journal of Unified Science*, 1939, 9.

person, his goals and fears, and his personality; "physiological" data, such as the person's being healthy or sick, strong or weak; finally, such "physical" actualities as the size of the physical area in which the person or a group is located.

It is utterly fruitless and merely a negative scientific treatment to put these facts into classifying pigeonholes. We need positive means of bringing these various types of facts together in such a way that one can treat them on one level without sacrificing the recognition of their specific characteristics. A way must be found to treat bodily changes, shift of ideology, and group-belongingness within one realm of scientific language, in a single realm of discourse of concepts. The question is "How can that be done?"

It can be accomplished by the use of constructs which characterize objects and events in terms of interdependence rather than of phenotypical similarity or dissimilarity. Thus, if one "characterizes an object or event by the way it affects the situation, every type of fact is placed on the same level and becomes interrelated with any other fact which affects the situation. The problem of whether or not one is permitted to combine, e.g., concepts of values with those of bodily weight, vanishes when confronted with the simple truth that both facts influence the same situation. [In the field approach], instead of picking out isolated facts, and later on trying to 'synthesize' them, the total situation is taken into account and is represented from the beginning. The field-theoretical approach, therefore, means a method of 'gradual approximation' by way of a stepwise increasing specificity. Picking out isolated facts within a situation may lead easily to a picture which is entirely distorted. A field-theoretical representation, on the other hand, can and should be essentially correct at any degree of perfection."

CHAPTER
12

EXPERIMENTAL STUDIES

By 1940, Lewin was accepted as one of the country's outstanding experimental and theoretical psychologists. He had already published the pioneer ideas on the use of mathematics in formal theory through his topological and vector psychology. He had brought into the vocabulary of psychological theory such concepts as field force, level of aspiration, life space, tension, and valence. He had devised experiments for such resistant phenomena as anger, conflict, decision, frustration, intention, satiation, and substitution.

"Psychologists," as Gardner Murphy recalls, "began everywhere to talk about aspiration level in the spirit of Kurt's pupil Hoppe, and the Zeigarnik effect related to memory for completed and uncompleted tasks." Then came the Barker-Dembo-Lewin study of dedifferentiation as a consequence of frustration, as well as the Lewin-White-Lippitt studies of authoritarian, laissez-faire, and democratic modes of organizing groups of boys. These soon became as well known, says Murphy, as Albert's rat (described by Watson) and the insight behavior of apes (observed by Köhler). It became clear to Murphy that "Lewinian psychology was rapidly elevated to a position of great importance."

The two studies Murphy refers to, on "Frustration and Regression" and on "Democratic and Autocratic Leadership," had implications for a wide variety of psychological problems, and Lewin and his colleagues approached them with their unusual theoretical and methodological sophistication. The first study, "Frustration and Regression," [1] did more than produce an objective verification of the hypothesis that regression occurs under conditions of frustration; it also added something of historic importance to the entire discipline of psychology.

Earlier studies, particularly Tamara Dembo's on anger done at the Berlin Psychological Institute, had shown that subjects who are frustrated in direct actions leading toward their goals sometimes seek roundabout routes and at other times give up temporarily or altogether. The Iowa experiments were designed to take the inquiry one step further. The study aimed to determine what the behavioral effects of frustration are and how they are produced. They considered this a question of major importance and designed the experiment to test the hypothesis that frustration effects in a variety of ways the level of both intellectual and emotional behavior. To accomplish this, they set out to compare the behavior of young children in a normal situation and in a frustrating one.

Erik Wright, who was part of the Iowa group, conducted a second experiment using a similar procedure and adding observations on the effect of frustration on the social relationship of children. To obtain this data, he conducted his experiment with 78 children in pairs, while Barker, Dembo, and Lewin observed their 30 children individually; the children ran from two to six years of age. Both experiments used play situations well within the everyday experience of small children and in which the youngsters could exercise constructive imagination.

The experimenters wanted to find out what frustration did to intellectual and emotional behavior, especially the constructive or creative qualities of children's activities. The basis for rating con-

[1] R. Barker, T. Dembo, and K. Lewin, "Frustration and Regression: An Experiment with Young Children," *University of Iowa Studies in Child Welfare*, 1941, *18*, No. 1.

structiveness was the richness of the play activity in which the child engaged. Thus the experimenters set up a continuum which ranged from free, simple, little-structured activity to imaginative, highly developed play. The former was rated of low constructiveness; the latter, high. Great care was taken to establish the best possible conditions for constructive play and for the establishment of a feeling of security among the children.

In the non-frustration phase of the experiment, each child was led individually into a room which contained conventional play materials and was left to play alone. The experimenter sat at a desk pretending to be absorbed in his own work but actually making records of the behavior he observed. At the end of thirty minutes, the experimenter walked to the middle of the room and lifted a wire-mesh screen which had closed off half the room. In the "just opened" section, there were a number of new, attractive, and exciting toys and the children were encouraged to play with them. They soon were duly absorbed and thoroughly fascinated. This part of the experiment was designed to develop highly desirable goals for the child which he could later be prevented from reaching. This was a prerequisite to creating frustration.

After the child had become deeply absorbed, the experimenter interrupted the play and led the child to the "old" part of the room. The experimenter then lowered the wire partition and fastened it with a padlock. The exciting toys were still fully visible to the child but were now physically inaccessible. The experimenter returned to his desk, leaving the child to do as he desired with the old toys. Thus began the frustration phase of the experiment. The situation brought out two easily recognized kinds of behaviors. The first related to accessible goals—playing with the conventional toys, talking, etc. The second related to inaccessible goals—trying to reach the toys behind the barrier, coaxing, complaining, making efforts to remove or break the wire partitions, etc.

Records of play for the two periods were then compared and rated for constructiveness. It was found, not surprisingly, that after the wire screen was lowered and locked, the children spent an average of more than one third of the time trying to penetrate the barrier or to escape from the room. A rating of the creativity of the children's various play activities disclosed that the "free" compared with the "frustrated" situations entailed a strikingly different level of constructiveness. As might be expected, the free period had the higher rate.

For the group as a whole, the experimenters found that the higher the level of frustration, the less creativity and the less time given to constructive play during the period. The experiment indicated that in frustration the children tended to regress to a surprising degree. They tended to become babyish. Intellectually, children of four and a half years tended toward the behavior of a three-year-old. The degree of intellectual regression varied directly with the strength of the frustration. Change in emotional behavior was also recorded. There was less smiling and singing and more thumbsucking, noisiness, and restless actions. Aggressiveness also increased and some children went so far as to hit, kick, and break objects. There was a 30 per cent rise in the number of hostile actions toward the experimenter and a 34 per cent decrease in friendly approaches.

Erik Wright, who conducted his experiment with pairs of children, reported differences in behavior when the two youngsters were close friends. In this situation, the two felt strong enough to attack the superior adult power. Thus, when physical attacks on the experimenter were considered, almost 90 per cent were carried out by strong friends and only 10 per cent by weak friends.

The authors summarized their main findings as follows: "Frustration as it operated in these experiments resulted in an average regression in the level of intellectual functioning, in increased unhappiness, restlessness, and destructiveness, in increased ultra-group unity, and in increased out-group aggression. The amounts of increase in negative emotionality were positively related to strength of frustration."

In another 1941 paper, "Regression, Retrogression, and Development," Lewin drew an important distinction between retrogression and regression. He described retrogression as "the return to a type of behavior characteristic of a previous stage of the life history of the individual," a going back to a less mature state which the individual had already outgrown. Regression, on the other hand, was "a change to a more primitive behavior, regardless of whether such behavior has actually occurred within the life history of the individual."

The autocracy-democracy study was the second of the noteworthy inquiries of this period that demonstrated Lewin's bold experimental design. Ronald Lippitt, telling of the inception of this study, says, "During the first month of the fall semester, a memorandum went to all new graduate students with suggestions by the professors for possible master's thesis topics. One of those listed under Dr. Lewin's name was a study of groups and influence structures. My undergraduate work at Springfield College had aroused in me a strong interest in problems of leadership, particularly the effect that different kinds of leaders had on children in character-building agencies. So I made an appointment to discuss this with Lewin. I was soon telling him about leadership and various group work situations I had observed or been involved in, and my idea about studying the influence of various kinds of leadership. He was almost immediately enthusiastic, and we soon got around to talking about autocracy and democracy. He encouraged me to write up a proposal for a study that would compare autocratic and democratic leadership of children's groups. It wasn't until some time later that I discovered that Lewin's original intent, when he had listed the topic, had been to start a mathematical study of the concept of groups as interdependent wholes, with an analysis of the idea of influence structures as one approach. But Lewin's style of fragmentary listening and enthusiastic projecting led to a blending of his thoughts and mine into a worthwhile field experiment."

During the next term, after Lippitt's thesis[2] was completed, Ralph White arrived at Iowa as a General Education Board postdoctoral fellow interested in political science. As Lippitt's experiment involved the kind of research White wanted to do, he worked

[2] "An Experimental Study of Authoritarian and Democratic Group Atmospheres," in Studies in Topological and Vector Psychology, *University of Iowa Studies in Child Welfare*, 1940, *1*, No. 16.

with Lippitt and Lewin to plan a broader experiment, using auto-cratic and democratic styles of group leadership. This was the first of a series of investigations elaborating upon the relationship between leadership, group atmosphere, and consequent group accom-plishment.

As Lippitt described the situation: "Kurt, Ralph, and I planned a more adequate complete experiment on autocratic and democratic styles. During the first or second meeting of the four clubs of eleven-year-old boys who had volunteered, Ralph, who had drawn the role of democratic leader in the first time period, behaved in a way that was quite different from the other democratic-leader roles as we had defined them. He was obviously getting quite a different effect in terms of responses of the children. Kurt's observation of this, as he stood behind the burlap wall and operated the movie camera, led to an excited gleam in his eye as he perceived a basic genotypic difference between the democratic pattern and what we labeled the laissez-faire pattern of leadership. So instead of correcting Ralph's style we moved it more toward a pure case of laissez-faire pattern and planned for other leaders to use the same role to get a more complete analysis of the dynamics of the difference. This shift is a good example of Kurt's creativity."

Lippitt and White,[3] working with small groups of Iowa City boys in 1938, sought to answer such questions as: What is the nature of democratic leadership? Can democracy be as efficient as a more authoritarian type of political organization? The primary objective, however, was to find out to what extent and in what ways the behavior of leaders shapes group behavior. To do this, two types of "leadership style" were considered: In the first style, the leader would automatically tell the group what to do and how to do it, would dominate the group, and would make all judgments as to whether progress was being attained. In sum, the experimenters set up the social atmosphere of the authoritarian leader. In the second style, goals and means for reaching them were left to the group to

[3] K. Lewin, R. Lippitt, and R. White, "Patterns of Aggressive Behavior in Exper-imentally Created 'Social Climates,'" *Journal of Social Psychology*, 1939, *10*, 271–299.

determine democratically. In both groups, the leader's relation to the members was held as constant as possible—friendly, but not particularly warm.

As Lippitt and White described it in their book-length report on the investigation:[4] "A small number of eleven-year-old children met after school to make masks and carry on other activities. They were divided into two groups of five each. They were led by the same person (Lippitt) and met eleven times, but with one batch he played a 'democratic' role and created a democratic atmosphere and with the other he played an 'autocratic' role. Five observers took continuous notes on the behavior of the leader and the children."

According to Lippitt, the data showed that the authoritarian leader usually initiated activity with an order, often disrupting ongoing activity by an order which started things off in a new direction not spontaneously chosen, and fairly frequently criticized the work. The experimenters reported that though "the groups behaved similarly at the outset, they rapidly became different, so that in the later meetings the contrast was striking. In brief, there was far more quarreling and hostility in the autocratically led group, and far more friendliness and group spirit in the one democratically led. The children in the autocratic group picked on scapegoats and showed other behavior that seemed too similar to certain contemporary dictatorships to be mere coincidence."

From this initial experiment, the differences seemed sufficiently striking to warrant a more exact and more detailed investigation. The following year, therefore, a second series of experiments was undertaken. This time, more groups were used; they were composed only of boys; and careful controls over membership and activity were exercised to make the clusters more comparable. It was also decided to add a third variation of "laissez-faire" adult behavior. This better-controlled experiment produced about six times as much evidence as the first. The study took into consideration the basic factor of child personality, and each child had the experience of both an autocratic and a democratic type of leadership. The

[4] R. Lippitt and R. White, *Autocracy and Democracy: An Experimental Inquiry* (New York: Harper & Row, 1960).

expanded experimental design also brought information on other matters—particularly on the characteristics of the transition periods.

Many of the findings of this study were striking. For example, in the autocratic atmosphere the boys were much more likely to lose initiative, to be restlessly discontented, to become aggressive and fight with each other, to damage play materials, and to function as individuals on their own with no concern for group goals or the interests of other members. In the laissez-faire atmosphere, there was much less work-centered behavior and discussion than under either of the other two varieties of leadership. Some boys who had been transferred to the laissez-faire from the authoritarian group became frightened and disturbed. Preference for democratic leadership was clearly expressed by all but one of the twenty boys in the four groups.

The autocratic setup created much discontent that did not appear directly but became noticeable in other ways. For example, the only four boys who dropped out did so during the autocratic leadership periods; more discontent was expressed during these periods although behavior stayed submissive. Autocratic leadership induced more demand for attention and more destruction of personal work materials and it suppressed individual originality. The propensity toward scapegoating became more noticeable.

Scapegoating was also in evidence under the laissez-faire conditions. The researchers attributed it to frustration brought on by too little leadership and to a feeling that there ought to be ground rules. The result was: vague feelings of inadequacy which somehow were relieved by ridicule of the less competent or less liked members of the group.

The experiments made evident a direct relation between group atmosphere and tension levels in the individual members of the group, and showed how the social atmosphere could affect their sense of interdependence and interaction.

To Lewin the results of the study were a source of real satisfaction, for they substantiated his own deeply felt belief in the superiority of the democratic system. "On the whole," he later wrote of the Lippitt-White results, "I think that there is ample proof that the difference in behavior in autocratic and democratic situations is not a result of differences in the individuals. There have been few experiences for me as impressive as seeing the expression on children's faces during the first day under an autocratic leader. The group that had formerly been friendly, open, cooperative, and full of life, became within a short half-hour a rather apathetic-looking gathering without initiative. The change from autocracy to democracy seemed to take somewhat more time than that from democracy to autocracy. Autocracy is imposed on the individual. Democracy he has to learn!' "

To Robert R. Sears, who headed the Child Welfare Research Station during a part of Lewin's stay, there was more than a little reaction formation in Lewin's interest in democracy. "The autocratic way he insisted on democracy was a little spectacular," Sears has observed. "There was nothing to criticize—but one could not help noticing the fire and the emphasis."

Alex Bavelas, who came to Iowa as the Lippitt-White study was being completed, suggested that people could be trained easily enough to be quite democratic, even though they were autocratic on their jobs, and that their behavior could be reshaped by using a number of different methods. Lewin asked him, "How would you do it?" Bavelas replied that he was not sure how, but that he was certain it could be done. Lewin repeated, "How would you do it?" Reluctantly, Bavelas sketched out some possibilities, and Lewin said, "Fine. Suppose you try them out." Ultimately, the ideas sketched by Bavelas became the basis for an extension of the autocracy-democracy studies to the field of industrial relations.

The Lippitt-White studies provide a representative model of how students and faculty teamed up to carry out Lewin's experimental designs. A number of colleagues assisted Lippitt and White, serving as observers, helping to analyze data, and acting as leaders in the various experiments. The inquiry was a cooperative product, another kind of Iowa *Quasselstrippe*. It indicated, too, Lewin's increasing concern with what was going on in the world around him, particularly in what happens to people under democratic and non-democratic conditions. The Lippitt-White studies were steps toward what came to be called "action-research"—the experimental use of social sciences to advance the democratic process.

Beatrice Wright says that "experiments like the frustration and the autocracy-democracy research take a good deal of time. It is much easier to run rats in mazes or to administer paper-and-pencil questionnaires in order to get large samples of data in short order. American psychologists in universities are too pressed to publish or perish, to get results quickly. Lewin's basis for tackling problems was always because they were significant and could be approached in conceptually meaningful terms. He was not constrained by criteria of speed, quantity, or statistical and experimental precision."

She adds that "Lewin's oft-quoted saying, 'There is nothing as practical as a good theory,' has sometimes been misinterpreted and used to discredit research that does not follow a precisely formulated theory or that is practically oriented. To be sure, theory was always an intrinsic part of Lewin's search for understanding, but the theory often evolved and became refined as the data unfolded, rather than being systematically detailed in advance. Lewin was led by both data and theory, each feeding the other, each guiding the research process. As for practically oriented research, Lewin's concern with social issues led him to value knowledge that could be applied to the social problems of the day. Research could be directed toward practical issues so long as it had the theory to guide it through all its stages. Indeed, if the theory were *good*, there would be nothing more practical."

A third crucial experiment carried out by the Lewin group—the so-called "Food Habits Study"—came about as a result of America's entry into World War II and of the friendship that had developed between Lewin and anthropologist Margaret Mead.

When the United States became involved in World War II, Margaret Mead was asked by M. L. Wilson, then Director of Extension in the U. S. Department of Agriculture, to serve as secretary for the Committee on Food Habits of the National Research Council. Wilson was the coordinator of the entire Federal Nutrition Program and had long dreamed of applying social science to problems of social change. The exigencies created by subsequent wartime food rationing provided the possibility of making his dream come true, and he asked anthropologists, psychologists, and sociologists to work with him on the Committee on Food Habits. The invitation to Margaret Mead to serve as secretary was part of the working out of his idea—and it would lead, through her, to Lewin.

It was on this basis, recounts Miss Mead, and in the knowledge that if social scientists were to participate in the coming war effort it was necessary to do a little field work in Washington, that she accepted the appointment. Characteristically, she doesn't remember whose idea it was which resulted in the eventual cooperation between the nutrition program in Washington and Kurt's graduate students at the University of Iowa.

Wilson was enthusiastic about Lewin. The two men worked out a design for a series of various kinds of studies which were relevant to the problems facing the Committee on Food Habits and which Lewin would conduct.

"The years in which I worked most intensively with Kurt were among his last at the University of Iowa," Mead relates. "Our committee had been requested to study and advise governmental agencies how to alter habits and tastes so that they would embody the findings of the new science of nutrition and also, during the wartime emergency, maintain the health of the American people, in spite of shortages and necessary shifts in types of food. As anthropologists, we came to the conclusion that our first task was to find out what American food habits were, what was the cultural setting within which different groups of Americans—those of foreign stock, those from different parts of the country—selected, prepared, ate, and enjoyed foods that kept them well or indifferently nourished. However, as a psychologist, Kurt's imagination turned first to experiment. This contrast was one which he and I kept constantly in play.

"Lewin set up a laboratory to work on the best psychological approaches to change, with food habits as the setting for the research, but his real interest, of course, was far wider even than how the people of the United States, or of the world for which we were also trying to plan, could learn to eat wisely and well.

"It was a lively group who always met my plane those days in

Iowa City, and if I come down at any prairie airport at sunset I can still recapture the sense of excitement and freedom, as I was greeted by a group of students whose personalities had been liberated by the atmosphere in which Kurt worked.

"I had to state our cultural hypotheses in forms which were intelligible to Kurt and his research group, who were oversensitive to individual differences and still skeptical about cultural differences. We wrestled far into the night over cultural formulations which would be derived from a study of New England and the Midwest: Specific formulations were then tried out in versions of the Bavelas test: 'What is a good meal for a boy to eat?' and 'Who would praise him for it?' From open-ended tests of this sort—psychological ones related to carefully constructed cultural hypotheses—we obtained new information about customs, finer differentiations of the maternal and paternal moral roles in the local Iowa version of American culture, and concrete details showing that Father presided over meat and butter, Mother over green vegetables and fruit juices, while desserts and soft drinks were wholly delightful and approved by no parent at all."

During the course of these studies, Miss Mead recalls, the concept later known as "group decision" was developed. Incongruous as it might seem that so significant a process should originate in a set of experiments on how housewives could learn to eat and serve so-called "variety meats," this was precisely where it began. Another set of studies had revealed that, though women claimed that their choice of meat to serve their families was imposed on them by their husbands, this actually was not the case. Indeed, it had been shown that the husbands had to eat what their wives themselves liked. All that would be necessary, therefore, to promote wider use of variety meats was to convince the housewives that they liked to eat them.

Other studies were conducted with carefully constructed groups of housewives or fraternity students on the use of such food items as whole-wheat bread or turnips. Miss Mead remembers the ill-fated experiment in which she was brought in as the "prestige expert from Washington to express publicly my high approval of turnips— which had no effect at all." But from these studies the experimenters learned that groups of people "can do a thing better when they themselves decide upon it, and also how they themselves can elect to reduce the gap between their attitudes and actions."

Margaret Mead's visits are remembered vividly by those who were at Iowa during the war period. "She and Kurt were fabulous together," remembers Sears. "Both could talk a mile or two a minute. When they sat down together, she would look worshipfully and silently at Kurt, and after a minute something he said would set her off, and he would start stuttering, 'but—but—but—' She would talk at him, and someone else would try to slow it down and say, 'Let's go after this—' They would just go at things and finally come out with some agreement."

CHAPTER

13

WIDENING CIRCLE

As Lewin's renown in America increased, invitations to lecture came from various academic institutions. He graciously accepted as many as he could and usually was overcommitted and overworked. In the spring of 1936, Lewin was asked to speak at the Menninger Clinic in Topeka, Kansas, and the nearby University of Kansas in Lawrence. Though Lewin was far from being a Freudian, he "showed ingeniously," as Feigl, who accompanied him, recalls, "how he could accommodate some psychoanalytic concepts within the frame of his psychological theory."

In his talk at the Menninger Clinic, Lewin stated that many of the concerns of topological psychology were shared by psychoanalysis —need, will, personality, and especially substitution. He also saw similarities between the topological and psychoanalytic approaches in that their center of interest lies in the problems of emotions and personality development. Both try to overcome the divisions between parts of psychology; both stress the psychological meanings of actions and objects, rather than just their physical appearance; and in both fields practitioners refuse to be content with mere descriptions and try rather "to deal with the causal interrelations of psychological phenomena."

Lewin went on to list their important differences, those that affected their methodology and the form and content of their theories. "Psychoanalytical ideas," he pointed out, "are based mainly on

132

the case study and a very special exploratory and therapeutic technique." Topological psychology, by way of contrast, employs all the accepted scientific methods, but it stresses especially the findings obtained through systematic experiments. Nor would topological psychology be satisfied with the method of proof employed by psychoanalysts for their theories. "It insists upon the much more rigid and higher standards of experimental psychology," he said, "such as have been developed in perception psychology."

The same lack of experimental precision, he felt, affects the content of psychoanalysis, which "has more or less consciously preferred richness of content to logical strictness of theory." To Lewin, psychoanalysis seemed speculative and intuitive, rather than logical and exact. "In other words," he said, "psychoanalysis is a *body of ideas*, rather than *a system of theories and concepts*." In its content, too, he contended, psychoanalysis most often confuses the problem by giving historical answers to systematic problems—a confusion of which topological psychology is free. Topological psychology distinguishes clearly between the two types of problems. In particular, topological psychology takes cognizance of the psychological environment—that is, it regards all psychological events as derived from the life space as a whole, and this, said Lewin, "includes both person and environment, whereas psychoanalysis deals mainly with the person."

He also felt that the very depth of historical coverage in psychoanalysis—especially in view of its failure to distinguish sufficiently between historical and systematic formulations—was a liability as well as an asset.

It is hopeless, Lewin argued, to try to establish any sort of laws in psychology without drawing on the experimental method. Though he conceded that the procedure of the psychoanalyst might be regarded as experimental in that the recovery of his patient "proved" his theory to be correct, Lewin did not recognize this as valid as evidence derived from experiments would be. "The superiority of the experimental method," he reiterated, "is based solely on two facts: it is a good way to disprove theories and it is highly self-correcting."

That psychoanalysis fails to distinguish sufficiently between historical and systematic problems seemed to Lewin to mean that it has much in common with the pure associationist approach he had disavowed in Berlin in the 1920's. "Both theories often answer the question 'Why does a person behave in a certain way?' by pointing to a similar behavior in his past." But topological psychology "strictly adheres to the 'principle of concreteness,' according to which only existing facts can influence behavior. This means that the psychological facts of yesterday have as little existence today as the psychological facts of tomorrow."

Lewin did not rule out the importance of the historical factor, which he judged to be essential to psychoanalysis, especially in its accounting for the present state of the person and his situation. But he looked at the historical aspects from a quite different point of view. They were valid "only if repetition of a situation leads to different behavior." "Not similarity but dissimilarity of effects in similar situations (or similarity of effects in dissimilar situations)," he noted, "has historical significance; it shows that some change of the person or the environment has occurred and that the similar situation has become, for historical reasons, in fact dissimilar. If one were to find the structure of the life space in a certain emotional state—for instance, in despair—to be essentially the same at different age levels, no historical explanation would be needed or even permissible."

The distinction between the historical and the systematic explanations of behavior was to Lewin absolutely basic. "If only the present state of the person influences his behavior today, as topological psychology claims, and if at the same time certain experiences and structures of the child have a direct influence upon the adult, as psychoanalysis claims, one would have to assume an immense rigidity of acquired structures within a living being." Then he noted that the extent to which the dynamic structure of the person remains unchanged during development and the way in which changes do occur constitute "one of the basic problems of psychology."

Next, Lewin told his listeners, he recognized a basic difference between the *concepts* of topological psychology and those of psychoanalysis. "Any attempt to deal scientifically with causal problems," he observed, requires the ignoring of directly observable phenomena and the introduction of such "intervening concepts" as force, libido, and drive, which can be observed only indirectly. Lewin found it impossible to treat such concepts with mathematical precision. He felt that they were derivations and conclusions "made more by feeling than by logic in the strict sense. If one asks the psychoanalyst whether the libido is an energy or a force," he generally gives the traditional and approved answer that "libido is directed energy." It would embarrass the users of such terms to take them too seriously, Lewin felt, or to ask "in what field the libido changed its locomotion; how the direction and the amount of change in direction can be determined; how the momentum of the libido is measured; and so forth."

But topological and vector psychology *are* able to "offer a variety of concepts which are mathematically strict, yet fully adequate to the nature of psychological processes, and which are not restricted to any particular school." For example, in the case of regression the close relationship which psychoanalysis finds between the present behavior of the adult and certain experiences in his childhood, Lewin continued, may be to a great extent "merely the result of the psychoanalytical method of revealing the person's history—that is, by free associations, dream analysis, and other procedures which, according to topological psychology, themselves depend upon the *present* state of the person; and all three might be consistent with one another in spite of the important differences between the actual history of the person and that revealed psychoanalytically." Lewin felt that the historical aspect of the problem of regression could be studied "only if one can establish the actual historical data independently," and he noted that psychoanalysis itself was coming around to this view.

"In summary," he concluded, "the psychoanalytical theory has developed a system of ideas unequaled in richness and detailed elaboration in the fields of needs, dreams, and personality." The case study method provides the psychoanalyst with access to the intimate history of the individual and his deeper personality layers "in a way unreached by other methods." But it does not provide opportunities for testing laws with the precision of the experimental method. Here it seemed to Lewin necessary to bring the problems involved "to a distinctly higher level conceptually. Topological and vector psychology, which in themselves are neutral to psychological schools, seem to be of decided help in this respect. Above all, it is necessary to distinguish historical and systematic problems and to eliminate historical answers to systematic questions." To accomplish this end, he agreed, cooperation between topological psychology and psychoanalysis "might prove fruitful."

Lewin spent two productive semesters at Harvard University, where he was a visiting professor during the spring terms of 1938 and 1939. Although the Harvard faculty of psychology wanted him joined closely to their department, he found himself most comfortable in the Harvard Psychological Clinic, where he held his seminars. The interests of the department were too abstract for him and too concerned with the elegant experiment instead of the realities of daily life. At the Clinic behavior was dealt with more directly. Harvard psychology at the time, with its galaxy of Gordon Allport, Edwin G. Boring, Karl Lashley, S. Smith Stevens, and Henry Murray, who headed the Clinic, was diversely fertile. Lewin found all of them congenial in one way or another.

Allport, a close friend, spent much time with Lewin promoting the concept of attitudes, trying to persuade him to accord it a more systematic place in his theory. He also urged Lewin, as had others, to import into his system various psychoanalytic concepts. Characteristically, Lewin listened courteously, conceded that there might be much truth in Allport's argument, and then, according to Allport, pleaded in his peculiarly winning manner, "Now, you don't mind, do you, if I represent the same phenomenon in a slightly different way?" "Whereupon," Allport recalls, "more often than not, he drew a Jordan curve. His restless intelligence seemed continuously to put forth pseudopods to engulf the thought of the other; but the prize once grasped was forthwith assimilated into the parent body of field theory. When Lewin took cognizance of the work of others, his response was an urge to reshape this thought into his own expanding system."

During part of his time at Harvard, Lewin lived alone at the Ambassador Hotel, where at one point he became ill and stayed in his room for several days. Learning of the illness, Allport arranged to have Lewin admitted to the Stillman Infirmary. He went to Lewin's room, bundled him up, and took him to the elevator. When the elevator door opened, there appeared a very frenzied gentleman who kept repeating, "How do you get out of this damned trap? I've been going up and down and can't make it behave!" The frantic gentleman was Bertrand Russell. "Between his hysterics and Kurt's delirium, I had a memorable elevator ride," declares Allport. "Needless to say, I did not attempt to introduce the two passengers."

Mason Haire adds to the picture: "Though the longest period during which I worked with Lewin was at M.I.T. after the war, I first met him at Harvard in 1939 when he was leading a seminar as a visitor. Quite a few people who worked with him later started with Lewin at that time, including Jack French, Dorwin Cartwright, John Harding, and Eliot Jacques. I think Lewin had a great deal to offer Harvard and wanted to be invited there. On the Harvard faculty, he seemed to get along best with Gordon Allport, though the relationship was difficult because their orientation was so different. Henry Murray and Lewin also had difficulties because they *were* more similar, though I'm judging this from the vantage point and distance of a graduate student. Stevens' 'operationism' was a way of letting the experiment intervene between the experimenter and the phenomenon, in the tradition of Boring. The idea was to get at the physical dimensions and not worry about epiphenomena. But Lewin was interested in going deeply into the study of the phenomenon, and so he was happier at the Clinic."

Gardner Murphy had been present when, during an earlier visit by Lewin to Harvard in 1936, Lewin and Henry Murray were comparing "systems." Lewin was, as usual, covering a blackboard—in the lecture room on the second floor of Emerson Hall—with his symbolizations of hodological and vector psychology. The air was heavy with chalk dust. "But how," asked Murray, standing before

137

the maze of lines and cross-hatchings, "can you deal with *qualitatively different* motives, vectors, goals?" Lewin chuckled. "Oh, in that event we use different colors of chalk."

"I was completely captivated by the very charm and convenience, both of the broad conceptualization and of the graphic representations," Murphy said. "In fact, in my first efforts to describe my own version of field theory, in a paper which appeared in the *Journal of Social Forces,* embodying what I had offered at the American Psychological Association in 1936, I used planes, surfaces, and subdivided areas in the manner of Kurt. I did not feel that the conception of 'psychological space' (or, as Stern put it, 'personal space') was well worked out; and Kurt and I once had a hot argument as to whether some of his diagrams gave us a sociological picture of persons interacting in a group and whether somehow the life space of each of the persons involved could be adequately represented in this manner."

Another invitation brought Lewin to the University of California in Berkeley during the summer of 1939. Being on the West Coast meant being close once more to Roger and Louise Barker, who had moved from Iowa, first to Harvard and then back to Stanford. Sears vividly remembers that summer when Lewin taught at Berkeley. Sears' wife, Pat, had just received her Ph.D. at Yale, writing a dissertation on "level of aspiration." John Gardner had won his degree at Berkeley with another "level of aspiration" study, and Sears had written several similar papers and had been working on "conflict."

"We were all filled with Lewinian empirical data," Sears recalls. "We attended a seminar Lewin held about once a week. I was brash and young and he was the great man, but he was very kind when we got into an exchange. One evening there was a crowd of fifty or sixty, and we were giving twenty-minute reports. The topic was 'aggression.' I was co-author of a paper on frustration and aggression published at Yale. I talked excitedly for a half-hour and summarized the position, emphasizing the theoretical formulations, and sat down. Then Kurt got up and started talking about his very different concept of 'aggression.' You would not have known it was the same phenomenon. Nothing he said sounded to me like 'aggression.' I got up after he had finished and said, 'Well, Kurt, this is all very well, but when you talk about disorganization of behavior, or whatever you call it, this isn't "aggression." ' He looked at me and said, 'On the contrary, that is "aggression." After I listened to you talk, I didn't know what topic *you* were talking about.' "

When the 1939 summer session at Berkeley ended, the Lewins went with the Barkers for a brief holiday to a cabin in the Sierra Madre mountains loaned to the Barkers by Louise's uncle. Robert Leeper, another member of the Lewin circle, joined them, and it was there that they first received the news that Hitler's armies had swept into Poland on September 1. The cabin had no electricity, but Kurt tuned in the car radio. Amid the shrieks and whines of its static, they heard the news. "This is it," Lewin told them. "This is the beginning, and it won't end in Poland."

Lewin was deeply pessimistic. During the years since his own escape from Nazism, he had often spoken about the blindness of those intellectuals who seemed unable to perceive that a holocaust was coming. He had increased the time and effort he spent trying to save family and friends who were still abroad, and often discussed with American friends the anguished dilemma that arose when suddenly, at last, everyone wanted to get out of Germany at once and it was not possible to bring them all. Neither Lewin nor his friends could possibly provide the large number of guarantors needed to bring to the United States all who wanted to emigrate from Germany. He had to make heart-breaking recommendations about priorities. A friend remembers of this period, "He was busy with endless correspondence about it. Gerti typed, and he dictated. And he walked up and down the floor."

Lewin's desperate efforts and the obstacles he encountered in trying to save his mother were typical of the experiences faced by many others. These have been documented by Arthur D. Morse in his book *While Six Million Died*.[1] Morse indicts government officials for failing to use the machinery at their disposal to rescue Jews from Hitler, and even going so far as to use the U. S. Government machinery to prevent the rescue of Jews.

[1] D. A. Morse, *While Six Million Died* (New York: Random House, 1968).

In December 1941, when all doors to America seemed closed, Lewin attempted to get a Cuban entry visa for his mother. The following extract from a letter he wrote me on December 5 describes his desperation:

I am in great trouble with the affidavit for my mother. We have sent something like $2,600 to Cuba and have the official receipts here. We have a photostatic copy of the wire sent to Germany by the Cuban government about September 10th or 20th but the Cuban consulate in Germany says that it has not received it. About four weeks ago, we finally got the Cuban government to send a second wire to the Cuban consulate in Berlin. Last Saturday I again had a wire, from the company in Amsterdam with which my mother deals, to the effect that the Cuban consulate has not received the visa. . . .

I know that people over sixty are sent wholesale from Berlin to Poland and that it is only a question of time before they will do the same thing with other countries.

But Lewin's exhausting efforts, reinforced by those of his friends, could not break through the long chain of State Department bureaucratic inaction. Sometime in 1943 his mother was shipped from Holland to a Nazi extermination camp somewhere in Poland. By mid-1944 he realized that his mother was dead.

At Milford, New York, Summer 1934. Left to right:
Alfred J. Marrow, Kurt Lewin, Fritz Heider.

A topology meeting, Duke University, 1934. Left to
right: John R. P. French, Jr., Esther Lewin, Karl
Zener, Horace Kallen (standing), Donald K. Adams.

Bryn Mawr, 1935. Left to right: Karl Zener, Kurt Koffka, William Stern, Molly Harrower, Tamara Dembo, Kurt Lewin, Genia Haufmann, Lawrence K. Frank, George Kreezer, Wally Reichenberg-Hackett, Grace Heider, Donald MacKinnon, David Krech, Lorene Wright.

Bryn Mawr, 1935. Left to right: Louise Barker, Roger Barker, Tamara Dembo, Herbert Wright, Lorene Wright, Lawrence K. Frank, Kurt Lewin.

Bryn Mawr, 1935. Left to right: Kurt Koffka, Theodora Able, Molly Harrower, Margaret Mead.

Kurt Lewin (left) and Kurt Koffka (right) holding a reluctant Edward Tolman for the photographer. Bryn Mawr, 1935.

At the World's Fair, New York, 1939. Kurt Lewin and (center) Monette Marrow.

C.C.I. meeting at the Plaza Hotel, New York, 1945. Left to right: Rabbi Irving Miller, Alfred J. Marrow, Rabbi Stephen Wise, Kurt Lewin, Charles Hendry.

At the Connecticut Workshop, 1946. Left to right: Frank Wright, Leah Gold Fein, Kurt Lewin, Kenneth Benné, Leland Bradford.

CHAPTER

14

ACTION RESEARCH
IN INDUSTRY

Lewin's concern for significant social problems of the day had originally led him, in his paper on Taylorism in 1920, to deal with the role of work in man's life. Though he recognized that the industrial setting was a bitterly controversial issue in the United States in the late 1930's, he did not hesitate to turn his attention to it when the opportunity arose in 1939. The occasion was the opening of a new manufacturing plant in a rural community in Virginia by the Harwood Manufacturing Corporation, of which I was an officer. The factory management faced many critical problems in trying to train three hundred inexperienced apprentices—people from the Virginia mountains—to meet the high standards of the production of the industrialized areas of the North. The trainees—mainly women with no factory experience—were eager to work, but on the job their work pace was slow and their output was low. After the customary twelve weeks of training required for reaching the skill level of an experienced worker, the local trainees produced only about half as much as apprentices doing similar tasks in northern plants.

Lewin was invited to visit the plant to meet with the staff to discuss the problem. Thus began a collaborative relationship that lasted for eight years. The plant manager reviewed the baffling human problems he was having. He explained that the employees' wages were higher than those they had been earning as domestics, farmworkers, or waitresses, that they felt good about their jobs, and yet the turnover was extremely high. Of immediate concern was that the workers were not producing enough and the plant was suffering heavy losses. The engineering department and the supervisory staff had tried all the known systems of rewards to increase production. At best the improvement was small. Continued supervisory pressure resulted only in an increase in the number of workers who quit their jobs.

In a problem-solving session that lasted all morning Lewin made a number of observations. One was that the employees' failure to meet management's requirements might be due to their feeling that the production goal set by the company was impossible to attain. The disparity between their own output—attained with great physical effort—and the production goals set by management was so great that the employees experienced no feelings of failure in not reaching it. There was nothing either inside or outside the plant to give the quota social reality.

Lewin suggested a number of methods to try to change the situation. The first was to stop putting pressure on individual employees. The second was to deal with workers as members of small groups rather than as individuals. Third, find some methods to give the group the feeling that the standard was realistic and could be reached. Lewin's recommendations were followed. The situation began to improve, but there were still too few workers meeting the company standard. Since Lewin had stressed how important it was for the employees to be confident that the goal could be met without strain, the management decided to take a step previously rejected. This involved offering jobs to experienced people who lived in other communities. A plant about forty miles away was closing and thus putting a large number of skilled workers out of work. Many of the latter were willing to take jobs at Harwood if the company could assure them of regular employment, help them find new places to live, and defray some of the moving costs.

In other circumstances these conditions might not have been

acceptable, since many members of the community where Harwood had its plant were unemployed. The town officials strongly opposed giving jobs to outsiders, but were persuaded to let the program be tried. About sixty highly skilled, experienced operators were added to the roster of Harwood employees and these newcomers were soon meeting management's production standards. For about two weeks the earlier employees remained at their low level of production. Then, slowly, they began to improve their output. Since the apparently unattainable goal was being reached, it began to look really practicable. What the experienced newcomers could do, the original trainees could also do.

Lewin made a number of visits to the plant. He was popular with production workers and supervisors alike—popular for himself and for his suggestions. Normally, these employees would have been suspicious of a foreigner, especially a psychology professor with no industrial experience who spoke English with a German accent. But Lewin won their confidence by his warmth, his understanding of their problems, and his good humor. They soon came to respect him for teaching them new ways of doing and thinking. His first baffled attempts to understand their southern drawl amused them; and they were flattered by the way he quickly adopted some of their expressions, such as the retort "That's snake oil" when he felt that an explanation was bogus.

Lewin actively encouraged the Harwood management to start a program of research and to employ Alex Bavelas, then at the University of Iowa, to plan and put into effect a series of small-group studies on human factors in factory management. This was agreed to and Bavelas launched a number of pioneering experiments. The earliest was aimed at discovering the effect of giving employees greater control over their output and an opportunity to participate in setting their own goals. The suggestions for this study came in part from the earlier food-habits experiments in which housewives had carried out decisions they had shared in making and in part from the autocracy-democracy study of Lippitt and White.

Group Decision

Bavelas began by holding meetings, lasting for about thirty minutes, several times a week with a small group of high-producing operators. The atmosphere was informal and no pressure was used. Everyone was encouraged to discuss the difficulties he would encounter if the group wanted to increase its daily production. The discussion revealed that people on the same job used different methods. These were examined and the advantages and disadvantages were analyzed. When the group suggested ways of overcoming the difficulties it anticipated, management agreed to help make the changes that were recommended.

The group was then asked to vote on the issue of increasing its own daily output. Each worker would decide for himself, but in the reinforcing context of the group setting. The group decided to lift output from the prevailing high ceiling of 75 units to 87 units, a level never before attained. It decided to reach the goal within five days—and did so. Later, the group raised its goal to 90 units, reached it, and later maintained it for five months, during which time other groups in the plant showed no significant increase.

This occurred because the act of deciding has the effect of linking motivation to action. Lewin explained, "Motivation alone does not suffice to lead to change. This link is provided by decisions. A process like decision making, which takes only a few minutes, is able to affect conduct for many months to come. The decision seems to have a 'freezing' effect which is partly due to the individual's tendency to 'stick to his decision' and partly to the 'commitment to a group.'" Lewin stated that a discussion would have an outcome different from a decision. To test this hypothesis, Bavelas compared the effectiveness of group discussion with group decision. He held separate meetings with two other groups of skilled operators. But here the agenda consisted only of discussion about raising production rather than making a decision to do so. He found that for the discussion group only a slight improvement followed. This seemed to confirm that the condition precedent to action is decision, that discussion by itself is not enough.

Self-Management

In another experiment, Bavelas studied the use of "pacing cards" as a way toward greater self-management in the work situation. He had a small group of workers plan their own hourly pace by means of such cards. So long as they kept at or above the required minimum quota, workers could plan their own hourly and daily work level. (They were on piece work, so the more they produced, the higher their earnings.) According to Lewin, the fairly constant output of a production worker is quasi-stationary. Production therefore could be increased by strengthening the forces tending toward higher levels or weakening the forces tending to push production down.

In this experiment, Bavelas found a marked increase in the output of the pacing-card group. It raised its production from a level of 67 units to 82 and stabilized at this level. The control group remained unchanged. Such a rise, Lewin observed, could not have been achieved by pressure methods, which bring on fatigue, aggressiveness, nervousness, and marked variation in output. But by diminishing the forces tending toward lower production by means of his pacing-card device, Bavelas was able to bring about a marked increase of output accompanied by relatively low tension—a necessary ingredient of stable production.

As is almost inevitable in a business enterprise, experimentation at Harwood had to be subordinated to practical factory needs. Promising research often had to be interrupted because of unexpected changes in production schedules or operating plans. Yet Bavelas, and then French, who succeeded him, were able to enroll many of the 600 plant workers and almost all of the plant's managers in one experiment or another over the years 1940–1947.

Leadership Training

In every industrial organization a main goal is to improve the rate of production. One means of doing this at Harwood was to train foremen for leadership. Appointed to their jobs because of their technical know-how, these supervisors already had the required mechanical skills. But leadership ability and style varied considerably from person to person. Could the supervisors' leadership skills be strengthened by new insights into their role as group leaders?

With the Lippitt-White study of authoritarian and democratic leadership as a point of reference, Lewin discussed with French setting up a new program of leadership training in which all levels of supervisory management would participate. Role playing, sociodrama, problem solving, and other action techniques were to be emphasized; lectures and discussions of theory would be few and brief.

The overall purpose of the leadership-training experiment was to equip the supervisors with more effective methods of winning cooperation, building trust, improving morale, and handling the disciplinary problems of their subordinates. Training these supervisors called for practices of self-examination, feedback, openness, confidence building, and group problem solving—all new in industry. The success of the experiment at Harwood encouraged French to employ many of the same techniques at the first session of the National Training Laboratories in Bethel, Maine, in 1947. Since then the leadership training methods begun in industry have become integral parts of sensitivity training programs.

Changing a Stereotype

French was aware that businessmen, although they pride themselves on being fact-minded, base any number of their personnel policies on stereotypes and not on scientific fact finding. A stereotype which confronted the Harwood management was the traditional attitude toward hiring older workers for machine jobs. The growing labor scarcity during World War II made it necessary to hire any workers who were available. But the suggestion that the policy be changed, and women over thirty years of age be employed, was vigorously resisted by supervisors at all levels. To overcome this attitude French held a number of staff meetings at which he offered objective scientific evidence that women over thirty could acquire the needed skills. Although the supervisors listened attentively and seemed impressed, their reluctance to hire older women remained as strong as ever.

French doubted that presenting more facts would change the supervisors' attitudes and decided that it would be necessary for the staff to discover the facts for themselves. Only in this way would the necessary insight be developed—the recognition of discrepancy between fact and belief. Toward this end, French suggested that top staff members undertake a research project of their own. If older workers were inefficient, it would be practical to determine how much money the company was losing by retaining the older women already on the job—women who, for the most part, had been given employment as hardship cases—as, for example, widows or women whose husbands were unable to work. French's suggestion was acted upon. The main cost factors considered were daily output, turnover, absenteeism, and speed of learning.

While French was to be available for counsel if wanted, the staff members were to conduct the project themselves. They determined the best methods of collecting data and made all other decisions. The project was theirs, not his. After a thorough study of the records over a period of several months, the results revealed surprisingly that the older women not only equaled but actually surpassed the younger women in work performance. Analysis of learning speed gave similar results: the older workers learned new skills more rapidly. Absenteeism and turnover comparisons also favored the older workers. Thus, on the basis of criteria of efficiency specified by the staff itself, women over thirty were as good as—if not better than—those under that age. The result was in sharp contrast to the

147

staff's expectations, but, the findings being their own, they trusted them.

This, however, was only winning half the battle. The task still remained not only of informing but—as it turned out—of convincing those members of the managerial staff who had not participated in the research. They continued to remain rigidly set against the employment of the older women. They too had to be re-educated. Before going into this phase of the project, the staff sought a sample reaction. They selected a representative forelady and asked her how one of the older workers in her unit was getting along. She answered that this woman was one of the mainstays of her assembly line. Similar queries about each of the eight older workers in her department of seventy workers brought similar glowing reports.

Since this forelady had expressed such satisfaction with the older workers in her department, she was asked if she'd be willing to use any additional women over thirty to fill still-open places in her unit. The suggestion shocked her; she rejected it. Her reason was that older workers would create problems and not solve them. They would take her time and only produce inferior quality. Women over thirty, moreover, were not strong enough to stand the pace.

It was obvious that the forelady's own satisfaction with the older women in her unit had no influence on her stereotype. Unaware of her inconsistency, she could be objective in evaluating specific individuals but not in her general view of the same matter. The older women she knew continued to be "exceptions." The vigor of her reaction made it apparent that the supervisors could not be won over as individuals and that re-education of the entire supervisory staff as a group would be required. This was undertaken, and later group decisions were reached recommending that an experiment be made in the training of new, older workers to see if they could make a record consistent with that of older women already in the plant. In this way, the idea of hiring older women workers gradually came to be accepted.

This experiment demonstrated that the manner in which an experience is introduced functions as a decisive factor. When the members of a group participate in a program to discover the facts about their own beliefs, the findings they make will stimulate changes in their conduct. The experiences they acquire—and share with others —as part of fact-finding research make possible the establishment of new behavior patterns which otherwise would be rejected.

French recalls that Lewin locked him in my office in New York and made him dictate an article [1] on this experience in changing the stereotype toward older workers—an incident which, French says, "illustrates his ability to see and appreciate a potential contribution even when he first heard it as only a casual anecdote. Who else would have been so ready to say, 'That ought to be published,' when it did not conform at all to the conventional methodological criteria?"

Overcoming Resistance to Change

One of the most serious managerial problems at Harwood during the years of Lewin's association was the resistance of production workers to changes in methods and job operations necessitated by competitive conditions, engineering progress, or consumer demands. When model changes occurred in the plant, as they did several times a year, it was necessary to transfer workers from old jobs to new ones. They were taken from jobs on which they were highly skilled and placed on new ones which required considerable time for the development of skill. Workers always resisted these transfers and they were times of frustration for both operators and management.

Evidence gained in interviews supported the judgment that the resistance to the change and the slow relearning were primarily motivational problems. Morale of the group appeared low, and many members were despondent. The interviews gave evidence of frustration, of loss of hope of ever regaining the former level of production, of feelings of failure, and of a very low level of aspiration. The frustration evidently was due to a "loss of face," em-

[1] J. R. P. French, Jr., and A. J. Marrow, "Changing a Stereotype in Industry," *Journal of Social Issues*, 1945.

bodied in the contrast between the previous high status and present reduced status.

Between 1940 and 1946 a number of small-group studies had been made to discover if it were possible to transfer workers more smoothly from old jobs to new ones, and if technological changes in job methods could be introduced without the usual manifestations of hostility and fall-off in production. These inquiries suggested that participation methods might provide solutions to the problem of overcoming resistance to change. An experiment along these lines was planned involving job changes.

An appropriate situation did not arise until the fall of 1947, after Lewin died. French, aided by Lester Coch, the personnel manager, was able to carry out the experiment as planned. The investigation called for introducing the required changes in jobs in three different ways, each involving a different degree of employee collaboration in working out details of the proposed new job assignments.

The first group did not participate in any way: the workers were told of the changes in their jobs, and the production department explained the new piece rate. The second group was asked to appoint representatives to meet with management to consider methods, piece rates, and other problems created by the job changes. The third group consisted of every member of the unit—not just the representatives. They met with management, took an active part in detailed discussions about all aspects of the change, made a number of recommendations, and even helped plan the most efficient methods for doing the new job.

The differences in outcome of the three procedures were clear-cut and dramatic. Average production in the non-participation group dropped 20 per cent immediately and did not regain the pre-change level. Nine per cent of the group quit. Morale fell sharply, as evidenced by marked hostility toward the supervisor, by slow-downs, by complaints to the union, and by other instances of aggressive behavior.

The group which participated through representatives required two weeks to recover its pre-change output. Their attitude was co-operative, and none of the members of the group quit their jobs.

150

The consequences in the total-participation group were in sharp contrast to those in the non-participating group. It regained the pre-change output after only two days and then climbed steadily until it reached a level about 14 per cent above the earlier average. No one quit; all members of the group worked well with their supervisors, and there were no signs of aggression.

The motivation and morale of each group was apparently proportional to the degree that it shared the decision making. French concluded that "the experiment showed that the rate of recovery is directly proportional to the amount of participation and that the rates of turnover and aggression are inversely proportional to the amount of participation."

Lewin had said that the constancy of the level of production at Harwood or at any similar plant could be viewed as a quasi-stationary process in which two types of forces are in gear: those component forces pushing production in a downward direction and those pushing production up. The difference in the strength of these forces makes the difference of production level between the participating and the non-participating group.

French pointed out that before the changes were introduced, each of the three groups had reached a level slightly above the production index of 60 units per hour, indicating that an equilibrium had been reached between the driving forces (such as the need to reach the quota) and the restraining forces (such as the avoidance of strain imposed by the difficulty of the task). With the job transfer, the component forces changed—but differently for the participating and non-participating groups. For the non-participating group, a new force pushing in the direction of restricting the level of output was created by the frustrations of the job transfer. Thus, it rejected the force toward higher production. On the other hand, the participating groups accepted both the new situation and the management-induced force toward higher production. In consequence, the additional forces working toward increased production were strengthened, hence the better recovery rate and the absence of aggression, grievances, and tension.

The Harwood studies just cited serve to illustrate how Lewinian methods helped shift the focus of industrial management from mechanistic engineering approaches to social-psychological concepts. The great interest in recent years in the humanization of industry stems in large measure from Lewin's emphasis on the dynamics of groups at work. Much of the recent research on the relationships between managerial approach, employee productivity, and job satisfaction is due to his influence.

While many people in industry would probably not recognize Lewin's name or be likely to have read his writings, the views that enlightened executives express are clearly recognizable to those who know of their origins as emanating largely from Lewin.

CHAPTER

15

TESTING THEORY
IN ACTION

When America entered World War II, the resources of the social and behavioral disciplines became an important part of the mobilization effort. The demand by many military and other government programs for professional advice forced the experts to evolve new ways of tackling problems and analyzing and reporting results. Moreover, these data and recommendations had to be communicated in a way which could be understood and used by laymen who had to act on them.

For many social scientists, the transition from safe academic work to an immediate concern with the hazardous application of research findings in making major policies was radical. But for Lewin and the majority of his colleagues, the transition was a logical consequence of the main thrust of their previous work. Thus they were readier than most others in the hastily improvised circumstances to investigate "real life" problems with more scientific rigor and confidence.

Lewin was limited in his early efforts because, not yet an American citizen, he could not get security clearance. But on January 5, 1940, he sent me a handwritten note saying, "I am a citizen! Hurrah!"

Soon Lewin and his group were taking up such questions as:

What was the state of morale and its probable future course both in enemy countries and on the home front? What techniques of psychological warfare would most effectively weaken the enemy's will to resist? What kind of leadership in military units was likely to be the most successful? How could more such leaders be found and trained? How could home-front consumption of foods in short supply be cut back and the use of more available foods be encouraged? How did human relations in office and factory affect war production in America's industries? What measures could be taken to care for and psychologically rehabilitate those injured in combat?

Solid answers to such questions, when translated into decisions, policies, and programs, might exercise a profound influence on the course and outcome of the war. All of them required seasoned judgment, based on factual knowledge in the behavioral sciences. Team effort was important, for, by its nature, the program usually required the contribution of more than one specialty or discipline. Little wonder, then, that the earliest, most continuous, and heaviest demand for aid was made on those who had had the most experience with psychological research in real-life situations and who were accustomed to working as teams: cultural anthropologists, such as Margaret Mead; public-opinion researchers such as Samuel Stouffer, Paul F. Lazarsfeld, and Rensis Likert; psychologists such as Murray and MacKinnon, who had worked in the Harvard Psychological Clinic and later played such an important role in the Office of Strategic Services (OSS); and Lewin and his Iowa group.

John MacMillan, of the Office of Naval Research, invited a group of social scientists—Lewin among them—to review research proposals and discuss general ONR policy. According to Rensis Likert, another member of the committee that was formed, "Lewin's ability to identify the major problems on which research was needed made him an invaluable member. Frequently when a methodology was inadequate he devised a procedure as well as a general theory of conceptualization to deal with the particular problem on which the research was being done. Lewin was much more interested in having significant research started on major social problems, even if the approach was crude, than on unimportant problems with nice, neat, precise methods. His willingness to move ahead even if the methods were tentative was a factor in the criticism aimed at him by some psychologists who held that his research had not adequately produced the large body of quantitative data required for his major conclusions. The soundness of his work, however, is amply demonstrated by the extent to which his central concepts have stood up as research on them and related problems has been undertaken in the two decades since his death."

All the experimental and other studies done for the OSS and ONR were related to the national emergency, to the practical requirements of the government departments which underwrote the research, and to the life of people in the local communities—a life vastly different from those psychological laboratories where abstractions called "subjects" performed tasks stripped of direct relationship to everyday life problems.

"There is little doubt," says Margaret Mead of this period of inquiry, "that coming to grips with the non-arrival of a shipment of lettuce involved in an experiment was an excellent setting for cooperation between anthropologists and psychologists and for the concept of 'action research.' The studies also offered many significant theoretical implications, and Lewin and his students and colleagues were on the alert for them. On some of these theoretical leads, such as those developed by Bavelas and French's studies of group performance at the Harwood plant, would someday be built many useful social procedures." She also remarked that Lewin's general program of action, plus his knowledge of how and why to experiment and of the relationships between experiments and theory, tied together the many and diverse topics which were investigated by the Iowa group.

Similarly, such seemingly trivial questions (from a research point of view) as to what would make a new drinking container most acceptable led to a series of experiments which defined the relationships between the beverage preferences of the user, various types of containers, and beverages.

One finding of this brief study, conducted by Festinger, was that the use of a new container is more acceptable if the type of beverage it contains is also new. This provided an interesting confirmation of a general principle in field theory and action research: that change of one kind of behavior is associated with changes of other kinds, and that it is important in bringing about change to look at the whole behavior system involved, rather than isolated actions or decisions.

During the war Lewin traveled frequently from Iowa City to Washington; he participated in many committees of social scientists, administrators, and military personnel working on a wide range of problems. Much of his labor—for example, advising the OSS on psychological warfare programs—was never documented in detail; some of the information concerning these activities is still classified. "But it is known," according to Lippitt, "that he made very creative contributions to the working out of the proper relations between psychological warfare, target setting, field operations, and evaluative reconnaissance."

His ability to grasp complicated ideas and to see complex relations was combined with a power of sustained concentration and an enormous enthusiasm for his work. The capacity of great scientists and artists to labor long hours is legendary; Lewin was one of them. He had a remarkable ability to keep a variety of projects, committees, experiments, and writing assignments going at once.

Those who worked with Lewin at that time believe that he was convinced that any psychological problem could be examined by means of experiment. He rarely failed to devise a way to test any thesis or to try out any hypothesis in the laboratory or in the field.

As the end of World War II seemed to be approaching, Lewin was completing nearly a decade of productive work at Iowa. The research output of his own students at Iowa, and students of his former students at other colleges and universities, on problems stemming from his own theory and research was enormous and diverse. Some idea of this can be gained from a glance at some of the titles of the published studies. In 1937, Herbert Wright published "The Influence of Barriers upon the Strength of Motivation," and Mary Elizabeth Keister, "The Behavior of Young Children in Failure," an experimental attempt to discover and modify undesirable responses to failure in pre-school children. In the following year, I published "Goal Tension and Recall," and 1939 saw the publication of Daniel Adler's "Types of Similarity and the Substitute Value of Activities at Different Age Levels," Adler and Jacob Kounin's "Some Factors Operating at the Moment of Resumption of Interrupted Tasks," and Lewin, Lippitt, and White's "Patterns of Aggressive Behavior in Experimentally Created 'Social Climates.' " In 1940 Lippitt brought out "An Experimental Study of the Effect of Democratic and Authoritarian Group Atmosphere"—a preliminary to the classic "autocracy-democracy" study; C. Anderson published "The Development of a Level of Aspiration in Young Children," and Sybille Escalona, "The Effect of Success and Failure upon Level of Aspiration and Behavior in Manic-Depressive Psychoses."

The following were published in 1941: Dorwin Cartwright's "Decision Time in Relation to the Differentiation of the Phenomenal Field," Jacob Kounin's "Experimental Studies in Rigidity," Barker, Dembo, and Lewin's "Frustration and Regression," and John R. P. French's "Disruption and Cohesion of Groups." In 1942, Roger Barker's "An Experimental Study of the Resolution of Conflict in Children" appeared, along with Beatrice Wright's "Altruism in Children and the Perceived Conduct of Others," Mary Henle's "An Experimental Investigation of Dynamic and Structural Determinants in Substitution," and Alex Bavelas's "Morale and the Training of Leaders."

In the last two years that Lewin was at Iowa, there came Lippitt and White's "The 'Social Climate' of Children's Groups," Cartwright and Festinger's "Quantitative Theory of Decision," Erik Wright's "Influence of Frustration upon the Social Relations of Young Children," and Jerome Frank's "Experimental Studies of Personal Pressure and Resistance"—the study on which he had been working when he first encountered Lewin at Cornell. These appeared in 1943. John R. P. French's "Organized and Unorganized Groups under Fear and Frustration" and "Level of Aspiration," by Lewin, Festinger, Sears, and Dembo, came out in 1944.

But Lewin was becoming increasingly restless. His attention centered more and more on group dynamics, experimental social psychology, and the process he termed action research. Psychology, he decided, needed to do more than just seek explanations of behavior. "We must be equally concerned," he said, "with discovering how people can change their ways so that they learn to behave better." This, he held, required experiments. He pointed out that "for thousands of years man's everyday experience with falling objects did not suffice to bring him to a correct theory of gravity. A sequence of very unusual, man-made experiences, so-called experiments, which grew out of the systematic search for the truth, was necessary to bring about a change from less adequate to more adequate concepts." [1] The same situation, he believed, was true in human affairs. Systematic scientific experimentation was needed to study social problems in small and large settings. But he doubted that such controlled field experiments could be carried out at Iowa.

Other factors were at work affecting Lewin's mood. His wartime travels produced psychological strains, since some Iowa colleagues showed resentment at his frequent absences and his "starring role." Some colleagues, besides disagreeing with his theories, criticized his consultant activities which forced him to neglect routine academic duties, such as attending faculty meetings. Finally, there were many Americans—"corn-fed, dust-bowl empiricists," in Allport's phrase —who were anti-theoretical and especially opposed to Lewin's emphasis on a philosophy of science. Many of these rejected Lewin because his approach did not emphasize large-scale testing and statistical analysis.

For his part, Lewin became skeptical about remaining in a conventional academic setting as his concept of the organization of action research developed. It could be best developed, he felt, if he presided over an autonomous institute affiliated with a university, but not subject to its routines. Of course, group dynamics and action research were debatable projects among his academic peers. Most preferred the non-activist tradition of academic psychologists and yearned to return to teaching, writing, and research in the security of Academe. So Lewin went his own way on his own work.

[1] K. Lewin and P. Grabbe, "Conduct, Knowledge, and Acceptance of New Values," *Journal of Social Issues*, 1945, *1*, 53–63.

His Washington assignments had placed him in a collaborative relationship with many non-academic people. The roles of practitioner and administrator (though he was not particularly efficient) gave him certain satisfactions. They offered a means of keeping in close touch with practical affairs and social issues. Moreover, certain problems were of great personal concern to him. Among them was a situation rather than a problem. He had been proposed by Horace Kallen, then Dean of the Graduate Faculty at the New School, as successor to the late Max Wertheimer who—together with Köhler—had been a colleague of Lewin's in Berlin.

To Kallen, it seemed that a fellow Gestaltist such as Lewin, who was a theoretician of great originality, an experimentalist, and a philosopher of the mind, would be the appropriate *"Nachwuks"* to Wertheimer at the New School. Outsiders, too, when Kallen broached the idea, were enthusiastic; but not Köhler, the other Berlin Gestaltist, then at Swarthmore. Lewin, the innovator, was too heretical for Köhler. Köhler's counsel was followed, and in spite of the efforts of Kallen and Gardner Murphy, Lewin was not invited to join the New School faculty.

The rejection caused Lewin a good deal of self-questioning—not because he was greatly concerned about the post, but because of the personal attitudes that came into play. He felt that for progress in his projects of action research and the dynamics of groups, Iowa was no longer an appropriate location. It was necessary to find a more fitting place and better opportunities, and he so advised several of his friends. He was especially concerned about his chance for unhampered inquiry and pursued his idea of an autonomous institute loosely attached to some university. The financing of such an institute would not, he realized, be undertaken by university authorities; it needed sources outside the conventional academic budget—from foundations, perhaps, and through personal contributions. And thus Lewin next turned his efforts toward a pursuit of funds for his institute.

CHAPTER

16

THE SEARCH
FOR HELP

At the beginning of his search for funds, Lewin first came to the Field Foundation, then headed by the late Marshall Field, Jr. Thinking I was acquainted with Field, he asked for an introduction. That I did not know the philanthropist did not deter Lewin once he had made up his mind that the Field Foundation was a potential source of help for his project. He phoned Mr. Field directly from my office while my attention was engaged in another matter. I returned to hear: "Mr. Marshall Field, please. Kurt La-veen speaking."

This unhesitating directness did not bring Mr. Field to the telephone, but it got Lewin an appointment with Maxwell Hahn, director of Field's foundation. Hahn's memory of his first meeting with Lewin is vivid. He describes him coming "shyly" into the rather modest offices of the Foundation in New York. "Unassuming and self-deprecating, Professor Lewin outlined convincingly his ideas for an institute to help democracy learn how to handle its group problems more efficiently and less prejudicially." Indeed, Lewin was so persuasive that Hahn insisted that his visitor join him at home for dinner and keep talking—an event, Hahn states, quite unheard of in foundation circles.

Soon after, Hahn went to Iowa City to evaluate Lewin and his ideas and came away confirmed in his initial impression. What especially caught his interest was a factory in which Alex Bavelas was working on an action-research experiment to improve employee morale. Hahn reported to the Foundation that Lewin merited its support.

"Although Kurt did not know it," Hahn comments, "he approached us when the Foundation's funds were extremely limited and had been overcommitted." Yet he undertook to provide Lewin a grant of $30,000 to be paid in two installments of $15,000 a year, the money to be used to set up the proposed center. This was in 1943.

The next year Lewin unexpectedly found an additional sponsor for his institute, the American Jewish Congress. Lewin at various times lectured to community organizations on minority problems and intergroup relations. He had published articles on these subjects. Some of these came to the attention of Rabbi Stephen S. Wise, then President of the American Jewish Congress, which had voted in the spring of 1944 to establish a research institute of exactly the kind Lewin was projecting. It was to be especially concerned with the causes of group prejudice and finding the methods that would be effective in eradicating them. Dr. Wise saw in Lewin the kind of scientist such a project would need and suggested that Rabbi Irving Miller, the Congress vice-president, explore with Lewin the possibility of his taking on this pioneer job.

It took Miller some time to reach Lewin, who was mostly in Washington and out of reach in the secret offices of the OSS. When Miller caught up with him by phone during one of his brief visits to Iowa, he agreed to see Miller after returning to Washington. Because of Lewin's relations with the OSS the encounter took on a cloak-and-dagger quality which today seems comic. Lewin said he would be arriving on an early train; the location of the OSS being classified, Lewin had Miller meet him for breakfast in the Savarin Restaurant of Union Station at seven o'clock of a hot July morning.

Lewin listened somewhat distractedly to Miller's proposition regarding the project of the American Jewish Congress to set up a research center for the study of community relations with a focus on group discrimination. A million dollars would be available for the study. Lewin suggested that he and Miller meet with me at my home in New York City the following Sunday. Miller agreed and Lewin telephoned me about the arrangement.

I was spending the summer with my family at a resort community on Long Island and invited the two there. Lewin promptly agreed but he had characteristically missed getting Miller's name (he referred to him in conversation as "this rabbi"), but somehow gave Miller the impression that the meeting would take place at the home of a man named Merril rather than Marrow.

Meanwhile, Lewin asked me to get him an account of the American Jewish Congress, about which he knew little or nothing. The report about its financial strength was not encouraging, though the Congress did have a notable history of social action. Organized in 1918, the Congress had among its founders Supreme Court Justice Louis Brandeis, Judge Julian Mack, Rabbi Stephen S. Wise, and other leading American Jews. In 1919, its representation had worked to have confirmation of the Balfour Declaration favoring establishment of a "Jewish national home" in Palestine written into the Versailles Treaty. In 1933 it had launched an anti-Nazi boycott and it had since been fighting Hitler and Nazism in every way it could. But it was only one among many Jewish organizations doing so. Although its leadership was distinguished, its resources were so small that they barely covered its budget. Various persons to whom I talked doubted that the American Jewish Congress would be able to raise the million dollars of which Rabbi Miller had spoken.

The report did not discourage Lewin. The Congress project appealed to him because its preoccupation with anti-Semitism came close to home to him, and because it could provide just the conditions he felt were necessary for the broad scale application of his conceptions of action research and group dynamics.

On the Sunday set for the conference, Lewin arrived early. He spent most of the pleasant sunny afternoon on the beach and finished off with a dip in the ocean. I remained on my porch waiting for Lewin's guest to arrive. As the afternoon drew to a close, I saw approaching a distant relative of mine by marriage, Rabbi Irving Miller. We greeted each other, each unaware that the immediate agency of our present encounter was Kurt Lewin. After a little chit-chat, Rabbi Miller said he had to run off; he was due at six o'clock at the home of some people and was already a few minutes late. He set off down the street.

About fifteen minutes later he came by again, this time with a worried look. He wanted to know if I knew the people who lived on that street. Being a summer resident, I didn't. Did Miller have the number of the house or the name of the family he was seeking? Maybe someone inside might know.

"I'm not quite sure," Miller replied. "I believe it's Merril. But there's no one by that name at the address I was given." So, frustrated, Miller began to tell about the man he had encountered in the Savarin Restaurant in Washington and how they had agreed to meet this day at a friend's house in Long Island.

"Are you talking about Kurt Lewin?" I asked.

"Yes," exclaimed Miller. "How did you know?"

Why I knew surprised him even more. And as we talked about it, Lewin came up wet from his dip.

In my library, where the three of us at last settled down to confer, Rabbi Miller was surprisingly realistic in his account of the project and ways and means. I was skeptical about it; there were the inevitable hazards in pioneering social research for an organization like the American Jewish Congress. It would want a quick payoff, whereas such studies are a long-range affair. I urged Lewin to hold off.

Lewin couldn't. He was eager to set up such a research center. "The idea of doing pioneer work in 'action research' that hopefully might provide an example big enough to revolutionize certain aspects of our social life," he wrote me shortly after the meeting, "is too attractive to be delayed. The stake is so high and so difficult that its attainment is more important than any other consideration." With his projected center for group dynamics well to the fore in his mind, this seemed a perfect chance to combine theory with action research. "I am ready to go to any lengths to find a productive solution," the letter continued. "Social action is part of the changing social world. Security, I realize, will have to be established every day anew. But I am ready to take the risk."

Lewin was aware that an organization like the American Jewish Congress could not receive community support unless its research program met community needs head on. "Pure" research hence would be out of the question. But in a separate statement of his design for a commission, Lewin delineated the combination of experiment and application he termed "action research." The combination was ideal, he declared, for scientists whose chief concern was geared toward action, toward changing the world while simultaneously contributing to the advancement of scientific knowledge.

Before he could start coupling theory with experiment, however, Lewin had to secure an academic location for the proposed center. He wanted it at a large university, preferably in a city troubled by the variety of vexing industrial, community, racial, and leadership problems he wished to study. The center would, of course, have to have the autonomy the project required, but its relations with the university's departments of social science, especially of psychology, sociology, and anthropology, would require close cooperation.

Five or six institutions seemed natural choices, but Lewin concentrated, as his friends advised, on two: the University of California at Berkeley and the Massachusetts Institute of Technology in Cambridge. California's Professor Edward Tolman and M.I.T.'s Professor Douglas McGregor undertook the task of urging the plan upon the presidents of their institutions.

Having stayed in Palo Alto in 1932–1933 and having spent the summer of 1939 in Berkeley, Lewin was enthusiastic about California's climate, especially because of the extreme severity of winters on the Midwest plains. His preference went automatically to the Pacific.

In August 1944, Rensis Likert arranged a dinner in the garden of the Cosmos Club in Washington, at which MacGregor and Lewin met to exchange thoughts about the idea of such a center at M.I.T. McGregor and Lewin were equally enthusiastic about the center and McGregor returned to Boston determined to win President Carl Compton's approval. Meanwhile, President Edward Sproul at

Berkeley found the idea promising, but needed time to think it through before asking the California Board of Regents to act on it. Carl Compton, M.I.T. president, responded similarly to McGregor.

At this time Lewin's position at Iowa was becoming difficult. His desire to set up a special kind of research center was no secret there, and many felt that he could not possibly discharge his duties at the Child Welfare Research Center and work at all the other tasks he was taking on. Iowa authorities wanted to be advised of his intentions.

Lacking a definite commitment from either California or M.I.T., Lewin's mind was not made up, but, with the Iowa people pressing him, he called Douglas McGregor at M.I.T. to ask for a definite yes or no. McGregor again got in touch with President Compton, and Compton, after a brief hesitation, answered "yes." Lewin was sent a formal invitation to set up the Research Center for Group Dynamics at M.I.T. His predilection for California's climate delayed his acceptance a day or two, but accept he did and gratefully. Two days later, Tolman called him with the word that President Sproul had mailed the formal invitation to set up the center at the University of California. But Lewin had already accepted M.I.T.'s offer and had begun to collect a staff and the balance of the money needed to support the institute.

CHAPTER

17

THE DYNAMICS UNDERLYING GROUP LIFE

At M.I.T., Lewin planned to link some of the work of the Research Center for Group Dynamics with that of the Commission on Community Interrelations of the American Jewish Congress. In his early work at the University of Berlin, Lewin had focused upon the individual in his social environment. After the early 1940's, Lewin contributed very little that was new to his already published theory of the "person." His energies were directed rather to the study of group processes. He was convinced that now it was possible to build up a body of knowledge and construct a general theory that would apply to any group—family, work, religion, community. To design experiments that should gather data about such diverse matters, he envisioned the study of such specific problems as how leaders are chosen, how group atmosphere is formed, how group decisions are reached, how the members communicate with one another, how group standards are established.

From Lewin's point of view, group behavior is a function of both the single person and the social situation. Neither the personality of the man alone nor the nature of the social situation by itself is adequate to interpret group behavior. Both variables must be understood. There were already a number of occupational disciplines in the United States that provided a favorable atmosphere for deeper study along these lines. This was particularly true of social group work, group psychotherapy, education, and industrial management —in all of which sufficient experience had been gained prior to World War II to persuade specialists in these fields of the need for more systematic and comprehensive observation of group functioning. While the needs were recognized, little significant research had been undertaken. Directors of social groups were among the first specialists to recognize that groups can be managed so as to bring about desired changes in the attitudes of their members. Recreational directors realized before most others that their techniques of dealing with club members definitely affected both the collective behavior and the personal conduct and attitudes of the rank and file. It was evident to a good leader that some methods were more successful than others, but often he had to depend upon intuition alone, or else he drew lessons from experience without thoroughly examining his methods.

Again, group psychotherapy strongly influenced the development of group dynamics. Although commonly associated with psychiatry, group psychotherapy did not actually come out of psychiatry and certainly is not limited to it today, as the formation and role of Alcholics Anonymous, for example, makes evident. Much in group psychotherapy does not derive from medicine or traditional psychoanalysis. Practitioners seek new insights from research in other human sciences of man, particularly in social psychology.

Students of progressive education also saw the need for studies of group behavior. This was stimulated by the educational philosophy of John Dewey. To carry out Dewey's theory of "learning by doing," teachers organized such group projects as student self-government and hobby-club activities. This called for the development of leadership skills and the collective setting of group goals. Teachers, like other group workers, had to learn how to guide children's clubs and teams and how to direct such extracurricular work toward productive ends. The teacher could be seen as a group leader who affected his students' learning not merely by his proficiency in his subject, but also by his skill at increasing their motivation, encouraging their active participation, and improving their esprit de corps. Lewin's pioneering research in group behavior thus drew upon the experience of educators in deciding upon and developing topics for research and in establishing a strong interest among social psychologists and teachers.

Finally, there was industrial management, or, more broadly, the management of people in large organizations, whether profit-making, governmental, educational or medical. All have the same responsibility to direct and coordinate the behavior of people. They share a common interest in finding new ways to get people to attain their potential and work at their best.

From the interaction of all these closely related and overlapping disciplines, group dynamics emerged as a definite field of study. What, then, is group dynamics? As the word "dynamics" indicates, it is a discipline which concerns itself with the positive and negative forces at work in human groups. The group modifies the behavior of its individual members. A person's role and rank in it, for example, may determine how others behave toward him: whether they treat him with deference or cause him unhappiness by excluding him. Groups exert on members influences which may be harmful or beneficial. A better understanding of the principles of collective behavior, therefore, might show how groups could be made to serve more socially desirable ends. Accordingly, Lewin advocated the scientific study of the group as a configuration of a variety of forces.

He undertook to employ the methods of science, as he conceived them, to study the dynamics of every kind of group. His first use of the term "group dynamics" in print was in a 1939 article in which he wrote that the purpose of his experiment "would be to give insight into the underlying *group dynamics*."[1] Lewin and his associates saw that in a group each member recognizes the other members as persons on whom he depends to a definite degree. The group is therefore a psychologically organic whole, rather than a simple collection of individuals. With this 1939 paper, Lewin began a

[1] "Experiments in Social Space," *Harvard Educational Review*, 1939, 9, 21–32.

series of articles expounding and discussing the dynamics underlying group life.

The gist of his theory might be stated as follows: A man who joins a group is significantly changed thereby. His relations with his fellow members alter both him and them. A highly attractive group can bring great pressure to bear upon its members; a weak group will not have as much moulding power.

To effect any sort of change in the goals or outlook of a group, a change in its equilibrium is necessary. To try to do this by appealing to members individually is seldom effective, as was learned by those of Lewin's associates who in 1940 began their experiments in industry. They discovered, for instance, that if a group sets the range or level of productivity in a factory, any attempt on the part of any single employee to deviate from that standard heightens the normal social pressure of his co-workers to push him back into line. The further he deviates from the norm, the stronger the pressure on him to conform to it.

When Lewin studied this problem at the Harwood plant in 1940, he concluded that it is futile to try to change any worker from one pattern to another unless the entire group to which he "belongs" is included in the change. Rather than disturb his relation to his group, the individual will as a rule take considerable risk, even at substantial financial sacrifice, to conform to his group. Thus the behavior of a whole group may be more easily changed than that of a single member. This willingness to stick together ("cohesiveness") is an essential characteristic of any group. Indeed, without it, it is doubtful that a group could be said to exist at all. Lewin defined "cohesiveness" as the resultant of the forces which keep members together— the positive forces of reciprocal attraction and the negative forces of reciprocal repulsion.

What renders a group cohesive? Among other things, that its activities must strengthen the individual's chance to achieve his own goals. Over a period of time certain standards develop in any group. These may include attitudes as well as actions. Each member expects the others to conform to the standards, but the extent of conformity varies directly with the degree of cohesiveness. What renders a group cohesive is, as Lewin pointed out, not how similar or dissimilar its members are—for example, in their attitudes—but how dynamically interdependent they are. Out of reciprocal dependence for the achievement of goals there arises a readiness to share chores and challenges, and even to reconcile personality clashes.

A group does not have to be composed of members who are greatly similar; it may be a "Gestalt"—a whole containing dissimilar parts. "For example," said Lewin, "a man, wife, and baby within one family may show greater dissimilarity to one another than the man to other men of his age and social class, or the woman to other women, or this baby to other infants. [2] Moreover, it is typical of well-organized groups with a high degree of unity to include a variety of members who are different or who have different functions within the whole. Not similarity, but a certain interdependence of members constitutes a group."

Lewin also pointed out that similarity can exist *without* interdependence just as it can exist *with* it. He remarked that dynamic wholes have properties which are different from the properties of either their parts or the sum of their parts. This did not mean to him that the "whole" is invariably more than the sum of its parts. The whole, he maintained, is not necessarily superior, nor does it add up to "more." His general formulation was simple, "The whole is different from the sum of its parts: it has definite properties of its own."

Lewin observed that a person is apt more often to be a member of a group to which he feels similar or to which he wishes to be similar than to groups upon whom his dependence is greatest.

Belonging is signified by adherence to the group code. Those who belong "obey." Thus group pressures regulate the conduct of the would-be deviant member. He stays among those with whom he feels he "belongs" even if their conduct seems unfair and their pressure unfriendly. To change his conduct or point of view independently of the group would get him into trouble with his fellow group members.

[2] Kurt Lewin, "Field Theory and Experiment in Social Psychology," *American Journal of Sociology*, 1939, *44*, 868–897.

Lewin's own identification with his adopted homeland was a true example of his theory of group belongingness. From his first days in the United States, Lewin was an American. He determined to learn English at once, although he never succeeded in completely losing his German accent. He never felt, as the French put it, *dépaysé*. Indeed, he astonished many of his friends with the thoroughness with which he made American customs and habits his own. I recall visiting the New York World's Fair with him in 1939; it was getting dark and we were growing hungry, but the Fair's restaurants were already crowded with dinner patrons. "Let's have a couple of hot dogs," Lewin said. "That's what we Americans eat on Sunday evenings in the summer!" Five minutes later that's what we were doing.

In his theory of group behavior, Lewin repeated his lifelong theme that acts cannot be understood on the basis only of the personality of the individual or only on that of the nature of the social environment. "Group behavior," he stated yet again, "is a function of both the individual person and the social situation." In the years that followed, he planned to build a new, realistic experimental social psychology that would help find solutions to major social problems. Both his work at M.I.T. and his assignment for the A.J.C. provided a daily life laboratory in which to test his theories of group dynamics. Lewin was excited and challenged by the prospect.

In an article published in 1945,[3] he described the objectives and ideology of the M.I.T. Research Center: "The Research Center for Group Dynamics has grown out of two needs, one scientific and one practical. In the field of social management, we are just awakening to the fact that a better knowledge is needed than day-by-day experience, tradition, and the memory of an individual or a social group can provide. We require understanding on a scientific level . . . There are increasing symptoms that leading practitioners in government, in agriculture, in industry, in education, in community life are becoming aware that the statement 'nothing is as practical as a good theory' holds also in the field of social management."

[3] Kurt Lewin, "The Research Center for Group Dynamics at Massachusetts Institute of Technology," *Sociometry*, 1945, 2, 126–136.

He then described his plan to have "the Research Center use whatever qualitative or quantitative psychological, sociological, or anthropological methods are needed for investigation. The main methodological interest, however, will be the development of group experiments and particularly change experiments. Such experiments can be carried out in the laboratory or in the field."

Lewin recognized that he was advocating an unusual blending of "pure" research and practical application and that there would be skepticism concerning its feasibility. As he put it: "One may ask whether this interrelation between theoretical social science and the practical needs of society will not lower the scientific level . . . Psychologists have recognized the necessity of a theoretical approach only relatively recently, and fear has been expressed that the preoccupation with the applied problems of the war will retard this development. The student of group life should be aware of this danger and of the still greater danger of becoming a servant of very one-sided social interests. We should, however, not try to set the clock back and retard a scientific step that is ready. We will have to look forward, and I am persuaded that if the scientist proceeds correctly, a close link with practice can be a blessing for the development of theory."

Lewin then continued: "One point should be seen clearly and strongly. There is no individual who does not, consciously or unconsciously, try to influence his family, his group of friends, his occupational group, and so on. Management is, after all, a legitimate and one of the most important functions in every aspect of social life. Few aspects are as much befogged in the minds of many as the problems of leadership and of power in a democracy . . . We have to realize that power itself is an essential aspect of any and every group . . . Not the least service which social research can do for society is to attain better insight into the legitimate and non-legitimate aspects of power.

"The Center would educate research workers in theoretical and applied fields of group life and assist in training practitioners. The main task of the Center would be the development of scientific methods of studying and changing group life and the development of concepts and theories of group dynamics."

CHAPTER

18

ACTION RESEARCH IN COMMUNITY AFFAIRS

With his characteristic commitment of time, energy, and enthusiasm, Lewin undertook the task of launching his two new and parallel commitments: the Commission on Community Interrelations (C.C.I.) for the American Jewish Congress (A.J.C.) and the Research Center for Group Dynamics at M.I.T. Each effort was typical of Lewin in action.

In laying the groundwork for the C.C.I. project, he made many trips from Iowa to the Atlantic Coast, taking the twenty-four-hour train ride repeatedly in order to go over plans with Lippitt, McGregor, Likert, French, Cartwright, and a number of other colleagues in New York and Washington. Of key importance was Charles Hendry, who was to become the first research coordinator for C.C.I.

The Hendry-Lewin relationship went back to 1940 when Hendry first learned of Lewin from an article in *The New York Times Magazine* on the Lippitt-White "autocracy-democracy" study. Fascinated by the story, he invited Lippitt, then teaching at Southern Illinois, to join the Research and Statistics Staff of the Boy

Scouts of America, of which Hendry was then the director. Lippitt accepted the invitation. Shortly thereafter, Hendry invited Lewin to serve as a consultant to the Boy Scouts' research program.

One day in the summer of 1944, Lewin phoned Hendry from Washington to "discuss a matter of urgent importance." He was coming to New York. Would Hendry meet him at Pennsylvania Station? Hendry did, then took him by bus to his apartment near Columbia University. Once settled down on the two-decker, Lewin quickly turned to business. "I shall never forget that ride," relates Hendry. "Lewin was bursting with exhilaration. Greetings, courtesies, and formalities completed, he opened his briefcase and produced a typewritten document, one obviously in the process of revision and refinement. Lewin insisted it be read then and there, atop the bus."

While Hendry strove to read amid the turmoil of traffic below, Lewin tried to protect the manuscript from the wind and to interject comments as if to underline the ideas. What Hendry was trying to read was the first draft of a memorandum to the American Jewish Congress on the establishment of C.C.I. It called for a broad program that would use scientific methods to search out the roots of anti-Semitism rather than its overt symptoms. "I was quickly aware," Hendry recalls, "that I held a precious document in my hands. I knew it then intuitively. I know it now in retrospect with deepened sensitivity."

Several weeks later, an eight-page letter, supplementing Lewin's outline in detail, came from Ronald Lippitt, who had left the Boy Scouts to join Lewin in the OSS. Lippitt listed (for the president of the American Jewish Congress) other considerations which he and Lewin had taken into account. "The American Jewish Congress," Lippitt quoted Lewin as saying, "is very anxious to make this an 'intercultural' project rather than a research on Jews." The whole idea was "to make very fluid the roles of researcher and practitioner." Lewin foresaw "promise of very significant adventure from all angles."

As in his earlier projects and programs, Lewin's optimism, energy, and enthusiasm were a driving force. Convinced that social science could be used in new and more effective ways to deal with practical problems of group and community life, he remained unmoved by arguments of those A.J.C. members who feared that social scientists would "try to tell people what to do" or by those "practical-minded" persons who brushed off social sciences as "merely common sense."

In a letter to Rabbi Wise, Lewin declared, "We Jews will have to fight for ourselves and we will do so strongly and with good conscience. We also know that the fight of the Jews is a part of the fight of all minorities for democratic equality of rights and opportunities, and that the liberation of the minorities will in fact be the greatest liberation of the majority. If we establish a Commission on Community Interrelations we do so with the knowledge that the Jews cannot win their fight without the active help of those groups within the majority which are of good will. It wants to work hand in hand with these groups. It will not try to use non-Jewish friends as a front to spare Jews from doing any part of the fighting that they themselves should do; but it will try to get positive cooperation between all groups in those areas of community living which count most."

Planning sessions were held in Cambridge, Washington, and New York during several months, with Lewin constantly on the go between the three cities. His physical endurance was a source of amazement to his associates. Hendry remarked, "I remember him saying one day that during the First World War he sometimes became so weary that he actually succeeded in sleeping while he marched in a column of soldiers." After one strenuous organizational day in New York, Lewin almost repeated this feat.

Lewin spoke often of the hopeful role of group dynamics and action research in human affairs. But he cautioned that the plans for it depended on discovering through scientific study the answers to such questions as the following:

Under what circumstances does a neighborhood which is open to Jews become all Jewish?

When does it stay "mixed"?

Which procedures in giving jobs to minority members serve to increase, and which to decrease, group tension?

175

Under what circumstances and to what degree is the building of self-respect among minority members a prerequisite for improvement?

How can one avoid the "shot-in-the-arm" effect, which improves intergroup relations for a while, only to have them fall back again to earlier or even lower levels?

What kind of training and education facilitates adjustment?

What problems develop in a community with the arrival of minority group members?

Which methods of dealing with these problems resolve them most readily?

Lewin was absorbed by these critical questions. He was now ready to make his laboratory "the individual," as seen in his groups, in his community. Tension, conflict, crisis, change—these were the targets upon which he trained his mind. His basic assumptions, hypothesis, and methodology could not be confined within the neat traditional boundaries of any specialized field, school of thought, or established system. His research undertakings were problem-oriented, cutting across and mobilizing the theoretical knowledge and the technical resources of all relevant disciplines.

He quickly began the task of assembling a staff for C.C.I. Charles Hendry was invited to serve as coordinator of research. With his acceptance, C.C.I., the first research organization of its kind, was in operation.

Lewin's letter of invitation to Hendry was a mixture of seriousness, light banter, and unconscious prophecy. "The whole thing will be an adventure," he wrote, "and I see you writing wonderful memoirs about it after your 80th birthday, with a lot of poetry and beautiful prose."

Lewin's acknowledgment of Hendry's acceptance, four days later, retained only the seriousness of the invitation: "I know that we will have to face an unknown number of obstacles, the most severe of which, I am sure, is hidden from us at present. The sailing for a while may be easier than I expect. But somewhere along the road, maybe in a half-year, maybe in two years, I am sure we will have to face major crises. I have observed this type of development in many research undertakings, and we will have to be unusually lucky if this time we avoid it. To my mind the difference between

· success and defeat in such undertakings depends mainly upon the willingness and the guts to pull through such periods. It seems to me decisive that one knows that such developments are the rule, that one is not afraid of this period, and that one holds up a team that is able to pull through."

It was during this period that Lewin announced to the staff that he had decided to change the pronunciation of his name. He stated that his children had difficulty explaining to their friends why the family name was spelled "Lewin" but pronounced "Laveen." To avoid further embarrassment to the children, he asked his colleagues to use the American pronunciation rather than the German.

But most of his associates found it difficult to shift from the familiar German pronunciation. Lewin himself often inadvertently reverted to calling himself "Laveen" and there was frequent laughter about it. The confusion continues to the present time, and colleagues of the Berlin and Iowa years and their students still alternate between "Lewin" and "Laveen."

Cartwright tells of the graduate student in his class who found the lecture on topology very difficult. Cartwright suggested that the student read the book *Principles of Topological Psychology*. Several weeks later the student reported back to him: "That book you recommended by the fellow Lewin is no easier to understand than that Professor Laveen you are always quoting."

CHAPTER

19

LAUNCHING
GROUP DYNAMICS
AT M.I.T.

While C.C.I. was being established, Lewin was also busy in Cambridge launching the M.I.T. Research Center for Group Dynamics and assembling its Advisory Board. At a dinner he gave for board members, President Compton spoke briefly about the future of the social sciences and the research Center for Group Dynamics. Compton described his pride in having the center on the M.I.T. campus, adding that he hoped no one would ask for at least three years what the name meant, why the Center belonged at M.I.T., and what sort of work it was doing.

In staffing the new Center, Lewin relied heavily on the membership of the Iowa City Hot-Air Club—a phenomenon on which Hendry too would remark early in his association with Lewin. Once a student-associate-colleague of Kurt Lewin, always so! And though President Compton might be unsure of what was to go on at the M.I.T. Center, Lewin was not. In an article published in the September 1945 issue of *Sociometry*, he outlined what he conceived to be the objectives of the institution.

He wanted to reach beyond the mere description of group life and to investigate the conditions and forces which bring about change or resist it. He meant to look at group life in its totality, not just at individual instances of it. He insisted that any research started at the Center would have to take into consideration *all* aspects of group behavior. In addition, any study put in motion would seek to employ new approaches, avoiding hackneyed methods as well as traditional categories and points of view.

The chief methodological approach would be that of developing actual group experiments, especially experiments of change, to be carried on in the laboratory or in the field. The importance of theorizing and conceptualizing was emphasized by Lewin. The Center was not going to concern itself with the mere gathering of data; indeed, he hoped that theorizing would steadily keep ahead of all data gathering. He felt it necessary that no field experiment be made until everything was "ready" for it, because the efficacy of field experiments depended so greatly on just the right social situation.

He wanted to make sure that his staff of experimenters were themselves an integral part of the situation they proposed to explore. Only as they themselves were involved in the planning and execution of data gathering could the experimenters attain the insight and interest required for success.

Finally, Lewin hoped to avoid any idea that the purpose of the Research Center was to train experts in "brainwashing" or "group manipulation." Experiments conducted by the staff and students at the Center should not only have for their purpose overcoming philosophical prejudices and technical difficulties; they should also be justifiable as honorable and necessary social procedures. "Group manipulation" would directly contradict the purposes of the Research Center for Group Dynamics, and Lewin wanted no part of it.

He also formulated his justification for locating the Center at M.I.T., rather than at a large university with a strong program in the social sciences and the humanities. "The main purpose of engineering," he declared, "is the release of human energies and the enhancement of man's power of dealing with nature—a goal for which the development of machines has provided the principal means. In the course of doing this, engineering has not completely overlooked the human element heretofore; but it has had a tendency to minimize it." To Lewin, a factory was much more than a structure of production lines; it was the "creation of a group with certain patterns of leadership, and any progressive factory management had to consider 'total culture,' which meant all aspects of group life."

Lewin and his family left Iowa City for good in September 1944. They spent four months in Washington, where Kurt finished his work with the OSS, and moved to Newtonville, Massachusetts, at the end of January. The family's household goods, much of it salvaged from Germany a decade or more before, preceded them on a moving van. They went last in the family automobile and spent a night en route at the Bronxville, New York, home of Charles Hendry and his family. Their arrival at the Hendry home was an occasion that the hosts have not forgotten.

The Lewin family car appeared in the Hendry driveway "loaded as one would load a covered wagon heading for the Western frontier of old." To Hendry's utter amazement, out of the car and from the midst of all its gear climbed Lewin, Mrs. Lewin, their two children, and "a huge dog." Hendry still cannot imagine where the dog had been "stowed away."

"Unusual efforts had been made because we were very proud to be entertaining so great a scientist and so warm a friend and colleague." But alas for the celebration! "At a crucial moment when water was required for the preparation of the dinner, Mrs. Hendry discovered that the pipes had frozen. Amateur efforts to thaw them almost burned down the house, and the meal finally proceeded only after water was borrowed from a neighbor. But Lewin being Lewin, the mishap went almost unnoticed in the merriment, enthusiasm, and warmth that his presence as usual generated."

Pioneers in Group Dynamics

Lewin hoped to get the new Center at M.I.T. into full operation by the fall of 1945. His newly appointed staff was asked to set up residence as quickly as possible. Marian Radke was the first, arriving about the same time as the Lewins. Festinger and Lippitt came a little later. Cartwright was the last, and the group celebrated with a festive get-together at the Lewin home Thanksgiving Day.

All five faculty members settled within a few blocks of each other in Newtonville, so that they could get together informally in the evenings for work and conversation. The following morning they usually commuted together to Cambridge. The staff Lewin had chosen were all under thirty-five years of age. All had worked with him at Iowa, and all had participated in one way or another in the research that laid the groundwork for the new Center. They shared a Lewinian point of view, but each brought a particular specialization in such things as personality development, intergroup relations, laboratory methods, action research, training in field experimentation, and survey techniques.

The famous Tuesday seminar, or *Quasselstrippe,* which the staff had been part of in Iowa, was re-established. The discussions initially centered on Lewin's developing ideas about group dynamics, his notions of social space as contrasted to life space, his involvement in expanding the theory of quasi-stationary equilibria to the process of social change, the growth of prejudice in young children, the origin of self-hate, and other practical social problems. Informal meetings were held almost anywhere and at any time of the day or night. Discussions took place while driving through heavy traffic, during evenings at the Lewin home, or on train trips between Boston and New York. The pace for Lewin was particularly hectic since he was carrying the major responsibility for organizing both the M.I.T. Center and the Commission on Community Interrelations in New York. The staff helped in such diverse activities as planning the research for both organizations and simultaneously establishing the doctoral training program at the university.

M.I.T. provided an ideal institutional setting for Lewin. Its flexibility with respect to administrative arrangements permitted him to design the Center's program as he thought best. He was comparatively free to pursue his interests wherever they might lead and he responded to this opportunity with great excitement. The Center was located in the Department of Economics and Social Sciences, which had little concern for disciplinary boundaries within the social sciences. This was perfect for Lewin, who, being eclectic about approaches to design and methodology, found this setting ideal for the varied research interests and preferences of his group.

Lewin worked closely with Professors Douglas McGregor, Charles Myers, and other faculty members of the Department of Economics and Social Sciences at M.I.T. Equally close working relations were established with Henry Murray, Gordon Allport, and others at Harvard. Several pre-doctoral students, who were also research assistants, soon arrived and joined the seminar sessions, which now grew to a dozen or more. The pre-doctoral group took about half of their courses at Harvard under an inter-university arrangement for graduate work between the two universities.

The offices of Lewin and his staff were close to each other and there was a great deal of running back and forth between rooms. Lewin frequently stuck his head into one of the offices and asked for help in writing a research proposal, interviewing a graduate student, or acting as host to some prominent visitor.

An increasing number of students came from the Harvard Graduate School to take courses at the new center at M.I.T., and Lewin was pleased when at the end of the first year he was able to get additional funds to add John R. P. French, Jr., to the faculty. French had studied under Lewin and, like the others, found it easy to adjust to the shift from student to colleague.

Among the faculty members relatively little interpersonal competitiveness was evident compared to what one might have expected. Lippitt believes that it was a combination of Lewin's leadership, and the cohesion generated by the sense of the importance of their mission, that reduced the frequency and intensity of interpersonal and role conflicts.

"Those of us who assembled in Cambridge at the end of the war to embark on this new venture thought of ourselves as pioneers," says Cartwright.[1] "We were members of an organization with no history or established tradition and with few precedents anywhere in the social sciences; we were committed to the creation of new

[1] D. Cartwright, "Some Things Learned," *Journal of Social Issues*, 1958, Supplement Series No. 12.

182

techniques of research and the utilization of established procedures in investigating new kinds of problems; we thought that the term 'group dynamics' could be made to refer to a reasonably coherent field of knowledge; we established a new program of graduate training for a Ph.D. in 'group dynamics' and we shared, in varying degrees, a rather uncommon view of the proper relation between social research and social practice."

The handful of people who made up Lewin's staff were aware that they were charting new territory and, indeed, carving out a whole new discipline in the behavioral sciences. But they were not without advantages. When the Center was established at M.I.T., few academic institutions existed with comparable experience in conducting organized research programs. M.I.T. had already developed administrative machinery making possible the organization of research projects involving large numbers of people. While financial support was always a problem, the Center did get support from such prestige organizations as the National Institute of Mental Health, the U. S. Air Force, the Field, Rockefeller, and Carnegie foundations.

Considerable attention was given to the proper relation between social research and social action. Ultimately, Lewin knew, the amount of support any research organization received would depend on the practical value of that research. At the same time, he and his staff were aware that too great a concern for immediate results could retard the scientific advances necessary for long-range usefulness. Lewin aimed to achieve the kind of balanced program at M.I.T. that took into account both the necessity of verifiable theory and the practical requirements of society. At the same time, Lewin did not hesitate to plan basic research which had no immediate application to real-life problems. The creation of an empirically verifiable theory, Lewin knew, was the essence of science; research, therefore, had to be guided by the need to develop an integrated concept of the processes of group life. Without a vigorous program of basic research, he felt, the other types of research would become sterile.

From this group's discussion six major "program areas" gradually emerged to give coherence to the total undertaking of the Center. The first area related to group productivity. Why were group enterprises so frequently inefficient or ineffective in getting things done? A series of experiments was subsequently begun to analyze the complex problems of the determinants of group efficiency. These included Lippitt's study, "The Strategy of Socio-Psychological Research in Group Life," Cartwright's "Psychological Economics," French's field experiments in "Changing Group Productivity," and Festinger's laboratory experiments on "The Role of Group Belongingness."

A second program area dealt with communication and the spread of influence, with much of the research deriving from a housing project for married student veterans at M.I.T. One study was conducted by Festinger, Stanley Schachter, and Kurt Back. Other studies in the area of communication were conducted by Lippitt, French, Gordon Hearn, and Morton Deutsch. "A Study of Rumor: Its Origin and Spread" was made by Festinger and Cartwright.

Social perception—closely related to communication—was a third area of investigation at the Center. One topic closely studied was the way in which a person's group roles and memberships affected the manner in which he saw social events. The nature of the process was studied by David Emery in a doctoral dissertation on industrial role and social perception; by Ronald Lippitt and David Jenkins, in terms of "Interpersonal Perceptions of Teachers, Students, and Parents"; by Harold H. Kelley in "The Warm-Cold Variable in First Impressions of Persons"; and by Albert Pepitone, on "Motivational Effects in Social Perception."

The field of intergroup relations, in which Lewin was already deeply involved through C.C.I., comprised the fourth major program area at M.I.T. Lewin sought to integrate the research at M.I.T. in this area with the work of the American Jewish Congress commission. He knew how inadequate society's ability was to reduce intergroup conflict. He was also deeply aware of how much more had to be known about the forces which produced conflict or harmony between different races and religions and how they could be controlled or directed. Action research offered a promising beginning, and Lewin offered a series of guidelines on the subject in a paper he wrote in 1946, "Action Research and Minority Problems." Lippitt and Radke discussed the problem in an article they did for the 1946 *Annals of the American Academy of Political and Social Science* entitled "New Trends in the Investigation of Prejudice."

The fifth program area dealt with group membership and individual adjustment. In his articles on the psycho-sociological problems of a minority group, on bringing up the Jewish child, and on self-hatred among Jews, Lewin had emphasized how personal self-esteem was influenced by the position in a status system of the group to which a person felt most strongly attached. If a person's racial, religious, or ethnic group was held in low esteem, he often had a low opinion of himself. Similarly, a high evaluation placed on a man's group by society as a whole tended to make him feel secure and worthy of approval.

Finally, the Research Center marked out the sixth area for study; the training of leaders and the improvement of group functioning. Of particular concern were the tasks of introducing change and of overcoming resistance to change. In his paper "Conduct, Knowledge, and the Acceptance of New Values" (written with Paul Grabbe), Lewin had pointed out that, while resistance to change arose almost inevitably when a modification of a group's customary procedures was attempted, it did not necessarily follow that change had to cause as much disruption as it often did. Much of the disruption was the result of inappropriate procedures in the effort to introduce change—for example, a failure to solicit the participation and planning of those whose jobs, responsibilities, or schedules were to be changed.

The role of the leader was recognized by Lewin as vital in the process of introducing changes needed to improve group life. At Iowa, Lippitt had done his experimental study of the effect of democratic and authoritarian group atmospheres, and Bavelas had also done a study at the Harwood plant which he discussed in his paper "Morale and the Training of Leadership." Both studies demonstrated that leadership skills could be identified and taught. At M.I.T. particularly promising results were obtained from experiments in training not single leaders but leadership teams in groups. Among those who participated in these studies were Lippitt, French, Kelley, Pepitone, Zander, and Pearl Rosenberg.

If Lewin was concerned with communication and the spread of influence as a problem in the behavioral sciences, he also recognized how essential it was for the advancement of science itself that there be a free flow of communication among scientists. While there was adequate communication within each discipline, there was little opportunity for a psychologist to know what political scientists were doing, for example, or for sociologists to be exposed to recent thinking in education. Lewin, therefore, encouraged his associates and students to take advantage of opportunities for personal interaction with colleagues in other disciplines by frequently attending meetings of related professional societies. The Research Center itself also sponsored a number of interdisciplinary conferences.

Lewin attracted to M.I.T. many brilliant students, among them was Simon Herman, who came from South Africa and who later went to the Hebrew University in Jerusalem, as Lewin himself had wanted to do many years back. Herman arrived in the United States to do his postgraduate work. He was intent on seeking out Lewin in the hope of studying under him. The two met in January 1945 in New York. Herman recalls "It was agreed that I would join him as one of his research assistants at the Research Center for Group Dynamics, which was then in its planning stage. To work under Kurt Lewin in that great experiment was an experience that profoundly influenced my understanding of the whole field of human relations."

From Canada came Gordon Hearn, a graduate of George Williams College, who left his post with the Y.M.C.A. in order to study with Lewin for his doctorate. Hearn's memories of the time he spent as a student at the Center provide another glimpse of Lewin in the teacher-student relation. Hearn had considerable experience in group work but little formal training in psychology. As he laughingly relates, "Lewin made my education a project for the entire faculty." In addition to his regular graduate courses, the new student received special tutoring in individual psychology from Radke and in group psychology from Festinger. Lewin himself set Thursday afternoons as his time for regular conferences with Hearn.

Teacher and pupil met out-of-doors to walk and talk up and down the banks of the Charles River. Lewin instructed his secretary that he was not to be disturbed during these meetings as he needed the exercise. But Hearn adds, "I suspect he knew I needed all the help I could get." The sessions were a sort of two-man *Quasselstrippe*, with Hearn telling Lewin what he was doing in the program, what ideas he was exploring, and what conceptual problems he was facing. As a rule, the pupil's exposition released a stream of creative suggestions and comments from the teacher. "I'd listen and build on the discussion, and when our walk was ended, I'd have a dozen new ideas to explore and new problems to tackle." Recognizing that his was a unique opportunity, Hearn always tried to make careful preparation. "A week later, when we resumed our walk, I'd be eager to show him what I'd done with the problems and questions he'd posed—and he was exploring some new train of thought. It was a memorable experience."

Another student was Morton Deutsch who first heard of Lewin while at C.C.N.Y. Lewin's *Dynamic Theory of Personality* excited him "enormously," as did J. F. Brown's *Psychology and the Social Order*, which articulated Lewin's theories of social psychology. Torn between social and clinical psychology, Deutsch arranged for interviews with Lewin and Carl Rogers. He met Lewin for breakfast on V-J Day in a hotel lobby in New York. Lewin was late and suffering from a severe sunburn. Deutsch remembers Lewin as "captivating and charming" as he described the Research Center at M.I.T. "His facial glow was not only from his sunburn," Deutsch reports. "He communicated an intense enthusiasm and the feeling of being engaged in work that was scientifically pioneering as well as socially significant. He was irresistible. M.I.T. was the place. I had to be there."

Deutsch did not regret his choice. At M.I.T., Lewin created a stimulating and fruitful atmosphere for graduate work. As soon as a student appeared, he was immediately involved in a research project in a colleague-like relationship with a faculty member and given considerable responsibility. "Friendly but sharp controversy about research and theoretical issues was the norm in the faculty-student seminar on ongoing research," Deutsch says. The sense of being part of an elite scientific group gave Lewin's graduate students at M.I.T. an unusual *élan*—a feeling created and sustained by Lewin's gentle but enthusiastic personality, his deep commitment to the relevance of science, and his way of thinking about psychological questions.

Harold H. Kelley chose to study with Lewin at the urging of Stuart Cook, Director of the Commission on Community Interrelations. Kelley, like the other graduate students, attended the weekly seminar given by Lewin. Though he had received his M.A. in psychology at the University of California in Berkeley, under Ralph Gundlach, and had had extensive experience in the Army working with Cook, John Lacey, and others, Kelley felt himself ill-prepared for what he recalls as the "exotic, specialized stuff that Lewin covered—topological and vector analyses, Aristotelian vs. Galileian modes of thought, and a whole new approach to research procedures. "I couldn't see the forest for the trees," Kelley now confesses. "I lacked perspective to realize the value of the studies, not for what they proved but for the problems they tackled and the questions they raised." Yet Kelley vividly describes as "exciting" interaction the planning sessions he attended while serving as Marian Radke's research assistant. "He imparted such enthusiasm to us about our own project that sparks seemed to fly as we discussed various possibilities."

Looking backward nearly a quarter of a century later, Kelley now believes that Lewin exerted "more influence on the directions of social psychology than any man before him." This influence, according to Kelley, was "not in terms of specific concepts or results—how could it be, if social psychology is to advance?—but in terms of level of theoretical analysis (the interpersonal and the socially relevant intrapersonal) and general approach (theory-guided experiments)."

John Thibaut was another research fellow at M.I.T. Before the war he had been a graduate student in philosophy at the University of North Carolina. Returning to Chapel Hill in March 1946 after military service, he took a reading course with J. F. Dashiell, the chairman of the Psychology Department. One day he told Dashiell

188

of his plans for continued study in psychology at Yale. Dashiell replied that he thought Lewin's new Research Center at M.I.T. would be more appropriate for him. Although Dashiell—an eminent figure in psychology—was a behaviorist and an "objectivist," he expressed great admiration for Lewin's work. "He convinced me on the spot and I mailed off a letter the same day asking for the application forms," Thibaut says.

At M.I.T. in the fall of 1946, Thibaut was assigned to Lewin as his research assistant. "Lewin talked and my job was to listen and later to set down as accurately as I could the content of what he had said. I was encouraged to question him and to develop further any of his ideas, but I don't recall that I was ever able to do much along those lines. On those afternoon walks he talked on a great range of topics in social psychology but he concentrated on the ideas of quasi-stationary equilibrium and of a psychological ecology—the first formulation of the ideas later published posthumously in his article 'Frontiers in Group Dynamics' in the first two issues of *Human Relations*."

Today Thibaut finds it hard to characterize Lewin's influence on psychology, not because it is difficult to find but because "it has been so pervasive." Whatever the trouble in describing the nature of Lewin's influence, Thibaut has said, "it is not so difficult to understand why he was influential. He had an uncanny intuition about what problems were important and what kinds of concepts and research situations were necessary to study them. And though he was obsessed with theory he was not satisfied with the attainment of theoretical closures but demanded of the theory that its implications for human life be pursued with equal patience and zeal."

Lewin rarely lost touch with former students. He maintained close contact with those on the staff of the Center and kept in touch with others through correspondence and intermittent visits. Roger Barker came to see Lewin from Clark University, Cambridge being much more accessible from Worcester than Iowa City. Alex Bavelas had joined the M.I.T. staff and often drove to Lewin's house in Newtonville to get his counsel on some of his own knottier problems. "We'd walk up and down in the snow in front of the Lewin house, Lewin talking and gesticulating and drawing excited diagrams in the snow. Lewin was not hesitant to look at a small thing, probably because he often saw in it a meaning that others had not seen. He was not insecure about anything and so didn't care whether it was a full-dress or half-dressed experiment. The point was that it was interesting."

Then there was always the family. Lewin had housed them in a big, rambling, quite old Newtonville cottage. Sundays he planned to spend with the family. Too often these Sunday plans were interrupted by the constant ringing of the phone and long telephone discussions. But Lewin always looked forward to these days at home—even though his work took most of his free time.

In sheer numerical terms, the output of published doctoral dissertations, experiments, and research reports at the Research Center for Group Dynamics at M.I.T. (many of them finished at the University of Michigan, to which the Research Center was transferred after Lewin's death) is formidable—some 125 papers in all. When added to almost as many published during the same period under Lewin's aegis at the Commission on Community Interrelations, the total is unprecedented among any group of psychologists.

In commenting on Lewin's influence as a teacher and intellectual leader during this period, George Mandler [2] declared that Lewin's students and associates at M.I.T. comprised "an honor roll of current psychology."

[2] G. Mandler, *Perspectus in American History* (Cambridge: Harvard University Press, 1968).

CHAPTER

LAUNCHING PROGRAMS OF COMMUNITY ACTION

Although the formation of C.C.I. was not formally announced until February 1945, a small staff consisting of Lillian W. Kay and Ronald Lippitt had been busy since September 1944 analyzing fundamental issues and making policy recommendations. Busy as he was at M.I.T., Lewin came to New York weekly to assist in planning a program that would not measure the effectiveness of methods already in use, but would work out and test new ways that might be better. He maintained that C.C.I.'s responsibility would not end with finding out what methods work; it also had to be concerned to see that its results were put into action. He suggested that C.C.I. should concentrate on problems that confronted the people who were engaged in fighting prejudice. It should carry on its studies in real-life situations where the results would be used. Finally, he stated that, whenever possible, C.C.I. should conduct its studies in cooperation with other agencies carrying on programs of action against prejudice. Lewin was pleased with the staff proposal to narrow their studies to three priority research areas. These were:

1. The conditions which improve the effectiveness of community leaders who are attempting to better intergroup relations. For example, what are the most effective and practical methods of training such leaders? What are the principles governing the choice of trainees? What can be done to promote the maintenance of the operating efficiency to which such leaders are brought as a result of training?

2. The effect of the conditions under which contact between persons from different groups takes place. For example, what conditions result in an improvement of attitude and in harmonious relations and what conditions bring about the converse? What conditions of contact result only in the formation of particular friendships as against the formation of friendly feelings toward other cultural groups taken as a whole? What conditions result in the formation of lasting favorable attitudes as against those susceptible to easy reversal in a prejudiced environment?

3. The influences which are most effective in producing in minority-group members an increased sense of belongingness, an improved personal adjustment, and better relations with individuals of other groups.

Lewin was less pleased with the staff's working conditions. At first it was assigned space in the New York City headquarters of the A.J.C. overlooking Central Park at Columbus Circle. But this grew crowded and forbidding as C.C.I.'s staff grew in size and complexity (for instance, when a distinguished advisory council of behavioral scientists was added to the permanent staff). New and better office space became an urgent need. It was supplied in the form of a loft at 50th Street and Broadway, which offered more space but hardly more attractiveness than the crowded office they were leaving. Then the staff had a piece of good luck.

Lewin persuaded his friend and fellow refugee Marcel Breuer, who had found a place with Walter Gropius in the Harvard School of Architecture, to take a look at C.C.I.'s loft and design its offices and furniture at a nominal fee. Breuer projected within the decrepit loft a layout with magnificent color combinations, specially built files, and a large library, honeycombed with shelving on all four sides and having a huge conference table in the center. Visitors from many distant places soon came to view the offices which Breuer had designed for C.C.I.

For its motto, Lewin proposed a quotation from the Hebrew sage, Hillel:

> If I am not for myself, who will be for me?
> If I am for myself alone, what am I?
> And if not now, when?

Lewin felt the lines had a special aptness. "In regard to research, the first and second lines say that we are ready to investigate ourselves, our ideals, and our conduct as seriously and as conscientiously as we are ready to investigate non-Jewish groups. Jews are a small minority, but the conduct of the Jewish child and adult, of the Jewish leader and follower, the Jewish businessman and rabbi, is at least as essential for Jewish fate and for the relations between Jews and non-Jews as is the conduct of any non-Jewish group. The last line of our motto says: The Commission means action, and action now. If we speak of research, we mean 'action research,' that is, action on a realistic level, action that is always followed by self-critical objective reconnaissance and evaluation of results. Since we like to learn rapidly, we will never be afraid to face our shortcomings. We aim at 'no action without research; no research without action.' "

Lewin's penchant for the symbolic representation of social forces had long been demonstrated on blackboards in the classroom. He now provided C.C.I. with a unique symbol, composed of a superimposed circle, crossed lines and an arrow. The circle, Lewin said, signified a community bound together in common interests; the crossed lines were the barriers—walls of prejudice, intolerance, and misunderstanding of cultural differences; the arrow represented facts in action research. This partnership was to be made available by the C.C.I. to all communities throughout the United States.

Stuart Cook came from the Air Corps to serve as co-director of C.C.I. One was needed in view of Lewin's multiplying responsibilities at M.I.T. and C.C.I.'s growing action-research program, which included opening offices in Boston and Chicago. Among the other psychologists who served full or part time were Alex Bavelas, Barbara Bellow, Milton Blum, Dorwin Cartwright, Isidor Chein,

Kenneth B. Clark, Morton Deutsch, Leon Festinger, John Harding, Marie Jahoda, Lillian Kay, Ronald Lippitt, Marian Radke, Gerhart Sanger, and Goodwin Watson. Like the other staff members of C.C.I., Cook quickly became caught up in the project's excitement and in Lewin's enthusiasm. Lewin saw the staff as a task force of behavioral scientists who could study ongoing events systematically and objectively, making recommendations for action as well as compiling research data. Hendry and Cook had the responsibility for carrying out the various studies.

Lewin never sought to assert his authority as C.C.I.'s chief architect and senior consultant. But Cook remembers that Lewin kept coming up with ideas for new projects which would have meant abandoning others already under way, and new approaches which would have required interrupting avenues of inquiry already opened. Much younger than Lewin, far less eminent and experienced, Cook occasionally found himself in the position of defending the operation against Lewin's enthusiasm. But he learned much from him at the same time.

One piece of wisdom that Cook says he has never forgotten grew out of a conversation with Lewin about a research proposal in which Cook listed the various aspects of the problem to be studied. Lewin offered the comment that when there were so many dimensions to a problem there was danger that the research would cover the minor aspects and never get to the major ones. "Sound research strategy," he said, "dictated looking for the variable aspect that would make a difference, coming back later to the others."

Lewin was learning too. For one thing, Stuart Cook remembers that Lewin was beginning to appreciate the difference between laboratory research (in which most of the time is spent thinking about and discussing the project's theoretical aspects while the actual experiment is done fairly quickly) and community research (in which the biggest and most time-consuming part of the job is building relations with community people and collecting data from them). "He learned too that there were inherent limitations in the results that could be expected, no matter how heavy the investment in time, money, and personnel."

194

Confronting the Social Issues

C.C.I.'s advisory council [1] which had originally met in Washington, continued to meet with the staff in New York to discuss a series of issues fundamental to the solution of problems of racial and religious prejudice. The issues they confronted were the ancient human problems of how people who are different from each other can live together without explosive conflict. Among the issues discussed were these:

1. *Assimilation versus cultural pluralism.* The idea of "acculturation without absorption"—particularly as it applied to the Negro—was a baffling one. A Negro leader who had been invited to attend one of the sessions startled his hearers when he said: "We Negroes want to break down barriers whenever possible; the Jews want to preserve many barriers. They seek to integrate but not to assimilate and they pride themselves on their separateness in many ways. We want to end separateness."

This difference in aims caused C.C.I. members to ask whether the Commission should consider minimizing racial and religious distinctions in certain areas while maintaining them in others.

a) Were there some areas in which each person should be regarded on his merits, irrespective of race or religion, and others in which Jewish distinctiveness should be maintained?

b) Would this justify encouraging the establishment of a separate Jewish medical association while at the same time fighting for Negroes to be admitted into the local medical society?

c) Would the definition of areas of separateness hurt or help the effort to reduce discrimination in other areas?

[1] The advisory council's membership included Gordon W. Allport, Harvard University; Nathan E. Cohen, New York University; Franklin Fearing, University of California at Los Angeles; Charles Johnson, Fisk University; Rensis Likert, Department of Agriculture, Washington D.C.; Howard Y. McClusky, University of Michigan; Douglas M. McGregor, Massachusetts Institute of Technology; Margaret Mead, American Museum of Natural History; Lois B. Murphy, Sarah Lawrence College; Fritz Redl, Wayne State University; Robert R. Sears, University of Iowa; Edward O. Tolman, University of California at Berkeley; W. Lloyd Warner, University of Chicago; Alfred J. Marrow served as Chairman of the council.

Two decades later the cry of "Black Power" and the development of the Black Nationalist Movement has shown how critical the issue was—and would increasingly become.

2. *"Separate but equal" versus integration.* It would be nine years before the Supreme Court issued its famous decision outlawing racial segregation in public schools. The decision was based in part on evidence submitted by Isidor Chein of the C.C.I. staff. In 1945, C.C.I.'s staff and advisers had been deeply divided over this issue, asking themselves: Should minority groups be urged to accept segregation as the price of immediate improvement in schools, hospitals, and housing; or should they risk indefinite delay by insisting on integrated projects? It was a question that would still divide the American community two decades later.

3. *Acceptance versus rejection of class stratification.* One of C.C.I.'s consultants, Fritz Redl, reported that experiences with interracial groups in boys' clubs indicated that middle-class white boys tended to accept middle-class Negro boys more readily than either "tough" whites or "tough" Negroes. Would it be sound policy, therefore, to acknowledge and work within existing stratifications in order to minimize racial differences? Would a black welder have more in common with a white welder than with a black psychiatrist?

4. *Other "minorities" versus "anti-Semitism."* The argument that Jewish problems were but one part of the much larger problem of disadvantaged minorities (which meant that democracy, rather than the welfare of the Jews, should become the central goal) was contrasted with the view that the problem of anti-Semitism was distinct from that of other minorities, so that interfaith committees on which Jews served should not end up, as they usually did, devoting all or at least most of their attention to black-white relations.

5. *Attacking "discrimination" versus attacking "prejudice."* Cities that introduced Negro employees on streetcars and buses as a *fait accompli* rarely experienced the kind of hostility that fre-

quently developed in communities where months of discussions were held with the aim of "preparing" people for planned changes in employment, housing, or education. Often white families who thought they would want to move out of housing projects when Negro families came in but were delayed in doing so, found in the interval that they liked their new neighbors. Such observations led some of C.C.I.'s advisers to suggest that if the pattern of racial segregation and religious discrimination could be changed swiftly and firmly, the new environment would take care of prejudiced attitudes; that is, an attack on behavior patterns would eventually change attitudes (rather than vice versa). Should C.C.I.'s goal, then, be legal action to remove institutionalized barriers between races and religions—quota systems in universities, blackballing in employment, housing discrimination—or should it concentrate on seeking to influence personal feelings and attack prejudices?

6. *"Direct"* versus *"incidental."* Some organizations focused directly on interracial or interfaith cooperation. Others, such as hospitals, universities, and labor unions, regarded these problems as incidental to their primary purposes. When should such groups draw attention to their interracial activities and policies? When should they ignore, or treat as entirely natural, the cooperation of different groups? When, if at all, was there need for an organization that focused directly on community inter-relations?

The C.C.I. advisory board recognized that there was much the staff had to learn and much to explore. But they understood that the staff couldn't wait for all the evidence. A beginning had to be made with the knowledge that was available. Such action would lead to more reliable knowledge. Action would become research, and research action. C.C.I. would not always be able to wait for research into "facts." They would have to rely on the application of certain postulates—postulates of group dynamics—to reduce community tension.

Working under Lewin's general supervision, Cook, Chein, and John Harding outlined four varieties of action research to carry out C.C.I.'s objectives, once the direction of these major policies was decided. They named these varieties of action research: (1) diagnostic, (2) participant, (3) empirical, and (4) experimental.

1. *Diagnostic* action research was designed to produce a needed plan of action. Here C.C.I. would step into an already existing situation (for example, a race riot or anti-Semitic vandalism), diagnose the problem, and recommend remedial measures. Unless the proposed cures were feasible, effective, and acceptable to the people involved, however, this design of action was often wasted.

2. *Participant* action research assumed that the residents of the affected community who were to help effect a cure must be involved in the research process from the beginning. They would thereby realize more keenly the need for the particular steps finally decided upon; at the same time their "ego investment" would support the remedial program. This type of action research—an example would be a community self-survey (see pages 214 ff.)—seemed to be most effective for a limited range of problems. It was useful in disclosing particular and local facts (not general principles) which could provide examples for other communities.

3. *Empirical* action research was primarily a matter of record keeping and accumulating experiences in day-to-day work, ideally with a succession of similar groups, such as boys' clubs. An inherent weakness of this procedure was that conclusions were drawn from experience with a single group, or with several groups differing in numerous ways, without test controls. Despite this handicap empirical action research could lead to the gradual development of generally valid principles as clinical medicine had already demonstrated.

4. *Experimental* action research called for a controlled study of the relative effectiveness of various techniques in nearly identical social situations. Of all the varieties of action research, the C.C.I. staff members agreed, the experimental had the greatest potential for the advancement of scientific knowledge. Under favorable circumstances it could definitively test specific hypotheses. It was, however, the most difficult form of action research to carry out successfully.

C.C.I. was officially launched at a dinner for a thousand guests held at the Plaza Hotel in New York. Lewin was the principal speaker and his talk was particularly significant for its reflection of his shift from theoretical psychology to action research. He began by outlining C.C.I.'s practical approach, Lewin pointed out that he was wary of what he described as "that type of so-called realistic policy which lives from day to day, patching up a hole here and applying a new coat there." He insisted that any constructive plan must include both long-range goals and day-to-day actions. Such a strategy should consider not merely the local situation and the peculiar constellation of events and personalities involved, but also the broader issues and the social forces behind them.

But contextual information, he pointed out, was not readily available. Statistics measuring such items as the distribution of Jews in various occupations (for example, the low percentage of Jews in banking) were on hand but statistics do not change anti-Semitic attitudes. Anti-Semites are never at a loss for a justification of their prejudices. A prejudice was reasonable to them, no matter how irrational it might seem to others. That "the forces of anti-Semitism are not rational does not give us the right to ignore them; nor does their irrational character place them outside the approach of science." Irrational behavior, Lewin felt confident, could be studied objectively and scientifically, but the studies must be in depth to be useful in any action program. Data must be assembled from every aspect of community life—economic, political, educational, cultural, traditional. They must include information concerning minority and majority, Jew and non-Jew, Negro and white.

Lewin maintained that C.C.I. must deal with minority problems as one of the crucial aspects of a developing democracy, as an issue that must be solved in a democratic spirit, if democracy was to survive as a way of life. True, each minority—Negroes, Catholics, Mexicans, Jews—had its own characteristic problem; but each should learn from the others. To Lewin a minority problem was meaningless without its counterpart "majority problem." "Every minority problem is, in fact, a majority problem," he stated. "The Negro problem is a problem of the whites, the Jewish problem, of the

Christian." Nevertheless, a condition for improving relationships between majorities and minorities called for altering the attitudes and certain aspects of the conduct of minority members. The alterations would be extremely difficult, inasmuch as members of minorities who are victims of discrimination tend to apply to themselves the unexpressed judgment of the majorities that minorities are inferior.

Many environmental forces served to develop in the children, adolescents, and adults of minorities a deep-seated antagonism toward their own group. Excessive submissiveness, feelings of guilt, extreme emotionalism, and other manifestations of ineffective behavior are the consequence. No group which is thus at odds with itself can live normally, much less happily, with other groups. Therefore, Lewin argued, it was hopeless to seek to cope with this problem in terms of individuals. The discrimination that individuals suffer is directed against them not as persons but as members of a group. Only by raising the members' esteem for the group character could relief come to them. More than twenty years later Martin Luther King would preach "black is beautiful" and Black Power advocates would demand that Negro history and Swahili be taught in the New York City schools.

Lewin realized from the start at C.C.I. that the research problems would not always be those he wished to select. He knew he would be responsible for overcoming social resistance to applying his findings. He would also have to hold in mind the community interest, for society neither supports nor makes use of research findings that do not meet community-felt needs. He perceived that he would have to state the problem not only in objective scientific terms but also in terms of the ways in which the community evaluates its problems. So his relationship to a community as a researcher would have to start with the community problems. At every step of his investigation he would have to bear in mind the attitudes of his lay collaborators and sponsors, as well as those of the general public. The research staff would have to consider the community as seriously as it took its own research.

CHAPTER

21

SOME MAJOR ACTION-RESEARCH PROJECTS

Two weeks after the first staff member was employed, C.C.I. was reluctantly involved in its first project, a case of vandalism in Coney Island. Efforts of Lewin to delay action were not successful. The A.J.C. insisted on C.C.I.'s help and thus the Coney Island project became C.C.I.'s initial "assignment." Others followed quickly. The Horace Mann School in New York asked for an evaluation of its intercultural program. This study included one of the earliest tests of the effectiveness of intergroup activity on the attitudes of participants. During the same period, three other inquiries were launched —two in Boston and one in a New Jersey industrial town—into the attitude of individual Jews toward their own group as measured by synagogue attendance, observance of dietary laws and religious holidays, friendship with non-Jews, attitude toward intermarriage, and affiliation with Jewish and mixed social clubs.

In Chicago, C.C.I.'s Midwest Regional office probed the roots of an attack on the Jewish center in Hyde Park, consulted with school officials concerned over Negro-white tensions in nearby Gary,

Indiana, and measured the impact of anti-Semitic speeches by Gerald L. K. Smith and his associate Arthur Terminiello.

C.C.I.'s programs drew considerable newspaper and magazine attention. Though not all the published articles were entirely satisfactory to Lewin and his colleagues in C.C.I., the pieces did provide the kind of public exposure that the Commission's supporters within the A.J.C. welcomed, and the social scientists on C.C.I.'s staff felt that the press was important in communicating their methods and goals.

Under Lewin's direction C.C.I. brought the A.J.C. intellectual prestige and greatly expanded influence. But, as Lewin had predicted, mounting demands for "fire-fighting" projects put an ever-growing load on the C.C.I. staff. Pressures were increasing to de-emphasize long-range scientific research in favor of direct and militant short-range social action. At the same time, the need for publicity (arising out of dependence on the public for funds, competition with other Jewish agencies, and criticisms from activists within the A.J.C. who did not understand the farsighted program C.C.I. was trying to set up) led to frequent policy changes. These distractions, plus a serious problem which arose concerning the financing of C.C.I., took their toll. The promised million dollars was not in hand; a large part of it had to be raised, and the A.J.C. demanded frequent cutbacks in the long-range program. One of the first casualties was Hendry, who resigned as C.C.I.'s research director in July 1946.

Lewin was distressed and wrote to Hendry on April 5, 1946. "I was very tired but went back to New York to fight the battle. If you and I, Stuart Cook, and Alfred Marrow would stick together through whatever comes, I feel we will win. There will be painful things to do, but they have to be done. You are well aware that absolute, long-range security for research is rarely ever found. In any type of action research in the social field, security can never be anything given on a legal contract level which one can 'have and forget about.' Social action is a part of a changing social world. Security in action research has to be re-established anew every day. I consider this crisis one of life or death for C.C.I., and I am ready to go to any lengths to find a productive solution for our basic enterprise. I for one am not ready to give up."

Lewin's skill at working with the leaders of the A.J.C. brought about a temporary solution to the harassing problems. The activities continued to expand and new projects were often undertaken before the manpower was available. But Lewin remained calm and confident. During the next five years more than fifty separate projects involving all four varieties of action research were carried out. The following are some of the most pertinent.

Gang Behavior

An "incident" between Jewish and non-Jewish teenagers on Yom Kippur was the basis for the first major C.C.I. study. A gang of Italian Catholic teenagers had disturbed the religious services of Yom Kippur at a synagogue in Coney Island. Though the incident had occurred before C.C.I. was ready to take on any assignments, the leaders of the A.J.C. felt that public interest in the event provided an unusual opportunity to demonstrate the value of a scientific approach to this kind of situation. They urged Lewin to take the event for his first action-research project. He agreed reluctantly, for at the time his staff consisted of only two persons. He assembled a task force including Jews, Protestants, Catholics, and Negroes. He drew them from group workers and psychologists on a part-time basis. All had been trained in research in human relations and were able to talk the language of both youths and grownups.

Their first step was to halt the legal action against the four young men arrested for creating the disturbance. The complaint was withdrawn and the boys were put in charge of the local priest and the Catholic Big Brothers.

C.C.I.'s next step was to canvass local attitudes and to involve as many citizens of the community as possible, since such participation would make action toward improvement more likely. A survey of representative community attitudes indicated that the disturbance had not resulted from organized anti-Semitism but was rather a symptom of an undirected, general sentiment of hostility. Aggression happened to turn on Jews on Yom Kippur because on this holy day the Jews were more conspicuous.

Nor was it an instance of delinquency that could be corrected by sending the juveniles to jail. The real problem, the survey disclosed, lay in the frustrations and disappointments which all the people in the community experienced every day of their lives; eliminating those would be the solution. This meant providing more and better housing, building recreational centers, improving transportation. Especially desirable were activities bringing together different racial and religious groups in a friendly atmosphere. These had to be planned.

The findings were brought to the attention of the Mayor's Committee on Human Relations and led to a promise to provide some of the needed facilities. C.C.I. was requested to continue to serve as consultant to the community and work closely with the gang that had started the Yom Kippur fight. Russell Hogrefe of the C.C.I. staff was assigned to this task. It took several months for him to win their confidence, and he then continued to work with them for a year.

The study had begun with three queries: (1.) Can the gang learn to behave in a way more acceptable to the community? (2.) Can the group's energies be redirected toward constructive activities? (3.) Can their negative attitudes of opposition and aggression be changed? At the end of a year, the answer to the first two questions was "yes." On the third, the findings were equivocal.

C.C.I. summed up the conclusions in a report [1] which indicated that the gang's relations with the adult world had vastly improved. The boys gave evidence of wanting to please adults, to whom they looked for recognition. Fighting had dropped off sharply. Energies were altered into constructive channels. Although there were no conspicuous changes of attitude toward the Negro and Jewish groups, aggression toward these groups had tapered off. Street fights with them had almost ceased. The gang's trend toward socially approved behavior was sustained. This implied significant changes. The ultimate measure of the success of the project was the fact that the changes endured after the consultant was withdrawn.

[1] B. Bellow, M. L. Blum, K. B. Clark, and others, "Prejudice in Seaside," *Human Relations* 1947, 98–120.

The group had become more and more self-sufficient and independent in maintaining its new ways. The upshot of this successful pioneer adventure in action research was to provide a pattern for an attack on the problems of a world of street gangs, cellar clubs, and ethnic rivalries which has since been adopted by many private and public agencies across the country.

Law and Social Change

Conferring with Lewin, the A.J.C. leaders took up the problem of *numerus clausus* in American colleges and universities. Lewin had expressed the view that discrimination often was the cause of prejudice, not the result of it, and that an alteration of behavior could bring a change of attitude. He held that if universities were required by law to admit students on merit and not on the basis of race or religion, the new practice would bring new and more favorable attitudes.

Lewin felt that the idea that "you can't legislate good will" is not always valid. There are many situations where legislation and law could be psychologically sound tools. Withdraw the support of the milieu from discrimination and you weaken its base. The object of prejudice is put in a new context, which may make apparent hitherto unnoticed traits that the prejudiced person has ignored. Legislation firmly enforced and supplemented with a broad program of community education could be highly effective in overcoming discrimination.

With this concept in mind, the president of the A.J.C. filed suit to challenge the *numerus clausus* maintained by the Medical School of Columbia University. The issue became a front-page story. The Medical School first denied that it had a quota for Jews but refused to open its selection system for inspection or to make a formal announcement of non-discrimination. The case was settled out of court when the University agreed to make available in the future the appropriate records, which would show whether or not there was a discriminatory quota, and to state publicly that all applicants would be judged without regard for race or religion.

This challenge to the quota system of a publicly supported private institution resulted in a revision of discriminatory policies by leading schools of higher learning throughout the country.

Integration of Negro Sales Personnel

Another and quite different critical issue was presented to the C.C.I. staff for action. To find the answer Gerhart Saenger and Emily Gilbert [2] set up a study which sought the facts about the department-store practice of not hiring Negroes as sales clerks because, as the store management put it, "our customers wouldn't stand for it." The researchers first interviewed store customers who had dealt with Negro clerks and others who had dealt with white clerks at work near Negroes. In addition, interviews were held on sidewalks with white persons in order to assemble street samples whose responses could be used as a control.

All respondents who showed signs of prejudice were asked directly whether they would continue to shop in stores that hired Negro salespeople. To the question "What would you think if all New York department stores hired Negro sales persons?" 64 per cent of the shoppers and 75 per cent of the street sample said they would approve. Of the group observed being waited on by Negro clerks, 20 per cent said they disapproved, whereas 21 per cent of the group observed with white clerks and 14 per cent of the street sample said they would resent being waited on by Negroes. The rest had no opinion.

Among the respondents were a dozen persons who expressed extreme prejudice and said they would not shop in a store which hired Negro sales help. But five of these had earlier been observed shop-

[2] G. Sanger and E. Gilbert, "Customer Reactions to the Integration of Negro Sales Personnel," *International Journal of Attitude and Opinion Research*, 1950, *4*, 57–76.

ping not only in such a store but at a counter served by a Negro! And two of them had themselves been waited on by the Negro!

The investigators concluded: "Whatever a customer's prejudice, it did not keep him from buying from Negro clerks. Customers accepted the situation they found in the store as a *fait accompli*, and, therefore, prejudice did not deter a person from accepting Negro sales help."

The results of this study confirmed that New York department stores were unduly apprehensive about the force of public prejudice against fair employment practices. Their fear that sales would be hurt was not supported by the evidence.

Group Loyalty

The active role taken by members of Lewin's M.I.T. staff in C.C.I. research is illustrated in a study by Festinger based on the belief that fellow members of the Jewish group were loyal to one another. This belief was demonstrated to be a mistaken one in an experiment on the "Role of Belongingness in a Voting Situation." Festinger brought together several groups of college girls from in and around Boston, strangers to one another, with an equal number of Catholics and Jews in each group. To each group he assigned two of his assistants, in the role of students. All of the girls in the experiment were identified by numbers only and were instructed not to reveal their names.

Then they were asked to nominate a "president" for their several groups on the basis of first impressions. They nominated by number and their voting was secret. (Festinger was able to identify each voter.) After the ballots were collected, it was announced—falsely— that the two assistants posing as college girls had been nominated. Then a vote was taken, but by design it was pretended that because of some confusion in the counting a second ballot would have to be held.

Between the first and the second ballot it was suggested in an offhand way that one candidate was Jewish and the other Catholic. (The two assistants posed alternately as Jew and Catholic to nullify personality differences.) The results showed that Catholics who had first voted for Jews tended to switch their votes to the Catholic candidate, but the Jews who had voted for the Catholic made no significant change. In personal interviews with Festinger, both the Catholic and the Jewish students had expressed liking for members of their own group. The Catholics alone, however, carried preferences through into action.

Integrated Housing

C.C.I. staff members had long recognized that just throwing people together—commingling Negroes and whites, Christians and Jews, Puerto Ricans and New Englanders—did not necessarily render their feelings toward one another kindlier. Lewin maintained that it was the manner in which the diverse people came together, especially whether or not they met as equals, which determined whether understanding improved or tensions heightened. What, Lewin asked, is the effect of opening public housing to all races and religions? Is it an antidote to the fear and hatred that exists among many of New York City's different ethnic groups? Does the quality of status defined by living together in the same building build healthier attitudes? Does one really know?

Lewin raised these questions at the time when public housing was being projected as a means of providing decent housing for slum dwellers. Negroes and whites were encouraged to rent space in the new projects, and their proximity offered fresh opportunities to observe interracial relations. A new concept in America's postwar culture, interracial housing offered two types of occupancy. One segregated Negroes and whites in separate buildings in a "checkerboard" pattern within the project. The other integrated all buildings on a first-come, first-served basis without regard to color.

To appraise the effects of these diverse situations, C.C.I. commissioned a study by two part-time staff members, Morton Deutsch and Mary Evans Collins. They selected four interracial housing projects,[3] two integrated, and two "checkerboard." Interviews were planned to draw out white attitudes toward the Negro neighbors and the whites' relations with the Negroes. These interviews were designed to probe deeply and lasted up to two hours. They were held with 100 white housewives and 25 Negro housewives. In addition, 24 Negro and white adolescent boys and girls were interviewed.

The results disclosed a sharp contrast in attitudes between the residents of integrated and segregated housing projects, even though the buildings matched in every particular of physical facilities, environment, and Negro-white ratios and differed only in occupancy patterns. In the segregated projects, resentments toward Negroes were much sharper and anti-Negro prejudice stronger; indeed, the white residents expressed a strong preference for still greater segregation.

On the other hand, where whites came to know Negroes as nextdoor neighbors, they shared a growing sense of common humanity which relaxed the tensions they had brought with them and replaced antagonism with friendliness. The change was expressed (among other responses) by their preference for more and more widely integrated housing. Also, they drew more closely together and became more genuinely good neighbors. The answers of housewives in the segregated projects, on the other hand, showed them to be more peevish, suspicious, and hostile toward others, including other whites.

The indication was that the manner in which people live together in a common dwelling can be a strong factor in shaping their relations as members of groups. Group cohesiveness and morale were higher in the integrated than in the segregated projects. White residents in integrated houses, despite initial forebodings, came to like living in them; many of them expressed pride in their building's "democracy."

[3] This study was planned with Lewin but carried out after his death.

Though even those well disposed toward interracial projects had been convinced that any Negro ratio going much above 50 per cent meant "trouble," the study found no valid evidence that ratios *per se* had any effect on good will. The most cordial relations seemed to exist in the integrated project with 70 per cent Negro occupancy.

The C.C.I. study by Deutsch and Collins was among the first using scientific methods to discover whether or not integrated housing is "workable." The evidence showed that it is.

Sensitivity Training—The Origin of the T Group

In the summer of 1946, Lewin directed another pioneering experiment of major social significance. The Connecticut State Inter-Racial Commission had asked him to help in training leaders and conducting research on the most effective means for combating racial and religious prejudice in communities. This led to the creation in 1947 of the National Training Laboratories, which, according to Warren Bennis, "have now grown to be an internationally recognized and powerful educational force affecting almost all of the social institutions in our society." [4] The original aims of this laboratory were to help people deal more effectively with complex human relationships and problems. Its method is usually called "sensitivity training" and sometimes "laboratory" or "group dynamics" training. Many authorities believe that it carries more promise for the amelioration of social problems than any current alternative.

It began in 1946 with a phone call to Lewin. The director of the Connecticut State Commission was troubled by his staff's inability to translate latent forces of good will in communities into overt endeavors to overcome various forms of bias. As Frank Simpson, the Commission's executive director, explained to Lewin, the Commission's efforts to implement the program had created serious doubts about its effectiveness.

Simpson's call came at a time when C.C.I. was troubled about its

---

[4] W. Bennis, *Journal of Applied Behavioral Science*, 1967.

own form and function. It was understaffed, with a high work load. Nevertheless, Lewin was determined to try out a new design for leadership training. Despite lack of money, know-how, and adequate staff, the help requested by the Connecticut State Commission was to be provided.

Lewin's own group at M.I.T. had already assembled a veritable stockpile of general ideas about group behavior from leadership studies with the Boy Scouts and in industry. These he believed were ready to be tested by experiments on community action. He proposed that the Connecticut training program be pre-designed as a workshop in which a "change" experiment could be conducted. The workshop was simultaneously to train its members, assemble observations on the whys and wherefores of the changes that developed in the trainees, measure their extent, and analyze the outcome. In sum, the workshop would simultaneously train the delegates and provide research data on what produced the changes.

The first task was to assemble a trained staff. As a hard core there were Ronald Lippitt, Leland Bradford, and Kenneth Benné, who headed a large team of trainers, observers, and researchers under Lewin's direction. With the three leaders, Lewin began to work out the design for the workshop to be held in June 1946 at Teachers' College, New Britain, Connecticut.

The program called for two weeks of training for forty-one hand-picked students, of whom most were professional educators or social-agency workers. Only a few were labor leaders and businessmen. About half the trainees were Negroes and Jews, with the sensitivities characteristics of both groups. What the participants were hoping to gain from the workshop was sought by means of interviews. Their expectations varied, but generally they hoped to develop greater skill in dealing with other people, more reliable methods of changing people's attitudes, insight into reasons for resisting change, a more scientific understanding of the causes of prejudice, and a more reliable insight into their own attitudes and values.

The workshop began with a program that encouraged discussion and decision by the entire group, launching at once the practice of initiating common activities. The staff treated the members as peers.

All were introduced in about three minutes. The leaders of the training and research teams briefly explained the recording equipment and the other data-collecting devices and how to use them. Fifteen minutes later the meeting became the workshop.

During their training period, most participants returned home for an evening's visit with their families. Those who remained on campus had nothing to do but sit around, and they asked if they might sit in on the feedback meetings in which the research staff (Deutsch, Murray Horwitz, Arnold Meier, and Melvin Seeman) reported on the unprocessed data they had collected in observing the three groups of trainees. Most of the staff feared that it would be harmful to have the trainees sit in while their behavior was being discussed. Lewin, however, saw no reason why the researchers should keep data to themselves, nor why feedback to the trainees should not be helpful. The result—in the words of Bradford—was like a "tremendous electric charge . . . as people reacted to data about their own behavior." Thus, the role of feedback in a T (training) group was discovered.

As Lippitt describes it,[5] "Sometime during the evening, an observer made some remarks about the behavior of one of the three persons who were sitting in—a woman trainee. She broke in to disagree with the observation and described it from her point of view. For a while there was quite an active dialogue between the research observer, the trainer, and the trainee about the interpretation of the event, with Kurt an active prober, obviously enjoying this different source of data that had to be coped with and integrated.

"At the end of the evening, the trainees asked if they could come back for the next meeting at which their behavior would be evaluated. Kurt, feeling that it had been a valuable contribution rather than an intrusion, enthusiastically agreed to their return. The next night at least half of the fifty or sixty participants were there as the result of the grapevine reporting of the activity by the three delegates.

"The evening session from then on became the significant learn-

[5] R. Lippitt, *Training in Community Relations* (New York: Harper's, 1949).

ing experience of the day, with the focus on actual behavioral events and with active dialogue about differences of interpretation and observations of the events by those who had participated in them.

"The staff were equally enthusiastic, for they found the process a unique way of securing data and interpreting behavior. In addition, the staff discovered that feedback had the effect of making participants more sensitive to their own conduct and brought criticism into the open in a healthy and constructive way."

In addition to these new, individual feedback sessions, the participants in each group spent about 18 per cent of their time appraising their own behavior. They held these sessions in the evening for an hour and a half.

When the workshop terminated, both staff and participants were satisfied that it had been a success. But the real test of the training's effectiveness was how well the trainees used their new knowledge and skills back home. Six months after they had gone back to work, they and their co-workers were interviewed. The responses disclosed that 72 per cent reported that they were using the new methods—role playing being the most frequently cited. About 75 per cent declared that they were now more skillful in improving group relations. They spoke also of their own increased sensitivity to the feelings of others and of their greater optimism about making progress. From every source came reports of changed performance in working with people, in planning action, in bridging the gaps between good intentions and actual behavior.

A consequence of the Connecticut leadership training workshop was the establishment the following summer of the National Training Laboratories (N.T.L.). It was housed in the Gould Academy, at Bethel, Maine, and financed initially by a grant Lewin obtained from the Office of Naval Research. Before the laboratory could hold its first session, Lewin died, never to know that this brainchild of his would become a permanent organization of national scope and that it would lead to some of the most significant contributions to the scientific study of human relationships.

Carl Rogers recently wrote that "sensitivity training is perhaps the most significant social invention of this century. The demand for it is utterly beyond belief. It is one of the most rapidly growing social phenomena in the United States. It has permeated industry, is coming into education, is reaching families, professionals in the helping fields and many other individuals." [6]

Bradford, one of the leaders at the 1946 workshop, and director and leading spirit of N.T.L. since its formation in 1947, believes that Lewin would have been "proud at the vast growth of sensitivity training as a technique and of the National Training Laboratories as a center of continuing research in the field. Lewin's great concept of creating "here and now" data, analyzing it, and using feedback remains the essential element in all the many variations of sensitivity training and encounter groups that have developed on every continent and in almost every land."

The Community Self-Survey—A Barometer for Bias

One of the most practical action-research projects was the Community Self-Survey of Discriminatory Practices. Psychologists know that emotional retraining is always a most difficult undertaking It is far easier to measure the extent of discriminatory conduct, for example, than to get action on it. It is this problem that Lewin and the staff had long discussed. How can facts be found in such a way that they will lead to action?

Lewin had frequently referred to the situation in most communities in which a few citizens were bothered by the existence of local discrimination and the majority preferred to think that conditions were satisfactory or improving. They chose to disregard the actualities. Many communities, when pressured by a minority for some action program, resorted to outside experts to develop information about where the prejudice was and what strength and form it took among them. But some had become aware of the shortcomings of

[6] C. R. Rogers, "Interpersonal Relationships USA," *Journal of Applied Behavioral Science*, 1968, 4, No. 3.

this approach. Few people cared about the experts' work, which was expensive, and public interest in it waned. Eventually the experts' report was delivered, filed, and forgotten. It rarely led to action.

Various urban communities put a considerable amount of pressure on Lewin and C.C.I. (mostly through members of the A.J.C.) to provide help. A particular problem was discriminatory practices in the community. C.C.I.'s small staff could not respond to all the requests for help in studying local discrimination, and those making the requests had only vague notions about the scope of the prejudice of which they complained and about where it was most widespread. It was necessary to create a dynamic nexus between fact finding and action. It was this search which led to the devising of the community self-survey.

Ideally a community self-survey would elicit genuine and significant participation on the part of citizens in this matter. Self reeducation is the goal, so that citizens are prepared, after a period of discovery and training, to play a more constructive role in rooting out discriminatory practices in their communities. What was wanted, Lewin stated to the C.C.I. staff, was a method that would:

1. Uncover the facts.
2. Show areas of greatest discrimination where countermeasures could be most effectively applied.
3. Provide an accurate measure of discrimination so that future surveys could indicate what progress had been made.
4. Cost little.
5. Get the kind of information that would enable discussion of what to do and how to do it.
6. Get community involvement so that action would follow fact finding. Residents would take seriously the facts that they themselves uncovered. Their findings should lead them to press for action because of their own energetic involvement.

To achieve these results, C.C.I. devised an Index of Discrimination. The Index could be translated as readily as a barometer reading. It established a procedure which carried research over into action. It was economical to set up and run, and it centered on people and organizations rather than on mere fact finding.

The place chosen for the pilot survey was called "Northtown." Located near New York City, "Northtown" had a population of 40,000—12 per cent of them Negroes, 9 per cent Jews—very much an "average" Eastern city. The Northtown survey took two and a half months to collect its data. It recorded a total of 409 interviews. Of these, 304 were family interviews (including 101 white Christians, 99 Negroes, 104 Jews); 35 were interviews with employers; 23 with real estate dealers; 20 with public and private school administrators; and 27 with functionaries in public accommodations and services. The data showed discrimination in every area investigated. That in itself was not surprising. But the intensity of discrimination and number of areas covered was an eye opener to most people.

Employment revealed the most glaring disparities. Earnings of Negroes were far less than those of whites with similar education. Negroes who attended only grammar school earned $1.08 an hour, whites $1.21. Housing showed Negroes at a most marked disadvantage. Comprising 12 per cent of the population, they were crowded into 5 per cent of the residential area.

In February 1948, the Northtown citizen committee reported its findings to representatives of all the sponsoring organizations. This project, which resulted in the development of a Barometer for Bias, represented a great step forward. A self-survey technique had been standardized; a measurement instrument, the Index of Discrimination, had been developed. The low costs involved would permit wide application of the techniques. (A self-survey the size of the Northtown program could be conducted for as little as $600, plus minor expenses necessary for professional and clerical service.)

The tools were now available for any community that wanted to roll up its sleeves and do its own job on discrimination. The Index of Discrimination would make it possible for communities to compare their practices with each other. It would also make possible annual self-assessment to measure the progress in their own community. Seventeen communities were soon conducting such self-surveys.

216

Handling Bigots

In another study C.C.I. addressed itself to finding out whether or not prejudice is encouraged to flourish in an atmosphere of silent acceptance. If, for example, a bigot feels free to make a remark in a department-store elevator or a crowded bus about "damned niggers" or "pushy Jews," does it indicate acceptance of bias if his listeners remain silent? Lewin believed that these incidents are not trivial, for most attitudes—good and bad—are most effectively spread through small face-to-face groups. The more intimate the group, the deeper the prejudice is planted.

What, then, could one do about public hatemongering of this sort? Should one challenge the bigot? Or did that do more harm than good? And if one challenged him, what should be said? And how should one say it? In an unusually complete experimental study,[7] a number of basically important facts were discovered.

The first big question facing the study was whether or not a bigot should be reprimanded. There might just be something in the common-sense formula so often heard: "It's best to mind your own business."

In the first set of experiments a number of different playlets were used, and in each instance the audience was carefully canvassed to discover whether it preferred to have the bigot ignored rather than answered as in the dramatization. To make sure that the bystander's preference with regard to answering the bigot was not influenced by the manner in which he was refuted or told off, two distinctly different manners were used: one, calm and quiet; the other, excited and militant. The experimental routine consisted of presenting three versions of an incident to each audience group: one without an answer to the bigot, one quietly answered, one angrily answered.

[7] C. Selltiz, A. F. Citron, J. Harding, O. Rosahn, and M. H. Wormser, "The Acceptability of Answers to Anti-Semitic Remarks," *International Journal of Opinion and Attitude Research*, 1950, *4*, 353–390.

The sequence of the versions was varied so that the order did not affect the choice.

Altogether, 199 experimental bystanders were tested in the pilot study. Of these, 65 per cent preferred the calm answer; 15 per cent, the excited, harsh answer; and 20 per cent, "no answer." This finding was completely confirmed by later experiments. Most significant, however, was the evidence that four out of five bystanders did not want to see the bigot go unchallenged. This meant that the individual who spoke up in public against stereotyped slurs on minorities could be assured that a typical group of bystanders would be on his side. A dignified manner of answering was preferred, but some kind of answer was definitely wanted by the group that overheard the remark.

This portion of the pilot study made it clear that "you don't remain silent." The problem then became: What kind of answer? To discover this, audience reactions were studied by a number of methods. There were 513 persons in this part of the investigation. A preference was expressed for using "American tradition" as against "individual differences." However, 80 per cent strongly preferred any answer at all to silence, and 68 per cent of the subjects preferred the calm, quiet manner. On the basis of these findings the investigators recommended that public slurs against minorities be answered by appeals based on either democracy or individual differences, and answered quietly.

CHAPTER

UNIFYING THEMES
AND THE
LAST DAYS

By the fall of 1946 the continuing C.C.I. studies of the nature and causes of tensions between people and the methods by which these tensions might be released had received wide recognition. The authoritative *Annals of the American Academy of Political and Social Science* published a special issue that dealt with the subject "Controlling Group Prejudice." Almost half the articles presented were by C.C.I. staff members or advisers, and Dr. Charles Johnson of Fisk University wrote, "The most significant recent undertaking in this field [group prejudice] is the Commission on Community Interrelations." Numerous other articles appeared in professional journals and in popular magazines.

Lewin, now more than ever, was in close contact with the "gatekeepers" of society. He and the C.C.I. staff were often called on to advocate policy, initiate action, and participate in setting goals for changing major social situations.

During this period Lewin was becoming ever more concerned with the problems of the Negro and the methods by which the attitudes of blacks and whites toward each other and, more important, the Negro's attitude toward himself could be changed. In a number of unpublished papers and talks, Lewin pointed out that the behavior of the American Negro is based on an image of himself that was shaped and transmitted over three centuries of collective history—and the first three years, or perhaps less, of his personal history. This self-image must be changed, he said, if the collective and personal history of the Negro were to take a new and positive direction.

He believed that the Negro who is determined to face the challenge of changing his self-image must have the courage to begin with the upbringing of his children; the courage to deal candidly with the black as well as the white causes of their condition and how to overcome them. But the Negro parent who seeks to raise his children's sights must improve his own self-image as well. Adults as well as children, confused by their status—as virtually all members of minorities are likely to be—feel unsure about themselves. They need help in defining their images of themselves as members of a group seeking a better future; in distinguishing between those situations in which the fact of their belonging to a minority culture is pertinent and those in which it is irrelevant; and in appraising what they share and what they do not share with the white culture.

Minority-group members, Lewin maintained, will rapidly learn to overcome their shortcomings if they can be induced to face them. It is neither healthy nor helpful, then, to meet shortcomings by crying "Prejudice!" Negroes can help themselves more, not less, by facing the statements that many of them are satisfied with low achievement, are apathetic toward self-improvement, have a high crime rate (especially for crimes of violence), often create disciplinary problems in school, fail to support their own organizations, and too frequently depend on the generosity of whites. Because he knows these statements are at least in part true, the Negro harbors a depressed self-image. To lift it he must recognize the reason for this partial truth, so that he may overcome it.

"To reverse self-segregation," Lewin said, "a minority should demand substantial sacrifices from its members. Sacrifice gives each member a greater stake in the group; he will not falter in a cause to which he has given so much of himself." Lewin's views add up to the simple proposition that people must have a hand in saving themselves; they cannot and will not be saved from the "outside." Interestingly enough, the same principle explains one of the basic rules of psychoanalysis: it does no good for the therapist to deduce the relevant facts and explain them to his patient; the patient must discover them for himself. When people are themselves involved in the findings, they cannot challenge them as inadequate or the collector as biased.

Lewin believed that the social scientists may serve principally as consultants or guides, so that the inquiry can be carried on with a high degree of technical competence. But the work must be done by the citizens themselves. Any group of people must help cure itself of its sickness on the basis of its own diagnosis and treatment. Self-help of this kind involves personal pride, trust, and feelings of self-growth. These tend to nullify and ultimately to dissipate the emotional blocks to change which sustain prejudice.

A research program tied to an action program can tell why one action is successful and another is not. When this is known, procedures can be designed to improve the successful action and replace the unsuccessful one. The tie-up with action, Lewin observed, keeps the research worker's feet firmly on the ground and serves to keep him sensitive to the real function of his findings as well as alert to their scientific reliability. The tie-up with research keeps the action-centered citizen alert to the dangers of operating in the dark without scientific instruments to guide him in assessing his accomplishment.

Despite the heavy responsibilities of C.C.I. and the Center at M.I.T., Lewin involved himself in yet another project in the last year of his life. This concerned the organizing of a research foundation to aid in the psychological rehabilitation of former residents of displaced-persons camps following World War II. Dr. Jacob Fine, a surgeon at the Harvard Medical School, had drawn Lewin's attention to the exigencies of camp life during the war and afterward which had made social (as well as, in many cases, physical) misfits of the displaced persons. Lewin, who responded immediately, proposed the establishment of an International Jewish Research Foundation on Human Relations with units in the United States and Palestine. The Foundation would conduct cooperative research with existing university institutes and international agencies. Dr. Fine began to seek the necessary funds.

In addition to his concern with this project, Lewin became deeply interested in the work of London's Tavistock Institute. It will be remembered that in 1933, on his visit to Cambridge, he had first met Eric Trist. In 1936 the two had met again at Yale, where Lewin took part in a seminar led by C. L. Hull. Trist had been deeply impressed by what he has described as the "poetic imagination" with which Lewin formulated his theoretical approaches. Trist subsequently used Lewinian theory in a number of studies during World War II. When the war ended he joined forces with the British psychologist A. T. M. Wilson in setting up programs for returned British prisoners of war.

Trist and Wilson prepared a proposal to the Rockefeller Foundation which led to the establishment of the Tavistock Institute in London. One of the Institute's first decisions was to put out an international journal for studies toward the integration of the social sciences. They wrote to Lewin asking whether he would consider establishing the journal in partnership between Tavistock and his group at M.I.T. Trist remembers their excitement when they received Lewin's letter saying that he would.

The partnership was first expressed formally in the founding of the journal *Human Relations,* and the Tavistock staff was happy when Lewin sent over the first two papers on "Frontiers in Group Dynamics." In the articles Lewin indicated his growing interest in the processes of social change. He said that he viewed group experimentation as a form of social management and that its practical task was to gain insight into people's desire for or resistance to specific changes. The attempt to change people's conduct, he observed, should be looked at as a quasi-stationary process. He cited, as an example, the level of discrimination in a community. There are usually social forces driving toward more discrimination. These include the interest of certain segments of the white population in protecting their jobs, as well as the ideas of biased white people about what is "proper" or "not proper" for Negroes. Opposed to these social forces were those resisting increased discriminatory practices, either out of fear of a black revolt or as a moral recognition that the existing practices were unfair. "It, therefore, becomes a matter of major importance," said Lewin, "for understanding and planning changes, to analyze carefully the opposing forces. Levels of conduct can be changed either by adding forces in the desired direction or by diminishing opposing forces." But Lewin cautioned, the effects can be very different between situations where the new level is brought about by increasing the forces which demand equality for the Negro and situations where the forces which oppose it are diminished. For, in the first situation, the new level would be accompanied by a state of relatively high tension and in the second by low tension. Since increase of tension above a certain degree goes parallel with greater fatigue, higher aggressiveness, higher emotionality, and lower constructiveness, it is clear that the second method is preferable to the high-pressure method.

Lewin considered the change process as having three steps: unfreezing, moving to the new level, and freezing at the new level. These could be achieved with existing techniques, but Lewin recognized that the problems of inducing change would require considerably more research than had yet been carried out. He expressed his optimism about the possibility of developing promising techniques for producing social changes that would be superior to the conventional methods and showed, by citing a number of action-research experiments, how this could be achieved.

Trist deeply laments that Lewin never spent the academic year 1947–1948 at Tavistock. But Lewin's influence on Tavistock has continued through the years. His field theory was used to shape the research design of the "Glacier Project," a pioneering study of group relations in a giant industrial organization—in this case, the newly nationalized British coal industry. Among the younger generation of British behavorial scientists, Trist believes, Lewin has been particularly important. "In the analysis of the environment and its causal texture; in research design and in following the course of a social process in detail; in his notion of the psychological time perspective, Lewin has profoundly affected the whole development of social psychology in the British Commonwealth, in Australia, and in India."

For Lewin, ever striving beyond his strength, the pace and demands of his activities began to take their toll. In the summer of 1946, when the Lewins spent a week at Martha's Vineyard with their friends Fritz and Grace Heider, the effect on him was evident. Both could see the building tension—and the onset of exhaustion. Brief as was the time they were together that summer, Grace Heider speaks of it as "frustration." The last years got "more and more frantic," she recalled. "More and more he was doing ten things at once."

Fritz urged his friend to slow down, and Lewin agreed, saying that he longed "to have again the old times." But even during that week at the Vineyard, the friends could hardly talk together because Lewin had a number of articles to finish. He was working on all of them at once—proofreading, writing through all hours of the night, coming for meals and then rushing away. The pressure seemed to crush his natural gaiety. Grace Heider recalls: "During this last period his playfulness was lost—you felt he was no longer capable of it, because he'd let himself get pulled in so many different directions that he was never inwardly at peace."

His friends were concerned but of two minds as to what ought to be done. There were those who wanted him to go on with bigger and better projects and those who wanted him to drop many of them and sit down and think more because they felt that he still was going to explore important new theoretical depths.

The change in Lewin impressed another friend from the old Berlin days. When MacKinnon saw him at the last meeting of the American Psychological Association which Lewin attended, he sensed that his ex-teacher's "ability to shift his energies and focus wasn't as clear as it had been before. He seemed to be preoccupied. You'd talk with him, but something would come to mind and he'd write it down or talk about something else. He was distracted by all these pressures and demands upon him. Lewin took on much more than any human being should have taken on; he was too generous of his time and energy, too busy, too involved with too many projects, too many people. It is almost surprising that he lived as long as he did."

On Monday, February 10, 1947, Lewin spent a typically busy day at the Center. After a hurried dinner at home he left for a meeting at the residence of Dr. Jacob Fine in Boston, where he was to speak. He told the small group of invited guests his reasons for supporting the proposal for the establishment of an International Jewish Research Foundation and the importance which he attached to a systematic program of social research for the rehabilitation of European Jewry. The audience responded to the idea with considerable enthusiasm.

Lewin had invited M.I.T. Research Fellow Simon Herman to accompany him to the meeting. Lewin had already asked Herman to consider a full-time position with the Foundation, to serve as liaison officer between interested groups in the United States and Palestine. Lewin had told Herman that he felt so certain that the project would materialize that he had personally refused an invitation from the University of California for the 1947 summer session so that he would be free to visit Israel and work on this new project.

On Tuesday morning, February 11—the last day of his life—Lewin met briefly with Herman again. He expressed considerable elation at the outcome of the previous night's meeting and asked Herman to write up the minutes of the proceedings and to join him for a further talk at five o'clock. Herman explained that he had set up a conference with some students for that hour and promised to phone Lewin that evening instead.

The rest of Tuesday was especially busy for Lewin. His agenda was overloaded with items that had to be taken care of before he left for New York the following day. His visit to New York involved meetings with important people on a number of pressing issues, and he hurriedly put together the ideas he planned to present. He also spent some time talking with Lippitt, who remembers that Lewin spoke about the mistaken notions of the therapist who perceives the challenge of creating persons who perceive themselves as ready and

225

expected to stand on their own feet once proper transference has been achieved. "The American culture ideal of the 'self-made man,' of everyone 'standing on his own feet,' " Lewin said, "was as tragic a picture as the initiative-destroying dependence on a benevolent despot. We all need continuous help from each other. This type of interdependence is the greatest challenge to the maturity of individual and group functioning."

During the late afternoon Lewin telephoned me. I was leaving for Florida the next day for a week's holiday. We talked for almost thirty minutes about matters at M.I.T. and C.C.I., and at the end of the conversation Lewin apologized for the long talk and whimsically promised that he would not interrupt the vacation with shop talk for "at least one day."

Probably because it was the day before Lincoln's Birthday, Lewin and Gordon Hearn were the only staff members at the Center late in the afternoon. At five-thirty, Hearn, preparing to leave, stopped by Lewin's office and saw him slouched in his chair, his head on his arms. Lewin looked up at him as he passed, asked him about his family (Hearn had been forced to leave them in Canada because of the postwar housing shortage in the Boston area), and deplored the continued lack of housing. They gossiped a bit and finally Hearn said good night. Lewin left for home a short time later.

That evening was "unusually peaceful and quiet," Mrs. Lewin relates. Late in the evening he complained of feeling ill. Mrs. Lewin phoned the family physician, who came immediately and after an examination expressed the belief that Lewin had suffered a heart attack. He planned to hospitalize Lewin early the following morning, but shortly after the doctor's departure, Lewin suffered another—and fatal—seizure.

In keeping with Jewish tradition, the funeral services were held as soon as family and intimates could assemble. Rabbi Maurice Pekarsky of the Hillel Foundation, a close friend, delivered the eulogy to the hastily assembled group of family, friends, colleagues, and students.

EPILOGUE

AN ENDURING
INFLUENCE

Lewin's life was a marked sequence of ironic contrasts. As a scientist he achieved notable success and international fame. He was the center of a wide circle of enthusiastic friends and collaborators who had the highest respect for him. He was invited to join in some of the most distinguished research projects as much for his qualities of human concern as for the brilliance of his mind.

Nevertheless, the psychology "establishment" always kept him on the periphery. No prestigious university offered him an appointment. (His significant work was done in odd settings, such as the Cornell School of Home Economics and the Iowa Child Welfare Research Station.) The American Psychological Association never selected him for any assignment or appointed him to any important committee, though he was a founder and president (1942–1943) of the Society for the Psychological Study of Social Issues.

Lewin's associates and students found him gay and congenial. His personal life, however, was a series of crises: the hardships of World War I, the struggle to establish his academic career in the 1920's, his troubled first marriage, the catastrophe of the Third Reich in the

227

1930's, the murder of his mother and other members of his family by the Nazis. Yet these ordeals never shook his faith in a better future. He met them as they came with characteristic fortitude, courage, and inextinguishable hope.

He was as gracious in his sufferings as he was silent about them. His pursuit of the truth about the hearts and minds of men caused him to subordinate his own pain to the service of other sufferers. Indeed, even after his death Lewin continued to inspire and renew the study of men's psyches. As Robert B. MacLeod states, "It is a tribute to the fertility of Lewin's ideas and to his genius for attracting colleagues of the highest caliber that after his death the group at M.I.T. did not dissolve. In accordance with the principles of group dynamics, the Research Center for Group Dynamics at M.I.T. generated their own leadership, loaded their covered wagon, and ventured west to the wilds of Michigan. Now, many years later, they are still young, vigorous, and productive." [1]

The first official recognition of his spreading influence was the setting up of an annual Kurt Lewin Memorial by the Society for the Psychological Study of Social Issues. The organization also held a memorial meeting for Lewin during the 1947 convention of the American Psychological Association at which three of his close associates—Gordon Allport of Harvard University, Edward C. Tolman of the University of California, and I—were invited to speak of his life and work in psychology.

Tolman, who spoke first, described "Lewin's emphasis on the ahistorical, contemporaneous, systematic determiners of behavior as an expression of a new and tremendously fruitful intellectual insight. . . . This emphasis on the importance of the contemporaneous signified that in order to mitigate the horrors of our world we can in large measure do so by inducing the appropriate field forces. We do not have to wait and start all over again with our infants and our infants' infants. We can begin here and now with ourselves, how-

[1] Robert B. MacLeod, presentation on behalf of the Kurt Lewin Memorial Committee, September 1, 1958.

ever unfortunate our personal histories may have been." Concerning the sharp criticisms of Lewin's postulations, Tolman spoke as he believed Lewin himself would have: "Far more important than any final precise evaluation of the details of Lewin's theoretical system was its extraordinary fruitfulness." Tolman reminded his audience of the excitement many had felt when they first learned of "Lewin's originality and courage in carrying out experiments under precisely controlled conditions on such problems as the effects of different types of leadership, of war morale, of eating habits, of worker productivity, and of intergroup conflict and community tensions." These experiments were, to Tolman, "one bright hope in an otherwise desperate social picture."

Gordon W. Allport offered additional testimony to the excitement that surrounded Lewin's work: "Genius and greatness seem always to generate controversy. Psychology is no exception and hence Lewin's was a most controversial figure. But Lewin had the advantage of rising with the floodtide of configuration and an awakening social conscience. The work of a genius seems always marked by a certain intellectual solitude. It sounds strange to say that Kurt Lewin was in any respect solitary. Nevertheless, his avoidance of the well-known paths of psychological science and his compulsion to strike off by himself were signs of a certain intellectual solitude. It was not that Lewin was asocial. On the contrary, more than most original thinkers, he exposed himself to the benefits of social facilitation—and inevitably won a circle of followers. As his own interests branched out to industrial psychology and public service, and his students took up important positions in war research, in clinics, and in community life, we heard less about an 'inner circle' and felt more widely in our national and professional life the wholesome impact of their work."

Allport pointed out that many Lewinian concepts that at first had seemed esoteric soon came to saturate the discourse of standard psychology. Among them Allport listed the dynamic power of unfinished tasks, escape from the field, the level of aspiration, differentiation, detour, time perspective, cognitive structure, levels of reality, barrier, rigidity, satiation, life space, marginal affiliation, group decision, change experiment. These are just some of the concepts that general psychology today has widely adopted. In the fields of personality and social behavior, there are no concepts as useful and as embracing as Lewin's twofold representation of the person as a differentiation region and as a point region in his life space.

In my turn, I described Lewin's aim as discovery of what determines changes in human relations. Such an aim, he had declared, is ideal for a scientist who integrates his role as scientist with his responsibilities as a citizen of a democratic society that must keep bettering its works and ways. The patterns of action research were developed primarily as ways of realizing this ideal, developed because Lewin was a socially conscious individual who believed that only science provides dependable guides to effective action and wanted his labors to be of maximum social usefulness as well as theoretical significance. I described the three areas of action which seemed to me to have shaped Lewin's career. The first was his interdependent style of life, his constant involvement in cooperative enterprises, and his continued collaboration with former students. The second was his persistent integration of theory and practical action, his uniting theory to ingenious experimentation, and even more his close coordination of seemingly abstruse hypotheses with the affairs of everyday life—something achieved by few other scientists. The third was his successful combination of scientific with personal and civic concerns, a combination Lewin brought to its highest point by his design and development of the method of action research.

When the memorial addresses were concluded, the Society for the Psychological Study of Social Issues announced the establishment of the Kurt Lewin Award, which would be given each year to the psychologist who made the outstanding contribution in at least one of the fields Lewin had created. The award was to be given at the annual meeting of the Society and the recipient would deliver the Kurt Lewin Memorial Lecture. The award and lecture have been annual events since 1947, and the award has come to be recognized as the nation's highest honor in social psychology. Of the distinguished social scientists who have won it, some are theorists, others experimenters, and still others pioneers in action research. Some are psychologists; some are not. But all are involved in the scientific study of social problems, as can be seen from the roster of the recipients and the work for which they were honored.

1948	George Brock Chisholm	"Social Responsibility"
1949	Edward Chace Tolman	"The Psychology of Social Learning"
1950	Gordon W. Allport	"Prejudice: A Problem in Psychological and Social Causation"
1951	A.T. M. Wilson (for Tavistock Institute of Human Relations)	"Some Aspects of Social Process"
1952	Gunnar Myrdal	"Psychological Impediments to Effective International Cooperation"
1953	Gardner Murphy	"Human Potentialities"
1954	Margaret Mead	"Cultural Discontinuities and Personality Transformation"
1955	None awarded	
1956	Otto Klineberg	"The Role of the Psychologist in International Affairs"
1957	Lawrence K. Frank	"Research for What?"
1958	Dorwin Cartwright (for the Research Center for Group Dynamics, University of Michigan)	"Some Things Learned: An Evaluative History of the Research Center for Group Dynamics"
1959	Fritz Heider	"On Lewin's Methods and Theory"
1960	Stuart Cook	"The Systematic Analysis of Socially Significant Events: A Strategy for Social Research"
1961	Robert MacIver	"Disturbed Youth and the Agencies"
1962	Theodore M. Newcomb	"Persistence and Regression of Changed Attitudes: Long-Range Studies"
1963	Roger Barker	"On the Nature of the Environment"
1964	Alfred J. Marrow	"Risks and Uncertainties in Action Research"
1965	Kenneth B. Clark	"Problems of Social Power and Social Change: A Relevant Social Psychology"
1966	Daniel Katz	"Group Process and Social Integration: A System Analysis of Two Movements of Social Protest"

1967	Muzafer Sherif	"If the Social Scientist Is to Be More Than a Mere Technician"
1968	Morton Deutsch	"Conflicts: Constructive and Destructive"
1969	Ralph K. White	"Three Not-So-Obvious Contributions of Psychology to Peace"

Lewin left his mark on the thinking of a whole generation of social scientists. He put his stamp on a whole discipline, giving it a name (group dynamics), a scope (action research), and a purpose that transcended psychology itself by setting as its goal not only the study of man but the betterment of society. Indeed, in an age of Black Power, urban decay, campus turbulence, bitter political turmoil, and talk of "participatory democracy," today's change seekers have a great deal to learn from Lewin's concepts and experiments.

So have today's psychiatrists. For as Cartwright points out, too, Lewin in his brief lifetime greatly advanced our understanding of the behavior and development of children, the nature of learning, the dynamics of social interaction, the determinants of effective leadership, and the requirements for social change.

It is for these reasons, too, that George Mandler has written that "social psychology, developmental psychology, and experimental psychology all changed significantly because Kurt Lewin wrote, because Kurt Lewin taught, and because Kurt Lewin was in the United States." Mason Haire points out that "no aspect of the field, whether it be social psychology in general, personality theory, or whatever, is the same for Lewin's having been there." In the years since his death, as we saw earlier, Lewin's varied contributions have continued to influence the work of his students and colleagues. Festinger comments that "95 per cent of today's social psychology is Kurt Lewin's and the research he inspired in group dynamics." MacKinnon remarks, "Group dynamics is today's culture and this all stems from Lewin." Gordon Allport discloses that "of all the psychologists I have known in person Lewin is most alive and prominent in my thinking." Sears voices the opinion that "Lewin was more responsible than anyone else, more than everybody else, for bringing the social and emotional behavior of children into the field of science." Margaret Mead adds that "Lewin and his group represented something wholly alive and significant for the whole country, for the whole of social science." Murphy writes, "Lewin had everything that went into the making of a great psychologist."

Lewin's influence continues to be felt in the generation of psychologists that followed and who did not know him during his lifetime. One of this group, typical of others, is Chris Argyris, who has written: "Lewin's work inspired me because it suggested a model that combined theory, empirical research, and relevance to reality. I vowed to work toward that goal. Today's students and younger faculty are striving to make their disciplines more relevant to critical life issues. All have much to learn from Lewin. For Lewin had the skill to integrate scientific rigor with reality and for this reason became the first major model of social scientist-activist of the highest quality. If more Lewins existed, we would not have to wonder if psychology had forgotten the humanness of human beings. I do not know of a better model for us to emulate. I am always bolstered, and my motivation is rekindled, by reading Lewin, the theoretician, researcher, and activist par excellence."

Another member of the group in the generation that followed is Warren G. Bennis. He writes: "I was never a student of Lewin's. I had known only colleagues and students of Lewin as my teachers and senior colleagues. I was always surprised when I actually read his work. Always a significant question, innocently explored with diagrams out of St. Exupery, and restlessly leading to such subjects as friendship, cultural differences in child rearing, leadership and its consequences, social change, and the origins of the philosophy of science. I thought that, like most charismatic men, his spirit would predominate rather than his mind. Only recently have I changed my mind about that. In putting together the revision of a book of mine, I rediscovered the extent to which I internalized his ideas and some of his methods. Several of the sections dealt with change and resistance to change: their intellectual forefather was Lewin. Several other sections cover subjects like power, authority, and social influence. Here, also, the intellectual legacy is Lewin. The sections on knowledge utilization similarly owe an enormous debt to Lewin. I used to think that Kurt Lewin was a giant metaphor with terrific influence on the family but with no, or little, substantive grasp over the activities of his inheritors. Now I have come to believe that we have so carefully disguised our identification to ourselves that we forget we are all Lewinians."

Allport once wrote: "Although Lewin never met John Dewey there was a community of spirit between the German-born psychologist and the American-born philosopher. Both were deeply concerned with the workings of democracy. Both recognized that each generation must learn democracy anew; both saw the dynamic relation between democracy and social science and the importance to social science of freedom of inquiry, freedom that only a democratic environment could assure. If Dewey could be termed the outstanding philosopher of democracy, Lewin was surely the major theoretician and researcher of democracy among the psychologists."

To his colleagues, too, Lewin was the archetypal innovator. Always most relevant for him was his conviction that psychology should never be divorced from life. Perhaps this is why Lewin so strongly stimulated the creativity of those who worked with him. Debates and disagreements were plentiful, as they must be where thought is free and advanced, but rarely did acrimony develop over the issues. Solving problems together called for the spirit of sportsmanship. What John Stuart Mill called the "morality of public discussion" was habit with Lewin and controveresy never degenerated into attacks on personalities.

Perhaps the word that describes Lewin more realistically than any other is "playful"—in the most significant sense of the word. That is, work was most fun for him when it was hardest. He had a zest for searching and seeking—working a problem this way, working it that, turning it upside down, inside out, left to right, right to left. He communicated a sense of enjoyment, in the spirit of one wanting freely to share his "play" with others.

Lewin had no strong desire to publish. He seldom put his own name on the studies he did with students. Sears pointed out that even though there are more references in the literature to research by Lewin and his primary students than to any comparable group in the fields of child personality and social psychology, Lewin's own name appears infrequently.

French puts Lewin in another perspective: "Somehow he seemed to be able to transmit to others a little of his own enormous creativity. I think those who worked most closely with him were not just carrying out his ideas; they were also stimulated to create new ideas and methods which then became part of Kurt's thinking."

Festinger believes that Lewin's greatest contribution "on the abstract level may have been the idea of studying things through changing them and seeing the effect. This theme—that in order to gain insight into a process one must create a change and then observe its variable effects and new dynamics—runs through all Lewin's work. To Lewin life was not static; it was changing, dynamic, fluid. Lewin's unfreezing-stabilizing-refreezing concept of change continues to be highly relevant today. His understanding of the importance of change was part of his philosophical approach to science and a basic ingredient of his 'metatheory.' As such, it helped change much of social psychology from art into science."

Dorwin Cartwright believes that the most dramatic development of Lewin's theory and method is "the response of society . . . to group dynamics. The strong influence of group dynamics is evident in education, industry, government, and in almost every aspect of group living—social work, religion, industry, public health, psychiatry, nursing, group therapy, the military establishment."

According to Adams, Lewin's paramount concern—the one which suffused many others—was *"vergleichenden Wissenschaftslehre."* Adams asked Lewin one day during the last year of his life, "When are you going to get back to the comparative science of sciences?" "I must do that," Lewin answered very soberly. "These things we are finding out will be discovered in five or ten years anyway, but this other might be fifty years away." The answer

235

suggested to Adams that Lewin's real business in life was the comparative science of sciences.

But psychologists concerned with social practice and social theory in organizational life find paramount the seminal work of Lewin in laying the foundation for much of their conceptual framework. Likert, Maier, and McGregor have emphasized the enormous influence of Lewin on their studies in industry. Clearly, Lewin's influence on the formation of theory was parallel. Heider's theory of interpersonal relations, Festinger's theory of cognitive dissonance, Cartwright and Harary's work on graph theory, all were in some degree shaped by their authors' association with Lewin. Tolman, himself a noted theoretician, expressed his debt by acknowledging that he "borrowed time and again from Lewin and absorbed his ideas into my very blood."

There are, of course, various alternatives to Lewin's concepts and methods. As Murphy observed, "One of the most common objections to Lewin's work was that he was concerned with present cross-sections of behavior, not with the history of how they came into being. The other main objections were that he had not really shown the non-utility of the reduction of wholes into definable units, that he had neglected individual differences, and that he had not shown that the topological (or any kind of graphic) portrayal of functions was more serviceable than the current verbal and conventional mathematical methods."

Murphy believes that Lewin could certainly have replied to all this: "Look at the new experiments and results which in point of fact did come from the new approach. And to this the observer can only add, not the new method alone, and not the specific individual alone, but the field relation of these two—and indeed their relations to the twentieth-century world and to the psychology prevalent in the world—is what gave field theory the vitality and the productiveness it achieved."

Heider, reviewing Lewin's contributions, remarks, "I get an impression whenever I try to understand Lewin's basic notions that they are, so to speak, visions not at all completely formulated and explicated, that they have a wealth of implicit meaning which has not yet been exhausted and that they are therefore still full of promise of further development."

Perhaps this is why Tolman wrote that in the future history of our psychological era Freud will be revered for his first unraveling of the complexities of the individual history and Lewin for his envisioning of the dynamic laws according to which individuals behave as they do.

APPENDIX

A BIBLIOGRAPHY OF THE
WORKS OF KURT LEWIN

"Kriegslandschaft." *Zeitschrift für Angewandte Psychologie,* 1917, *12,* 440–447.

"Die psychische Tätigkeit bei der Hemmung von Willensvorgangen und das Grundgesetz der Assoziation." *Zeitschrift für Psychologie,* 1917, 77, 212–247.

"Die Verwandtschaftsbegriffe in Biologie und Physik." *Abhandlungen zur theoretischen Biologie,* 1920, *5,* 1–34.

"Die Sozialisierung des Taylorsystems." *Praktischer Sozialismus,* No. 4, ca. 1920.

"Kindlicher Ausdruck." *Zeitschrift für Pädagogische Psychologie,* ca. 1920.

Der Begriff der Genese in Physik, Biologie und Entwicklungsgeschichte. Berlin: Julius Springer, 1922.

"Die Verwechslung von Wissenschaftssubjekt und Psychischen Bewusstein in ihrer Bedeutung für die Psychologie. I and II." *Psychologische Forschung,* 1922, *1,* 47–65; and *ibid.,* 1922, *2,* 66–140.

"Über den Einfluss von Interferenz auf die Intensität obertonfreier Tone." *Psychologische Forschung,* 1922, *2,* 328–335.

"Über einen Apparat zur Messung von Tonintensitäten." *Psychologische Forschung,* 1922, *2,* 317–326.

"Das Problem der Willensmessung und das Grundgesetz der Assoziation: I & II." *Psychologische Forschung,* 1922, *1,* 191–302; and *ibid.* 1922, *2,* 65–140.

"Über die Umkehrung der Raumlage auf dem Kopf stehender Worte

238

und Figuren in der Wahrnemung." *Psychologische Forschung*, 1923, *4*, 210–261.

"Über Idee und Aufgabe der vergleichenden Wissenschaftslehre." *Symposion*, 1925, *1*, 61–94.

(with K. Sakuma) "Die Schrichtung monolularer und binocularer Objekte bei Bewegung und das Zustendekommen des Tiefeneffekts." *Psychologische Forschung*, 1925, *6*, 298–357.

"Idee und Aufgabe der vergleichenden Wissenchaftslehre." *Sonderdrucke des Symposion*, 1926, *2*, 61–93.

Vorsatz, Wille und Bedurfnis (mit Vorbemerkungen über die psychischer Krafte und Energien und die Struktur der Seele). Berlin: Springer, 1926.

"Filmaufnahmen über Trieb- und Affektausserungen psychopathischer Kinder (verglichen mit Normalen und Schwachsinnigen)." *Zeitschrift für Kinderforschung*, 1926, *32*, 414–448.

"Ein verbesserter Zeitsinnapparat." *Psychologische Forschung*, 1926, 7, 273–275.

"Ein zahlender Chronograph." *Psychologische Forschung*, 1926, 7, 276–281.

"Gesetz und Experiment in der Psychologie." *Symposion*, 1927, *1*, 375–421.

Gesetz und Experiment in der Psychologie. Berlin-Schlachtensee: Welt-kris-Verlag, 1927.

"Die Entwicklung der experimentellen Willens- und Affektpsychologie und die Psychotherapie." *Archiv für Psychiatrie*, 1928, *85*, 515–537.

"Die Bedeutung der Psychischen Sattigung für einige Probleme der Psychotechnik." *Psychotechnische Zeitschrift*, 1928–1929, *3*, 182–187.

(with H. Rupp) "Untersuchungen zur Textil-Industrie." *Psychotechnische Zeitschrift*, 1928, *2*, 8–23, 51–63.

"Zwei Grundtypen von Lebensprozessen." *Zeitschrift für Psychologie*, 1929, *113*, 209–238.

"Les Types et les lois de la psychologie." *Pour l'Ere nouvelle*, 1929, *8*, 251–252.

"Gestalttheorie und Kinderpsychologie." *Werdende Zeitalter*, 1929, *10*, 544–550.

Die Entwicklung der experimentellen Willenpsychologie und die Psychotherapie. Leipzig: Herzel, 1929.

"Die Auswirkung von Umweltkraften." *Proceedings of the 9th International Congress of Psychology*, 1929, 286–288.

"Kindliche Ausdrucksbewegungen." In W. Stern (ed.) *Psychologie der Frühen Kindheit*. 6th ed. Leipzig: Quelle und Meyer, 1930. English translation: *Psychology of Early Childhood*. New York: Holt, 1930.

An address given in February 1931 at a convention on problems of the Montessori method. *Die Neue Erziehung*, 1931, *2*, 99–103.

Die psychologische Situation bei Lohn und Strage. Leipzig: Herzel, 1931.

"Ersatzhandlung und Ersatzbefriedigung." *Bericht über den XII Kongr. d. dtsch. Ges. für Psychol*. Hamburg: 1931, pp. 382–384.

"Der Richtungsbegriff in der Psychologie. Der spezielle une allgemeine hodologische Raum." *Psychologische Forschung*, 1934, *19*, 249–299.

"The Conflict between Aristotelian and Galileian Modes of Thought in Contemporary Psychology." *Journal of Genetic Psychology*, 1931, *5*, 141–177.

"Environmental Forces in Child Behavior and Development." In *A Handbook of Child Psychology*. Worcester, Mass.: Clark University Press, 1931. Pp. 94–127.

"Vectors, Cognitive Processes, and Mr. Tolman's Criticism." *Journal of Genetic Psychology*, 1933, *8*, 318–345.

"The Psychological Situation Attending Reward and Punishment." *Shr. Psychol. Pedag.*, 1933, *1*, 31–76.

"Théorie des Schwachsinns. Hommage au Dr. Decroly par les Usines réunies Scheerders van Kerchove à St.-Nicholas-W." Belgium, 1933.

"Psycho-Sociological Problems of a Minority Group." *Character and Personality*, 1935, *3*, 175–187.

A Dynamic Theory of Personality. New York: McGraw-Hill, 1935.

"Some Social Psychological Differences between the United States and Germany." *Character and Personality*, 1935, *4*, 265–293.

"Psychology of Success and Failure." *Occupations*, 1936, *14*, 926–930.

Principles of Topological Psychology. New York: McGraw-Hill, 1936.

"Psychoanalysis and Topological Psychology." *Bulletin of the Menninger Clinic*, 1937, *1*, 202–212.

(with R. BARKER and T. DEMBO) "Experiments on Frustration and Regression in Children." *Psychological Bulletin*, 1937, *34*, 754–755. (Abstract.)

"Carl Stumpf." *Psychology Review*, 1937, *44*, 189–194.

"Experiments on Autocratic and Democratic Atmospheres." *The Social Frontier*, 1938, *4*, No. 37, 316–319.

"The Conceptual Representation and Measurement of Psychological Forces." *Duke University Contributions to Psychological Theory*, 1938, *1*, No. 4, 247.

(with R. Lippitt) "An Experimental Approach to the Study of Autocracy and Democracy: A Preliminary Note." *Sociometry*, 1938, *1*, 292–300.

(with R. Lippitt and R. White) "Patterns of Aggressive Behavior in Experimentally Created 'Social Climates.'" *Journal of Social Psychology*, 1939, *10*, 271–299.

"When Facing Danger." *Jewish Frontier*, 1939.

"Reply to Dr. Garrett." *Psychology Review*, 1939, *46*, 591–595.

"Field Theory and Experiment in Social Psychology: Concepts and Methods." *American Journal of Sociology*, 1939, *44*, No. 6, 868–897.

"Experiments in Social Space." *Harvard Educational Review*, 1939, *9*, No. 1, 21–32.

"Formalization and Progress in Psychology." *University of Iowa Studies in Child Welfare*, 1940, *16*, No. 3, 7–42.

"Intelligence and Motivation." *Yearb. Nat. Soc. Stud. Educ.*, 1940, *39*, No. 1, 297–305.

"Bringing up the (Jewish) Child." *The Menorah Journal*, 1940, *28*, No. 1, 29–45.

"The Background of Conflict in Marriage." In M. Jung (ed.), *Modern Marriage*. New York: S. S. Cross, 1940. Pp. 52–69.

"Analysis of the Concepts Whole, Differentiation, and Unity." *University of Iowa Studies in Child Welfare*, 1941, *18*, No. 1, 226–261.

"Personal Adjustment and Group Belongingness." *Jewish Social Service Quarterly*, 1941, *17*, No. 64, 362–366.

"Regression, Retrogression, and Development." *University of Iowa Studies in Child Welfare*, 1941, *18*, No. 1.

(with R. Barker and T. Dembo) "Frustration and Regression: An Experiment with Young Children." *University of Iowa Studies in Child Welfare*, 1941, *18*, No. 1, xv and 314.

"Self-Hatred Among Jews." *Contemporary Jewish Record*, 1941, *4*, No. 3, 219–232.

"Democracy and the School." *Understanding the Child*, 1941, *10*, 1–7.

"Field Theory of Learning." *Yearb. Nat. Soc. Stud. Educ.*, 1942, *41*, part 2, 215–242.

(with A. Bavelas) "Training in Democratic Leadership." *Journal of Abnormal and Social Psychology*, 1942, 37, 115–119.

"Time Perspective and Morale." In G. Watson (ed.), *Civilian Morale*, second yearbook of the S.P.S.S.L. Boston: Published for Reynal & Hitchcock by Houghton Mifflin, 1942.

"The Relative Effectiveness of a Lecture Method and a Method of Group Decision for Changing Food Habits." Mimeographed.

Committee on Food Habits, National Research Council, Washington, D.C., 1942.

"Changes in Social Sensitivity in Child and Adult." *Childhood Education*, 1942, *19*, 53–57.

"A Profile Measure of Morale." *Psychological Bulletin*, 1942, *39*, 449. (Abstract.)

"Psychology and the Process of Group Living." *Journal of Social Psychology*, 1943, *17*, 113–131.

"Forces behind Food Habits and Methods of Change." *National Research Council Bulletin*, 1943, No. 108, 35–65.

"Cultural Reconstruction." *Journal of Abnormal and Social Psychology*, 1943, *38*, 166–173.

"Defining the 'Field at a Given Time.'" *Psychology Review*, 1943, *50*, No. 3, 292–310.

"The Special Case of Germany." *Public Opinion Quarterly*, 1943, 7, 555–566.

"Authority and Frustration—Studies in Topological and Vector Psychology, III." *University of Iowa Studies in Child Welfare*, 1944, *20*.

"Constructs in Psychology and Psychological Ecology." *University of Iowa Studies in Child Welfare*, 1944, *20*, 1–29.

"The Solution of a Chronic Conflict in a Factory." *Proceedings of the Second Brief Psychotherapy Council*. Chicago, Ill.: Institute for Psychoanalysis, 1944. Pp. 36–46.

(with T. DEMBO, L. FESTINGER, and P. SEARS) "Level of Aspiration." In *Personality and the Behavior Disorders*. New York: Ronald Press, 1944. I, 333–378.

"Dynamics of Group Action." *Educational Leadership*, 1944, *1*, 195–200.

"Constructs in Psychology and Psychological Ecology." *Studies in Topological and Vector Psychology*. University of Iowa, 1944. III, 1–29.

"Jewish Education and Reality." *Jewish Education*, 1944, *15*, No. 3.

"A Research Approach to Leadership Problems." *Journal of Educational Sociology*, 1944, *17*.

(with PAUL GRABBE) "Conduct, Knowledge, and Acceptance of New Values." *Journal of Social Issues*, 1945, *1*, 53–63.

(ed., with PAUL GRABBE) "The Problems of Re-education." *Journal of Social Issues*, 1945, *1*, No. 3.

"Action Research and Minority Problems." *Journal of Social Issues*, 1946, *2*, 34–46.

"Behavior and Development as a Function of the Total Situation." In

L. Carmichael (ed.), *Manual of Child Psychology*. New York: John Wiley and Sons, 1946. Pp. 791–844.

"Research on Minority Problems." *The Technology Review*, 1946, *48*, No. 3.

"Problems of Group Dynamics and the Integration of the Social Sciences: I. Social Equilibria." *Human Relations*, 1946.

Psychological Problems in Jewish Education. New York: Jewish Education Committee, 1946.

"The Research Center for Group Dynamics at Massachusetts Institute of Technology." *Sociometry*, 1946, *2*, 126–136.

"Frontiers in Group Dynamics: I. Concept, Method and Reality in Social Science; Social Equilibria and Social Change." *Human Relations*, 1947.

"Frontiers in Group Dynamics: II. Channels of Group Life; Social Planning and Action Research." *Human Relations*, 1947.

"Group Decision and Social Change." In T. H. Newcomb and E. L. Hartley (eds.), *Readings in Social Psychology*. New York: Henry Holt, 1947.

"Studies Towards the Integration of the Social Sciences." *Human Relations* (Tavistock Institute of Human Relations), 1947, *1*, 1–140.

Resolving Social Conflicts. New York: Harper's, 1948.

"Cassirer's Philosophy of Science and Social Science." In Paul Arthur Schilpp (ed.), *The Philosophy of Ernst Cassirer*. New York: Tudor Publishing Co., 1949.

Field Theory in Social Science: Selected Theoretical Papers. Dorwin Cartwright (ed.). New York: Harper & Row, 1951.

"Intention, Will, and Need." In D. Rapaport (ed.), *Organization and Pathology of Thought*. New York: Columbia University Press, 1951. Pp. 95–151.

Group Decision and Social Change. G. E. Swanson, T. M. Newcomb, and E. E. Hartley (eds.). New York: Holt, 1952.

(with R. Lippitt and R. White) *Autocracy and Democracy: An Experimental Inquiry*. New York: Harper & Row, 1960.

APPENDIX

B

THE BERLIN EXPERIMENTS

Bluma Zeigarnik's classic experiment [1] on the recall of uncompleted tasks—the first corroborative experiment on the structure of tension systems—was undertaken from 1924 to 1926 with 164 child and adult subjects. The 18 to 22 tasks were simple ones: listing cities, solving riddles, stringing beads, counting backward. The subjects were permitted to complete half of these tasks; the other half were interrupted before completion. Some time later, each subject was asked to recall as many of the tasks as he could. The results were striking: uncompleted tasks were recalled over completed ones by a margin of 1.9 to 1. In confirmation of the preferential recall of uncompleted tasks, Zeigarnik also found that unfinished tasks were remembered first more than three times as often as the finished ones.

Zeigarnik theorized that motivation for a satisfying performance of the tasks arose from three sources: (a) the strength of the goal tension developed by a need to achieve the goal of completion; (b) the subject's personal ambition or drive; and (c) the "obligation" to do as the experimenter requested. In many instances, Zeigarnik reported, the subject resisted interruption; this in itself was evidence of the impulse to satisfy one or all of these quasi-needs.

The possibility that emotional stress caused by the interruption had influenced the superior recall of the unfinished tasks was examined in a subsequent test. Here the subjects were interrupted in one third of the

[1] B. Zeigarnik, "Über Behalten von erledigten und unerledigten Handlungen," *Psychologische Forschung*, 1927, *9*, 1–85.

tasks; permitted to finish another third; and interrupted and then permitted to complete the final third. The results showed that recall among the second and third groups—in both of which the subjects were permitted to finish the tasks—was almost identical, indicating that the critical factor was not interruption but incompletion. By preventing completion of the tasks, the experimenter had blocked the subjects' only natural means of releasing the tension system. Thus, the tensions not only demanded release by means of completion; they were also being reproduced in recall. Recall clearly had the role of indicator for the still-unreleased tension.

Zeigarnik concluded that, by refusing to allow the tasks to be completed, she had prevented the only natural release of the tension system. These tensions not only drove in the direction of completion but were assertive in reproduction, an indicator for the driving tension. The superior memory value of the interrupted tasks was due to the energies existing at the time of questioning rather than to those at the time of interruption.

The existence of the quasi-need generated by the intention to perform was the first experimental confirmation of Lewin's theory of psychic dynamics. Lewin recognized that the construct of a system in tension for representing psychological needs presupposed a field theory. Conceptually, he wrote later, tension referred to the state of one system relative to the state of surrounding systems. Zeigarnik's findings demonstrated a tendency for change in the direction of equalization of the state of neighboring systems. It was typical of Lewin's approach to scientific experiment that, rather than seeking more exact quantitative measurements, he encouraged his students to try new independent variations from the basic assumptions and test them experimentally with the purpose of corroborating them.

Maria Ovsiankina [2] undertook a series of further experiments in 1927 aimed at correlating the release of tension to the reaching of a goal and linking an intention to a need in a state of hunger. If Lewin was correct in hypothesizing that a need for a certain goal carried with it a corresponding force causing a tendency to reach the goal, then it could be expected that as long as the goal was not reached attempts would be made to reach it. Ovsiankina sought to create experimental conditions

2 M. Ovsiankina, "Die Wiederaufnahme von unterbrochenen Handlungen," *Psychologische Forschung*, 1928, 2, 302–389.

that could determine the strength of the tension, not by testing recall, but by measuring the subjects' spontaneous resumption of the tasks.

As in the Zeigarnik experiment, Ovsiankina set her 125 subjects a number of specific assignments to carry out, thereby creating a group of tension systems striving for discharge and seeking behavior that would bring release. Ovsiankina's procedure was similar to Zeigarnik's except that (a) her interruptions were for the most part "accidental" (rather than deliberate, as with Zeigarnik), and (b) she introduced a free period shortly after the interruption, lasting from two to eight minutes, while she busied herself with other matters. Ovsiankina studied what happened during this interval.

Of the tasks which the subjects thought were "accidentally" interrupted, 100 per cent were spontaneously resumed. Of clearly "deliberate" interruptions, 82 per cent were resumed. Analysis of the subjects' actions during the free period showed that the resumptions came in greatest number when the breaking off took place just before a task's completion. Also, resumption occurred most readily when the subject had been working hard at the task, or had a special aptitude for it, or was highly ambitious.

Commenting on Ovsiankina's findings, Lewin wrote: "The frequency of resumption signifies that, as long as the need is not satisfied, a force corresponding to the valence of the goal should exist and lead to an action in the direction of that goal." It is this force which creates the strong tendency to take up again an interrupted task.

Vera Mahler's [3] 1930–1931 experiment sought to determine the effect of quasi-needs or tensions by measuring the recourse to substitute actions when the original task could not be completed. The substitute value of any given action, she postulated, could be measured by the decrease in the frequency of resumption of the original task. If completion of the substitute task satisfied the original goal tension, the subject would not return to the first task. Ratios could thus be established comparing various types of substitute activity in terms of their effectiveness for this purpose. Of particular interest to Mahler was the question whether an unreal substitute action could produce genuine satisfaction of needs or quasi-needs.

Working with a group of 155 adults (mostly students) at the Psy-

[3] V. Mahler, "Ersatzhandlungen verschiedenen Realitatsgrades," *Psychologische Forschung*, 1933, *18*, 26–89.

chological Institute, and a second group of 35 children ranging in age from five to ten years, Mahler created a tension system by giving the subjects a task that was interrupted before completion. She then invited the subjects to finish the task in a different manner by means of a substitute completion. To test the degree to which various kinds of substitute actions released the tension of the original system, she offered her subjects the opportunity to finish interrupted activity by thinking about it, talking about it, and doing it differently. If the original interrupted task consisted of punching small holes to make a word on a piece of paper, one substitute activity would offer the subject the opportunity to finish the word by writing it or saying it.

Generally speaking, she found that a "real" or "action" substitute task—that is, a physical act—was more effective in releasing the tension caused by the interruption than an "unreal" substitute such as merely talking or thinking about it. Thus, after a substitute completion of the task through action, spontaneous resumption dropped 86 per cent; when the substitute completion consisted of talking about the task, spontaneous resumption dropped only 33 per cent. (Mahler also found that the degree of reality for either action or speech varied from task to task. Thus, in tasks such as counting squares, speech assumed a higher reality than did action as a substitute activity.)

A major factor in the effectiveness of the substitute was whether or not the original goal was attained in essence. The goal might be either external (the specific performance asked for by the experimenter) or internal—that is, an inner goal set by the subject for himself. If this internalized goal was essentially reached by means of the substitute performance, the tension was discharged and resumption of the action was relatively less frequent. For example, the task of stringing beads was given to children and to adults. The inner goal of this action for the children (as distinguished from the goal set by the experimenter) was to make a necklace they could put around their necks. The substitute task—talking about the necklace or imagining what the necklace would look like if put together with a variety of beads—did not lead to a release of tension, as indicated by the high voluntary resumption of this task (83 per cent). On the other hand, the inner goal for the adults was to design a tasteful pattern of beads; this could be done even if only part of the task had been completed. None of the adults who carried out the substitute task resumed stringing the beads.

Mahler also found a significant difference between tasks in which there were problems to be solved (such as calculating or figuring) and realization tasks (requiring the production of visible work). In pure problem tasks, no resumption occurred after the substitute completion in the form of talking—indicating that the tension had been released. In activities which involved both problem-solving and realization tasks, release of tension did not occur after a substitute completion by means of talking or thinking; only after a substitute action did the resumption rate go down.

Mahler concluded that it was not possible to assign permanently to one type of substitute completion a fixed and definite degree of reality independent of the original task. The major factor in determining the substitute value of any action was whether or not the individual's goal was reached. Lewin explained this by theorizing that the substitute value of one activity for another depended upon a communication between the two underlying need systems in such a way that satisfying the one also satisfied the other. While substitute activities of higher degrees of reality generally had greater replacement value, it was the relation of the substitute act to the inner goal of the original activity that was decisive. As Lewin put it, "Substitute satisfaction occurs only when this inner goal is in sufficient degree attained by the substitute activity."

Sarah Sliosberg [4] studied the effectiveness of substitutes in terms of make-believe vs. realistic situations. Working in a real-life situation with children three to six years old, Sliosberg first offered them chocolate cookies, then substituted gray cardboard pieces of the same size and shape. Some 60 per cent of the children rejected the substitute object altogether; 20 per cent accepted the cardboard—but as a plaything, rather than something to eat; another 20 per cent of the children put the cardboard into their mouths, then returned it, saying, "It's only paper."

However, when the same children were offered the cardboard substitute for chocolate cookies to be fed to their dolls, while at play, 55 per cent of them fully and immediately accepted the substitute and fed it to their dolls. Another 25 per cent took the cardboard after some hesitation. No children here rejected the cardboard entirely—as 60 per cent had done in the real-life situation.

Sliosberg observed that the child's treatment of the substitute de-

4 S. Sliosberg, "Zur Dynamik des Ersatzes in Spiel und Ernstsituationen," *Psychologische Forschung*, 1934, *19*, 122–181.

pended on how strong his need was to occupy himself with the original. When this need was strong, the substitute was rejected without exception. The child was apparently firmly tied to the existing situation. Once the child's original interest had lagged (corresponding to satisfaction of his need), rejection of the substitute occurred less frequently. The child was freer in his actions and more readily able to make the transition to a lesser degree of reality.

Gita Birenbaum's [5] experiment on the strength of the factors that determine the forgetting of an intention was concerned chiefly with the connection between certain tensions and the total activity of the person. Her study tested subjects for the frequency of forgetting an intention, the influence of the emotional factor involved (including the subjects' attitudes toward the experimenter), and the influence of the psychic environment—that is, the effect of positive and negative valences— on forgetting.

After creating a rather informal situation and asking a number of general questions, Birenbaum asked each of her subjects (psychology students) to solve a number of written matchstick problems and to sign each answer sheet. Ostensibly, the signatures were needed to help the experimenter keep her records in order; actually, however, it was the signing of each sheet that was the intention being tested. A set of five problems was given the subjects. After a pause of five to ten minutes, a second set of five similar problems was given. During the pause the experimenter engaged in small talk with her subjects.

Birenbaum discovered an unusually high rate of forgetfulness among her subjects in signing the sheet for the sixth problem—that is, the one immediately following the pause. Quickly, however, the subjects remembered to sign the papers and by the time the eighth problem was completed, all had remembered to sign the sheet. The intention of signing the sheets was carried out in the following percentages:

First set of problems: 80, 100, 100, 100, 100
Second set of problems: 20, 90, 100, 100, 100

The unusual degree of forgetfulness in carrying out the intention immediately after the pause was significant. In the control group, where no pause took place, there was no such drop. Nor did the forgetting

[5] G. Birenbaum, "Das Vergessen einer Vornahme," *Psychologische Forschung,* 1930, *13,* 218–284.

appear to have any connection with ability to remember; the rate of execution of the intention was restored to 100 per cent with the eighth problem, despite the fact that additional time had elapsed since the last execution in the fifth problem.

In a second test series, the subjects were told that the sixth problem was a "critical" one. This in turn was followed by five additional problems of various types (such as building words, naming cities, tracing a figure), each of them different and all of them quite different from the first five matchstick problems and from the sixth "critical" one. All 37 subjects signed all the papers after performing the first five tasks—a showing of 100 per cent. With the sixth ("critical") problem, the accomplishment ratio fell to 40 per cent and, with the new and different tasks, never rose above that level. The intention of signing the sheet was carried out in the following percentages:

> *First set of problems:* 100, 100, 100, 100, 100
> *Second set of problems:* 40, 20, 40, 40, 0, 0

Birenbaum had also divided her subjects—rather arbitrarily, as she admitted—by personality type into three groups. Among her first group (which she labeled as "naive-quiet"), 89 per cent of the intentions were carried out. The second group, described as "controlled," had a great deal of trouble after the "critical" sixth problem; their average in signing the sheets was only 70 per cent. The third group, whom Birenbaum called "naive-excited," was livelier than the others and felt the test situation more intensely. Their signature record was only 42.8 per cent.

Birenbaum attributed the differences in results solely to the subjects' behavior types. She also concluded that emotional factors could change the inner tension systems of her subjects: greater tension would result, for example, if the task had a connotation of success or failure. While the emotional stress created by the task did not affect motor activity, the task in its emotional context no longer was connected with the earlier experiments but became a totality of its own. When the emotion was so deeply felt, the subject's new psychic area would have a different center and the signature was most frequently forgotten. Thus, intentions or purposes corresponding to a main task or a central need were almost never forgotten. Forgetting depended essentially upon whether and how deeply the tension system corresponding to the intention was rooted in the main task. The more significant a part of the central need system, the greater the chances of carrying out the intention. In Birenbaum's experiment, intention was most frequently forgotten when it was isolated from the subject's other activities and unrelated to his psychic needs; intention was most frequently carried out when it figured as part of a larger, more coherent sequence of activities.

Another of Lewin's students, Ferdinand Hoppe, [6] aimed to investigate the factors which influence goal-setting behavior by measuring the effect of success or failure on raising or lowering the level of aspiration. A thorough investigation of a few cases (he used only 10 subjects), Hoppe felt, would be more valuable than a broad statistical study in determining what kind of dynamic problems were involved and which concepts could be used to represent them.

Hoppe set his subjects a number of tasks—dart throwing, ring tossing, puzzle solving, arithmetic. A wide range of achievement levels was offered: "tough," "easy," or "no improvement." As soon as the subject had reached an initial level of performance, he was asked: "What score are you going to try for next?" If, for example, the subject succeeded in placing six rings on a moving belt, he might decide to try for eight on the next round. This goal of eight now became his level of aspiration. If in seeking to reach eight he scored only six, he would experience a feeling of failure on reaching a level that had been regarded as a successful performance earlier. Frequently the subject would set a lower goal for his next attempt.

Hoppe's first finding was that the experience of success or failure was not bound to any specific accomplishment, but rather was linked to a goal or ideal that served to measure whether or not the action had the character of an achievement. He also found that the level of aspiration shifted directly with the level of performance; an experience of success gave rise to a higher level of aspiration on the next attempt. One success after a series of failures, however, was generally not enough to affect the factors in goal-setting behavior that influenced the decision to raise the level of aspiration. Upon failure, the level of aspiration was generally lowered or the action discontinued. In no instance observed by Hoppe was the level of aspiration lowered after success and raised after failure.

[6] F. Hoppe, "Erfolg und Misserfolg," *Psychologische Forschung*, 1930, 1–62.

Hoppe thus found that an individual's level of aspiration was not constant but rather shifted and changed with the degree of the success or failure, the previous course of events in the experiment, the special structure of the assignment, and the individual's personal characteristics.

Lewin believed that the concept of level of aspiration was of great importance in learning. "Whether or not a person will learn a certain activity," he wrote, "is deeply influenced by his trying or not trying to do so. Therefore the factors which determine the level of aspiration are of basic importance for learning. A child may permanently keep his level of aspiration too high or too low for his ability. Good students tend to keep their level of aspiration slightly above their past achievements, whereas poor students tend to show excessively high or excessively low levels of aspiration. Failure frequently leads to rationalization, emotional outbreak, overpersisting, or rapid discontinuance."

S. Jucknat's [7] experiments (with a far larger number of subjects) on level of aspiration sought both confirmation and refinement of Hoppe's findings that a person will experience a feeling of success or failure only when a goal or other norm is present. Jucknat was particularly interested in how likely—and how great—a shift in goals was to occur as an aftereffect of success or failure.

The success series in his experiment was composed of ten different maze puzzles of increasing degrees of difficulty but all solvable. The failure series consisted of ten unsolvable problems. By informing his subjects of the degree of difficulty of each task, Jucknat was able to determine the subject's level of aspiration before he set to work. Then, by arbitrarily creating experiences of success and failure, he was able to produce more refined and detailed data on the effect of such experiences on the aspiration level.

Jucknat's experiment bore out Hoppe's findings, but also indicated that the kind of success experienced also affected the aspiration level. After a weak success (for example, a maze completed with the help of the experimenter), only about half the subjects raised their expectations, while many actually lowered theirs. After an easy success, however, almost every subject (96 per cent) raised his sights. The degree of the success also affected the degree to which the level of aspiration rose. After barely succeeding, for example, the subject's next task was

[7] S. Jucknat, "Leistung, Anspruchniveau und Selbstbewusstsein," *Psychologische Forschung*, 1937, *22*, 89–179.

usually either one step up or one step down; after an easy success, on the other hand, the subject might jump several steps upward in selecting the next maze to complete. Jucknat found the same pattern in the failure series, in which the subjects lowered their aspiration level in proportion to the degree of the failure experienced.

Tamara Dembo,[8] in her study of the genesis of frustration and anger, based her experiment on the assumption that the affective processes could be understood only by tracing the relations of an individual occurrence to the total course of events and the total situation. The dynamics of anger thus took on specific meaning only when the field forces of the whole determining situation were known. Dembo aimed at discovering those forces.

Her first task was to search for ways that anger could be induced in an experimental situation. She asked her subjects: "Have you been angry lately? Do you know why? What did you do then?" Typical answers were: "Yesterday I was in a hurry to get home and the bus didn't stop for me. Was I mad!" Or "I tried to prove something to a friend of mine but he just wouldn't listen. I got so mad I began to scream." Or "I couldn't get any work done all day. By the time I had been interrupted for the three hundredth time, I found myself yelling at the whole office."

Seeking a factor common to all these responses, Dembo developed what appeared to be a workable hypothesis: if a person tried to reach a goal but failed despite his best efforts, he became angry. Closer examination, however, showed that this hypothesis was not universally valid. Anger was not always the consequence when a person failed to reach a desired goal. Why, then, did failure to achieve one's aim cause anger in one instance but not in another? Presumably, the non-appearance of anger indicated lack of a strong desire to reach the goal. Common sense said that frustration increased in proportion to the intensity of the desire that was unsatisfied. Yet here too it was wrong to generalize. Sometimes an obstacle barring the way to a vitally important goal did not cause an emotional outburst; at other times a trivial blocking of an unimportant action caused violent anger.

Dembo took for her point of departure Lewin's postulate that behavior is determined by the momentary structure and state of the behav-

[8] T. Dembo, "Der Anger als dynamisches Problem," *Psychologische Forschung*, 1931, *15*, 1–144.

ing person and by his psychological environment at that particular moment. According to this theory, a person engaged in a triviality could react violently to frustration because—in this field, at this moment—meaningless objects had received a special significance.

Dembo set herself three tasks: (a) to discover the dynamics of anger; (b) to analyze the changes that occur when a goal is unattainable; and (c) to discover the effect of barriers on the various choices between alternatives of behavior. Between 1925 and 1928, she undertook 64 experiments with 27 subjects, each lasting one to two hours. She assigned each subject a specific task which, though apparently capable of achievement, was in fact impossible. Thus, the subjects were told to throw wooden rings around the necks of bottles fifteen feet away until ten consecutive successes were registered—an impossible feat, to all intents and purposes, yet apparently capable of achievement.

A second task required the subject to reach for a flower some distance away without moving his feet outside the area where he was standing. When the subject found a way to do it, he was then asked for a second solution. Most subjects were able to find both without great difficulty. They were then asked to figure out a third way, although in fact no additional way was possible. The subject's efforts to come up with one more answer were encouraged by the experimenter. Indeed, Dembo insisted on a third solution. The consequent frustration brought on a series of angry reactions, remarkable both for their intensity and for the wide range of their outward manifestation.

Dembo described the experimental situation as one in which a force vector is working on the subject in the direction of a positive valence. Concerning the force vector, two questions have to be considered: what are the conditions of its appearance and what are the real occurrences (thoughts, questions, actions) by which it manifests itself?

It can be assumed, Dembo reasoned, that the vector becomes manifest for one of the following reasons:

(a) The subject, having committed himself to the experiment, feels obliged to do what the experimenter demands. Even when it seems pointless to go on looking for a solution, the insistent request of the experimenter pushes him to keep on trying.

(b) The task in itself is interesting. The subject enjoys testing his skill at finding a way out of a seemingly hopeless situation.

(c) The difficulty of the task challenges the subject. He feels personally involved with the task he has undertaken and it becomes im-

254

portant to him to avoid failure and to be skillful and ingenious enough to succeed. He wants to solve the problem quickly and correctly so that he will show up well in comparison with others.

Dembo found that there was no uniform pattern in the subjects' responses to the experimental situation. Sometimes an explosive emotional outburst was preceded by a weak expression of petty annoyance. In other instances, the subjects offered substitute solutions (throwing the rings on a nearby object or deliberately walking out of the square to reach the flower), either before or after frantic efforts to succeed. At still other times, substitute solutions might be followed by an abandonment of the task altogether. In a few instances, an emotional (occasionally even physical) attack on the experimenter followed a rest period or a "failure." Sometimes fantasy solutions were suggested: "Fill the room with water and swim to the flower," one subject proposed.

In summary, three kinds of activity followed this frustration-producing situation: actions in the direction of the task-goal; escape movements; and aggression against the experimenter.

The actions in the direction of the goal assumed one of several forms: real solutions or variations such as leaving the field; unrealistic solutions such as hallucinatory or daydream solutions due to the difficulties and the conflict of tensions within the real field; or substitute actions, relating closely to the subjects' level of aspiration.

The experimental procedure had been arranged so that the social field of forces would be dominated by the experimenter. Struggles with the experimenter developed frequently among the subjects, who often gave evidence of a temporary liberation from the task-field (and thus a destruction for them of the prevailing field of forces).

Dembo's pioneering experiment on the genesis of anger was significant confirmation of Lewin's theory that behavior was a function of the total situation. It showed that the effect which a need had on the structure of a life space depended on the intensity of the need. It demonstrated the impact of fields of force in a conflict situation in behavior. Finally, it underscored the difference between activities with substitute "valence" and those with genuine substitute value.

Anitra Karsten [9] approached the problem of a system in tension by investigating the phenomenon of psychical satiation—a term coined by

[9] A. Karsten, "Psychische Sattigung," *Psychologische Forschung*, 1928, *10*, 142–154.

Lewin. Her experiment sought to confirm the hypothesis that an individual's turning away from an activity after numerous repetitions was due to a progressive lowering of the tension level that led to the original action. Her study was an investigation of how repetitions of the same activity could cause the subject to reach the point of reluctance to continue, and how rapidly this satiation appeared.

She asked her subjects to make short strokes with a pencil, draw figures, read poems, etc., until they lost all desire to continue, at which point they were free to stop. The chief criterion of satiation in the experiment was this spontaneous stopping.

Karsten found that satiation following constant repetition of a task was not due to muscular fatigue. By conferring a new and different meaning on what was essentially the same task—that is, by embedding it in another whole—a satiated subject could be led to begin anew. For example, after becoming satiated with making pencil strokes in a three-five pattern, the subject was asked to change the pattern to four-four. The change considerably diminished the satiation although the physical effort remained the same; indeed, the change had the same effect as transferring to a totally new activity. Karsten also reported that satiation came more rapidly if the activity was performed without any measure of progress or sign of advancement; such unawareness of achievement led to disintegration and errors.

Lewin noted that Karsten's results provided "an impressive demonstration that repetition by no means always brings with it an improvement in performance." What was more likely to occur with repetition was a gradual change in the originally positive valence to indifference and at last into a negative valence.

Karsten's study demonstrated that the treadmill repetition of a task without measures of progress or signs of advancement robbed the subject of any sense of achievement and that such unawareness brought disintegration and mistakes. She noted, too, that repeated actions with little ego involvement did not induce satiation as readily as actions with either pleasant or unpleasant connotations. To Lewin, this was an instance of a general law according to which both agreeable and disagreeable activities must lead to satiation more quickly than relatively neutral repetitions.

This theory offered an interpretation of why women's fashions change more rapidly than men's. "The velocity of satiation," according to Lewin, "depended on the degree to which an activity was psychologically central (as against peripheral)." Style in clothing is relatively central to women and relatively peripheral to men. Hence, women's fashions satiate more rapidly and changes follow more frequently.

Sara Fajans [10] (with the help of Vera Mahler) carried out a series of experiments during 1928 and 1929 with some 140 children ranging in age from six months to six and one half years. They sought to determine how significant a factor distance was in establishing the strength of a valence, especially where the psychological distance corresponds to the physical distance.

The children were offered objects with a positive valence—a chocolate bar, a rattle, or a doll—at different distances, but always so that they were unable to reach it. The investigators then observed the kind of effect (and its duration) that the object had on each child. They found it easy, even in infants, to recognize the nature of the child's response—that is, whether the child turned toward or away from the object, and whether it was active or passive toward it. Marked differences in the children's behavior were found between the near-experiment and the far-experiment. In the near-experiment, the child continuously exhibited a lively and active turning toward the desired thing; in the far-experiment, the turning toward was brief and consisted chiefly of looking at—rather than reaching for—the object.

The same infants turned toward the goal object a total of 96 seconds in the first near-experiment as compared with 26 seconds in the first far-experiment. Some 53 seconds were spent in the first near-experiment in direct active turning toward; in the far-experiment, the average of this type of activity was only 5 seconds. Finally, the experimenters found that the duration of all periods of turning toward was so much greater in the first near-experiment than in the far-experiment that it completely overpowered the effect of the temporal sequence of the first two experiments. This was true not only on the average but also for each individual infant in the two groups. In the second experiment as well, the lesser distance of the goal object greatly enhanced the effect of the valence.

Commenting on Fajans' study, Lewin noted that one cannot assume that psychological distance corresponds to physical distance; also that

[10] S. Fajans, "Die Bedeutung der Entfernung für die Stärke eines Aufforderungscharakters beim Säugling und Kleinkind, *Psychologische Forschung*, 1933, *17*, 215–267.

"the mere knowledge of something (e.g., the geography of a foreign country or immediate family affairs) does not necessarily change the child's life space more than superficially. On the other hand, psychologically critical facts of the environment, such as the friendliness or unfriendliness of a certain adult, may have fundamental significance for the child's life space without the child having a clear intellectual appreciation of the fact . . . With the gradual extension and differentiation of the child's life space, a larger environment and essentially different facts acquire psychological existence."

Lewin's students had unusually wide latitude in choosing their particular fields of study. Sara Forrer,[11] for example, decided to investigate Ovid Decroly's method of teaching retarded children to read. Decroly's way of reinforcing the printed word with actions that would strengthen the memory process was an ideal topic for inquiry in terms of Gestalt psychology. The Belgian teacher had postulated that children retain sentences more easily than single words and words more readily than single letters. Lewin stated, in referring to Forrer's experiment, that "the findings confirm the marked advantage of the 'global' method of reading and writing. To a child taking no joy in learning to write an alphabet, a change of valence (attractiveness) occurs more quickly when he is allowed as soon as possible to write meaningful communications in sentence form."

Somewhat more closely related to Lewin's researches were the experiments of Georg Schwarz [12] on habit, particularly on finding the factors causing backsliding to an older habit and other automatic actions which occurred contrary to the will of the subject himself. With Lewin's study of association as his point of departure, Schwarz examined the conditions which caused a change in a "performance habit" to become more difficult for the subject.

He first developed a habit in his subjects; then he introduced changes which made relearning necessary. His experiments indicated that a tendency to relapse to the first habit arose when the new task figured only as an item in a larger configuration of performances. When the

[11] S. Forrer, "Eine Unterschung zur Lese-Lein-Methode Decroly," *Zeitschrift für Kinderforschung*, 1934, *42*, 11–44.
[12] G. Schwarz, "Ueber Rückfälligkeit bei Umgewöhnung," Teil I, *Psychologische Forschung*, 1927, *9*, 86–158.

258

subject took his task as his principal goal, reversion to the first habit did not occur.

The significance of the series of empirical studies done under Lewin's guidance in Berlin has been remarked by many historians of the behavioral sciences. There has been criticism as well, particularly to the effect that they were carried out with relatively small numbers of subjects. Lewin admitted that a greater number of cases would probably have added to the reliability of his findings. He agreed that "of course, additional confirmation is always desirable." But he pointed out that his own results had stood up well when his experiments were replicated by others and that, more important, the exactness of measurement was paramount only in some cases. In testing the effect of an intention, for example, Ovsiankina found that about 80 per cent of all interrupted tasks were resumed. There was some merit in trying another group of a hundred interruptions, Lewin wrote. But whether the percentage of resumption was 75 or 80 or 85 was of minor importance. "To prove or disprove the theory of tension systems," he wrote, "it seems much more important to find a variety of derivations from this theory which should be as different as possible from one another, and to test as many as possible of these derivations, even if this test should be rather crude quantitatively at the beginning."

APPENDIX

THE TOPOLOGY GROUP—1935

D. K. Adams (Duke)
Dan Adler (Iowa)
Carl E. Anderson (Iowa)
Roger Barker (Illinois)
T. L. Bayne (Cornell)
Jerome S. Bruner (Harvard)
Claude Buxton (Swarthmore)
Malcolm Campbell (N.Y.U.)
Dorwin Cartwright (Harvard)
Robert C. Challman (Columbia)
Charles Cofer (Brown)
Richard S. Crutchfield
  (Swarthmore)
Tamara Dembo (Iowa)
Karl Duncker (Swarthmore)
Sibylle Escalona (Framingham)
Maurice Farber (Iowa)
W. W. Flexner (Cornell)
F. S. Freeman (Cornell)
David Goldknopf (N.Y.U.)
Mary M. Gordon (Iowa)
Eugenia Hanfmann (Chicago)
Fritz Heider (Smith)
Mary Henle (Bryn Mawr)

George Humphrey
  (Queen's Univ.)
Helen Jennings
  (Hudson Training School)
Olaf Johnson (Iowa)
Sigmund Koch (Iowa)
Jack Kounin (Iowa)
D. Kretch (Colorado)
P. J. Kruse (Cornell)
Kurt Lewin (Iowa)
Mrs. Lewin
H. S. Liddell (Cornell)
Ronald Lippitt (Iowa)
Marion Long (Cornell)
Boyd McCandless (Iowa)
Donald K. MacKinnon
  (Bryn Mawr)
Dr. Macmillan (Cornell)
Norman Maier (Michigan)
Alfred J. Marrow (N.Y.U.)
Neal E. Miller (Yale)
Gardner Murphy (Columbia)
Lois Barclay Murphy
  (Sarah Lawrence College)

260

Edwin Newman (Swarthmore)
Dr. Oeser (Scotland)
R. M. Ogden (Cornell)
M. R. Pekarsky (Northwestern)

T. A. Ryan (Cornell)
Robert Sears (Yale)
Mildred Spicer (Cornell)
E. C. Tolman (California)

APPENDIX

D

IOWA STUDIES

C. ANDERSON, "The Development of a Level of Aspiration in Young Children" (1940), developed a scale of maturity of aspiration for children between two and eight years, using activities such as throwing a series of rings over a stick and knocking down tenpins with a ball. The study found that when pressure is brought to bear on a child in the form of offering a reward, the level of aspiration (the degree of difficulty chosen) will decrease. When it is impossible to lower the level of aspiration, the maturity of aspiration may regress.

D. L. ADLER, "Types of Similarity and the Substitute Value of Activities at Different Age Levels" (1939), studied the relation between certain cognitive processes and substitute value at three age levels. After interruption of the original task, the child had to finish a second task which was physically identical to the interrupted one. For the younger age levels, although they could see the similarity between the tasks, the children found no substitute value in building a house for Mary rather than for Johnny. For the older children too, when the attention was mainly on the similar concrete object (e.g., one house vs. another), there was low substitute value; however, a categorical approach (e.g,. stressing housebuilding as such) gave the similar activity considerable substitute value.

D. L. ADLER and J. KOUNIN, "Some Factors Operating at the Moment of Resumption of Interrupted Tasks" (1939), found that the presence of uncompleted work of another person does not lead (or only rarely leads) to spontaneous completion by children.

A. MARROW, "Goal Tension and Recall" (1938), investigated the effect of praise and condemnation in a competitive situation on the Zeigarnik quotient. In both cases, the quotient rises, apparently indicating that the strength of the force in the direction of spontaneous recollection is a function of the intensity of the need.

H. F. WRIGHT, "The Influence of Barriers upon the Strength of Motivation" (1937), found no increase in speed with decreasing distance from a goal when the situation involved nursery school children pulling the goal (a marble) toward themselves. The study also indicated that a difficulty may increase the need for an object behind a barrier: the child will prefer (everything else being equal) a toy which is slightly more difficult to reach.

M. E. KEISTER, "The Behavior of Young Children in Failure: An Experimental Attempt to Discover and to Modify Undesirable Responses of Preschool Children to Failure" (1937), found it is possible to change the reaction of nursery school children to failure through proper training. The increase of persistence and the decrease of rationalization and of emotional and destructive reactions showed a certain amount of transfer to different areas of activity.

R. BARKER, T. DEMBO, and K. LEWIN, "Frustration and Regression" (1941), showed that the constructiveness of play of a five-and-a-half-year-old child may regress to the level of a three-and-a-half-year-old as a result of frustration.

R. BARKER, "An Experimental Study of the Resolution of Conflict in Children" (1942), studied the way in which children make choices between more or less agreeable or disagreeable foods and found that the choice time increases with the intensity of the conflict. The decision time is longer in choices between two negative than between two positive valences.

B. A. WRIGHT, "Altruism in Children and the Perceived Conduct of Others" (1942), studied five- and eight-year-old children when they had a choice of keeping a preferred toy or giving it to someone else. The other child (who was not present) was either someone unknown or a best friend. The five-year-old children consistently kept the preferred toy, irrespective of who was to receive it; whereas among the eight-year-old children the degree of altruism varied with the subject and with the recipient—where the recipient was a stranger, more altruistic choices were made. The eight-year-old children whose choices were either all altruistic or all egoistic arrived at a decision more quickly than those who sometimes made one type of choice and sometimes the other. The children judged other persons to be altruistic or egoistic to the same degree as they themselves were.

D. CARTWRIGHT, "Decision-Time in Relation to the Differentiation of the Phenomenal Field" (1941), measured the discrimination of figures and meaning, and found the decision-time to be longest if the forces in opposite directions were equal.

D. CARTWRIGHT and L. FESTINGER, "A Quantitative Theory of Decision" (1943), elaborated and quantified the previous study.

S. ESCALONA, "Effect of Success and Failure upon Level of Aspiration and Behavior in Manic-Depressive Psychoses" (1940), found that extreme decision retardation is typical of certain types of depression. Also, the level of aspiration at a given time depends upon the strength of the valence of success and failure and upon the probability of success at that time.

J. KOUNIN, "Experimental Studies of Rigidity" (1941), compared the satiation and co-satiation of normal seven-year-old children with twelve- and thirty- to forty-year-old feeble-minded persons of the same mental age. The velocity of satiation and the degree of co-satiation decrease with chronological age, apparently, even if the mental age is the same.

M. HENLE, in "An Experimental Investigation of Dynamic and Structural Determinants of Substitution" (1942), addressed herself to the significant problem of finding some principles by which one can predict beforehand what tasks will and what tasks will not substitute for each other.

M. E. WRIGHT, "The Influence of Frustration upon the Social Relations of Young Children" (1943), found that friendship between two children increases in certain situations of experimenter-induced frustration. This might be interpreted as an attempt to increase their own power relative to the power of the experimenter.

264

R. Lippitt, "An Experimental Study of the Effect of Democratic and Authoritarian Group Atmospheres" (1940), investigated the adaptation of children to the cultural atmosphere created by the group leader. The feeling of group-belongingness (as expressed, for instance, by the use of the term "we" more frequently than "I") is stronger in democratically administered clubs.

K. Lewin, R. Lippitt, and R. White, "Patterns of Aggressive Behavior in Experimentally Created 'Social Climates'" (1939), found that, on several occasions, one of the group members was attacked as a scapegoat in the autocratic groups.

A. Bavelas, "Morale and the Training of Leaders" (1942), found that the degree of cooperation between children in a day camp increased after their adult leaders were retrained from autocratic to democratic leadership techniques.

R. Lippitt and R. White, "The 'Social Climate' of Children's Groups" (1943), in experiments with ten-year-old children, tested the effect of induced needs during the presence and absence of the inducing power field. They found that the amount of work output in an autocratic group atmosphere dropped very decisively within a few minutes after the leader left the room. This was in contrast to a democratic group atmosphere, where the work had been chosen and planned by the group itself and where the work output was unchanged when the leader left. In this context, the observers distinguished two types of reaction to autocracy: aggressive and apathetic. They believed that the readiness of an individual to accept autocracy in the club depended partly upon the home background and whether the child was more oriented toward "boy values" or "adult values."

J. Frank, "Experimental Studies of Personal Pressure and Resistance" (1944) found, in an experiment with college students, that the step-by-step method is more efficient in coercing a person to eat than the attempt to make him go the whole way at one step. It also found the effectiveness of the power field for creating induced forces to be greater if the distance between the persons is smaller.

J. R. French, "The Disruption and Cohesion of Groups" (1941).

J. R. French, "Organized and Unorganized Groups under Fear and

Fustration" (1944), studied adaptation to group atmospheres in experiments with college freshmen.

K. Lewin, T. Dembo, L. Festinger, and R. Sears, "Level of Aspiration" (1944), indicated that the experience of success or failure depends on the level of performance within a frame of reference. This frame of reference may be a goal set for that action, past performances, or the standards of a group. A feeling of success will prevail if a certain level, related to the dominant frame of reference, is reached.

APPENDIX

E

C.C.I. PUBLICATIONS

ABOUT C.C.I.

KURT LEWIN, ALFRED J. MARROW, and CHARLES E. HENDRY, *Accent on Action: A New Approach to Minority Group Problems in America.* Mimeographed, 1945. 14 pp. Presents a point of view on integrating research and community action in the fight against prejudice.

HAROLD P. LEVY, *Pushing Back the Barriers.* Reprint from *Better Times,* May 10, 1946. 4 pp. Describes some early C.C.I. projects, particularly the preliminary work on incident control.

TRACY S. KENDLER, *The Research Program of C.C.I.* Mimeographed, May 1949. 2 pp. Describes the problems investigated by C.C.I. and their relationship to the overall program of the American Jewish Congress.

WILLIAM SCHWARTZ, *Questions and Answers about C.C.I.* Mimeographed, June 1950. 9 pp. A discussion of the work of C.C.I. presented in question-and-answer form. Each of C.C.I.'s major research projects is described briefly.

GENERAL METHODS OF IMPROVING INTERGROUP RELATIONS

MILTON L. BLUM and CLAIRE SELLTIZ, *The Seminar as a Method of In-Service Training.* Reprint from *The Journal of Educational Sociology,* *19,* No. 7, March 1946. 9 pp. Describes a seminar in which public school and Hebrew teachers studied the intergroup relations of their students.

GOODWIN WATSON, *Action for Unity.* Pamphlet. *Jewish Affairs* pamphlet series, *1,* No. 5, April 1946. 23 pp. A summary of the book *Action for Unity.* This pamphlet is based on a nation-wide survey carried out in 1944–1945 which analyzed a number of major strategies for the improvement of intergroup relations.

GOODWIN WATSON, *Action for Unity.* New York: Harper's, 1947. 165 pp. Compares and evaluates methods of combating prejudice and building good intergroup relations.

MAX WOLFF, *Working Together.* Mimeographed, 1947. 7 pp. This statement is intended as a guide to the American Jewish Congress chapter in initiating and/or participating in projects of community-wide interest. The methods are applicable by any group interested in community action projects.

MAX WOLFF and SYLVIA CHARLOW, *Discussion Guide based on "Action for Unity," by Goodwin Watson.* Mimeographed, March 1948. 23 pp. A step-by-step program guide to be used in discussing the book *Action for Unity* and developing an understanding of anti-minority problems and some ways of coping with them.

CLAIRE SELLTIZ, *The University and the Fight Against Prejudice.* Mimeographed. This article appeared in the *Standard, 34,* No. 6, March 1948. 4 pp. Discusses some research findings on the effects of education on prejudice. It closes with a plea for colleges to avoid setting up discriminatory barriers in the admission of students and for them to undertake research in the field of intergroup relations.

MAX DEUTSCHER, *An Evaluation of a High School Intercultural Education Program.* Mimeographed. Paper read at the annual meeting of the Eastern Psychological Association, April 1948. 5 pp. A brief report on the effects of an integrated biology and social studies course on the attitudes of the participating high school students.

C.C.I. REPORT #1, *A Report on the Problem of Changing Neighborhoods.* December 1953. Mimeographed. 16 pp.

COMMUNITY SELF-SURVEYS

MARGOT HAAS WORMSER and STUART COOK, *The Use of the Community Self-Survey in Combating Discrimination.* Mimeographed. Paper read at the annual meeting of the American Psychological Association, September 1947. 11 pp. Describes the theory and techniques used in community self-surveys of discriminatory practices.

JOHN HARDING, *Community Self-Surveys: A Form of Combating Discrimination.* Reprint from *Congress Weekly, 15,* No. 9, March 5, 1948. 4 pp. Describes and compares alternative ways of conducting self-surveys.

CLAIRE SELLTIZ and SYLVIA CHARLOW, *Barometer for Bias.* Reprint from *Congress Weekly, 15,* No. 21, June 11, 1948. 3 pp. Brief summary of methods used and illustrative findings from the Northtown community self-survey.

Lewis G. Kay, *Northtown Report.* Mimeographed. This article appeared in *Congress Weekly, 16,* No. 17, May 9, 1949. 2 pp. Brief description of action taken in Northtown following the community self-survey of civil rights.

Claire Selltiz and Margot Haas Wormser (eds.), *Community Self-Surveys: An Approach to Social Change. Journal of Social Issues, 5,* No. 2, Spring 1949. 65 pp. This journal issue contains the following articles: "Introduction," by Stuart W. Cook; "The Northtown Self-Survey: A Case Study," by Margot Haas Wormser; "Some Basic Principles of Self-Surveys," by John Harding; "Some Technical Problems of a Self-Survey," by Claire Selltiz; "A Comparison of Different Types of Self-Surveys," by Benjamin W. Lambert and Nathan E. Cohen; "On Evaluating Self-Surveys," by Isidor Chein.

Margot Haas Wormser and Claire Selltiz, *Community Self-Surveys of Discriminatory Practices: A Summary of a Program of Research.* Mimeographed, July 1949. 9 pp. Summarizes C.C.I.'s work in the development and study of community self-surveys dealing with discriminatory practices.

Margot Haas Wormser and Claire Selltiz, *Community Self-Surveys: Principles and Procedures.* Mimeographed. This material also appears as Chapter 19 in Vol. II of *Research Methods in Social Relations,* by Marie Jahoda, Morton Deutsch, and Stuart W. Cook (New York: Dryden Press, 1951). 39 pp. Discusses crucial factors in the development and application of self-survey techniques to the problem of assessing the status of civil rights within a community.

Margot Haas Wormser and Claire Selltiz, *How to Conduct a Community Self-Survey of Civil Rights.* New York: Association Press, 1951. 271 pp. This manual is intended to provide help with the technical problems of conducting a self-survey. Securing broadly representative sponsorship, constructing interview schedules, securing and training interviewers, analyzing data and reporting findings are all discussed.

Claire Selltiz, Margot Haas Wormser, and John Harding, *How to Conduct a Community Self-Survey of Civil Rights. Supplement One: Interview Schedules and Related Material.* Mimeographed, November 1951. Contains interview schedules and related materials for each area of community life which may be covered in a self-survey.

Claire Selltiz, Erna Benjamin, John Harding, and Margot Haas Wormser, *How to Conduct a Community Self-Survey of Civil Rights. Supplement Two: Analysis Plans.* Mimeographed, November 1951. 163 pp. Gives detailed instructions for analysis of data gathered through each interview schedule presented in *Supplement One: Interview Schedules and Related Material.*

INCIDENT CONTROL: TECHNICAL PAPERS

JOHN HARDING, ABRAHAM F. CITRON, and CLAIRE SELLTIZ, *Personal Incidents: A Study of the Effectiveness of Various Types of Answers to Anti-Minority Remarks.* Mimeographed. Paper read at the annual meeting of the American Psychological Association, September 1947. 7 pp. Reports the results of a study of alternative ways of answering anti-Semitic remarks.

ABRAHAM F. CITRON and JOHN HARDING, *An Experiment in Training Groups of People to Answer Anti-Minority Remarks in an Effective Fashion.* Mimeographed. Paper read at the annual meeting of the American Psychological Association, September 1947. 8 pp. Reports results of research on training people to answer anti-minority remarks.

ABRAHAM F. CITRON, RUSSELL HOGREFE, and JOHN HARDING, *An Experiment in Training Volunteer Trainers.* Mimeographed. Paper read at the annual meeting of the American Psychological Association, September 1948. 4 pp. Describes an experiment in transmitting the skill of effectively answering anti-minority remarks via the process of training trainers selected from organized social groups who in turn subsequently train their fellow group members.

ABRAHAM F. CITRON, ISIDOR CHEIN, and JOHN HARDING, *Anti-Minority Remarks: A Problem for Action Research.* Reprint from the *Journal of Abnormal and Social Psychology*, 45, No. 1, January 1950. 28 pp. Describes an experimental program for determining the effectiveness of various types of answers to anti-minority remarks.

CLAIRE SELLTIZ, ABRAHAM F. CITRON, JOHN HARDING, OTTO ROSAHN, and MARGOT HAAS WORMSER, *The Acceptability of Answers to Anti-Semitic Remarks.* Mimeographed, and reprinted from *International Journal of Opinion and Attitude Research*, 4, No. 3, Fall 1950. Mimeographed, 35 pp; reprint, 37 pp. Reports a series of experiments on the acceptability, to audiences, of various methods of answering anti-Semitic remarks.

ABRAHAM F. CITRON and JOHN HARDING, *An Experiment in Training Volunteers to Answer Anti-Minority Remarks.* Reprint from the *Journal of Abnormal and Social Psychology*, 45, No. 2, April 1950. 18 pp. Report of an experiment in which six groups of volunteers were trained to answer anti-minority remarks.

JOHN HARDING, ABRAHAM F. CITRON, and ESTELLE KING, *An Experimental Study of Answers to Anti-Negro Remarks.* Mimeographed. Published in the *Journal of Social Psychology*, 1951. 18 pp. Reports an experiment to determine whether changes in attitude occurred when subjects were presented with an anti-Negro incident and various answers.

JOHN HARDING, *An Experimental Study of Answers to Anti-Negro Remarks*. Mimeographed. Paper read at the annual meeting of the American Psychological Association, September 1951. 4 pp. Compares experimental results on answers to anti-Negro remarks with findings on answers to anti-Semitic remarks.

INCIDENT CONTROL: POPULAR ARTICLES

ABRAHAM F. CITRON, *Voices for Democracy*. Reprint from *Congress Weekly*, *13*, December 27, 1946. 3 pp. Discusses the significance for democracy of public incidents involving slander of minority groups and gives the results of research on effective action against such incidents.

ABRAHAM F. CITRON and JOHN HARDING, *Answering the Bigot: A Summary of the Incident Control Project*. Photo-offset, 1949. 7 pp. Summarizes a series of projects on the development and communication of effective ways of responding to anti-minority remarks.

ABRAHAM F. CITRON, *Objection Sustained: An Introduction to Incident Control in Private Situations*. Photo-offset, 1949. 12 pp. Describes problems posed by bigoted remarks made in conversation among associates and a rationale for answering such remarks.

INCIDENT CONTROL: TRAINING AIDS

ABRAHAM F. CITRON, *Stand Up and Be Counted among the Voices for Democracy*. Mimeographed, 1948. 7 pp. Gives a step-by-step account of how to set up a community-wide institute for training volunteers to answer public slurs against minority groups.

ABRAHAM F. CITRON (compiler), *Readings in the Psychology of Prejudice*. Mimeographed, 1948. 22 pp. This collection contains excerpts from a small list of standard works on the psychology of prejudice. The material was prepared for volunteers who lead programs on the topic of answering anti-minority remarks.

ABRAHAM F. CITRON, *Directions for the Demonstration of the Personal Incident Project*. Mimeographed, January 1948. 15 pp. Step-by-step instructions for public presentation in dramatic form of the results of research on answering anti-minority groups.

ABRAHAM F. CITRON, *Common Questions Asked of Demonstrators*. Mimeographed, 1948. 3 pp. A compilation of questions related to anti-minority incidents. A training aid for the use of volunteers who train groups to answer public slurs against minority groups.

ABRAHAM F. CITRON, *Answers to Some of the More Important Questions Asked of Demonstrators*. Mimeographed, January 1949. 8 pp.

A compilation of answers to questions raised in relation to answering anti-minority remarks.

ABRAHAM F. CITRON, *Common Incident Situations.* Photo-offset, 1949. 12 pp. Summarizes the incident control project and goes on to cite common incident situations and the way in which they were handled.

ABRAHAM F. CITRON, *The Incident Control Project and the American Jewish Congress Program.* Mimeographed, January 1949. 12 pp. Describes the philosophy of the incident control project and the way it fits into the general program of the American Jewish Congress.

EFFECTS OF INTERGROUP CONTACT

RUSSELL HOGREFE, MARY C. EVANS, and ISIDOR CHEIN, *The Effects on Intergroup Attitudes of Participation in an Interracial Play Center.* Mimeographed. Paper read at the annual meeting of the American Psychological Association, September 1947. 6 pp. Reports a study of eight- to fourteen-year-old children brought together in an interracial play center each Saturday for eight months.

STUART W. COOK, *Some Psychological and Sociological Considerations Related to Interracial Housing.* Mimeographed. Statement made in behalf of the Committee for Fair Housing before the City Commission of Jersey City, N.J., November 1947. 3 pp. Summarizes the implications for housing policy of research on the effects of segregation.

CLAIRE SELLTIZ, STUART W. COOK, and JOHN HARDING, *Problems of Intergroup Contact: A Definition of a Research Area.* Mimeographed, February 1951. 8 pp. Outlines the dimensions of a research program aimed at discovering the conditions under which face-to-face contact between different racial and religious groups creates favorable intergroup relations.

MINORITY GROUP MEMBERSHIP: THEORETICAL ANALYSES

ISIDOR CHEIN, *Group Membership and Group Belonging.* Mimeographed, 1948. Report to International Congress on Mental Health based on discussions of the preparatory commission on minority group integration in the U.S.A. 13 pp. Surveys the problem of multiple group membership and wider group loyalty.

ISIDOR CHEIN, *Some Comments on the Needs of Jewish Youth.* Mimeographed. Paper delivered at the annual conference of the National Association of Jewish Center Workers, July 1948. 3 pp. Discusses the needs of Jewish youth arising from their membership in the Jewish group.

ISIDOR CHEIN, *The Problem of Belongingness: An Action Research Perspective.* Mimeographed. This article appeared in the *Jewish Cen-*

ter Worker, May 1948. 4 pp. Discusses the problems of Jewish youth growing out of varying degrees of identification with the Jewish group. Research possibilities for shedding light on these problems are briefly noted.

ISIDOR CHEIN, TRACY S. KENDLER, and CAROL COAN, *Discussion Guide on Raising Jewish Children*. Mimeographed, 1949. 9 pp. Guide for a discussion course covering such questions as: parental goals for their children; problems children and parents face; the significance of parents' attitudes and practices.

ISIDOR CHEIN, *A Psychologist's Notes on the Impact of Current Trends on Jews*. Mimeographed. Paper read at the National Conference of Jewish Social Welfare, June 1949. 4 pp. Presents psychological considerations involved in assessing the effect of current trends on the lives of Jews.

TAMARA DEMBO, *The Problem of Jewish Identification*. Mimeographed, April 1951. 4 pp. Discusses Jewish identification as part of the general problem of multiple group membership.

ISIDOR CHEIN, *The Faulty Educational Model*. Reprint from *Congress Weekly, 18*, No. 3, January 15, 1951. 4 pp. Presents a critical review of the basic assumptions of Jewish education as it is now practiced in America.

ISIDOR CHEIN, *Jewish Education and Personality Growth*. Mimeographed. Paper read at the First National Conference on Jewish Education, January 1951. 3 pp. Discusses psychological problems of Jewish education. The relevance of personality growth to Jewish content is examined in some detail.

ISIDOR CHEIN, *Education and Knowledge*. Mimeographed, November 1951. 6 pp. Discusses the difference between real knowledge and pseudo knowledge and methods by which Jewish education can promote the former rather than the latter.

ISIDOR CHEIN, *The Need for Jewish Knowledge*. Mimeographed, 1951. 4 pp. Argues the existence of a basic need among Jews for Jewish knowledge and discusses ways in which Jewish education can foster this need instead of discouraging it.

MINORITY GROUP MEMBERSHIP: EMPIRICAL STUDIES

JACOB I. HURWITZ, *On Being a Jew: Perceptions, Attitudes, and Needs of Jewish Children*. Mimeographed. This article appeared in *The Jewish Center Worker*, May 1948. 7 pp. A brief description of a study of Jewish children. Discusses problems encountered, communication between the subject and the majority group, and values derived from membership in own group.

ARNOLD M. ROSE, *The Negro's Morale: Group Identification and Group Protest*. Minneapolis: University of Minnesota Press, 1949.

153 pp. This book describes how Negroes feel toward other Negroes and toward themselves. It also discusses the reactions of Negroes to discrimination and the way in which these reactions influence Negro-white relations.

ISIDOR CHEIN, WILLIAM SCHWARTZ, ABRAHAM F. CITRON, and MARGOT HAAS WORMSER, *Description of the Issues in the Experience Survey of Jewish Educators and Group Workers*. Photo-offset, March 1950. 22 pp. Describes the issues raised in the experience survey on problems in preparing Jewish youth for their dual role of membership in the Jewish and general communities.

ISIDOR CHEIN, WILLIAM SCHWARTZ, ABRAHAM F. CITRON, and MARGOT HAAS WORMSER, *Interview Schedule: Experience Survey of Jewish Educators and Group Workers*. Mimeographed, March 1950. 22 pp. Schedule used by interviewers on problems in preparing Jewish youth for their dual role of membership in the Jewish and general communities.

ISIDOR CHEIN and JACOB I. HURWITZ, *The Reactions of Jewish Boys to Various Aspects of Being Jewish*. Mimeographed, 1950. 42 pp. This monograph reports a study of the way Jewish boys feel about their Jewishness, identification with the Jewish group, relationships with non-Jewish peers, personal and social adjustment, and receptivity to Jewish cultural programs.

MARION RADKE, *The Meaning of Minority Membership to Jewish College Students*. Mimeographed, 1951. 36 pp. Reports one of a series of studies which have as their objective the investigation of the meaning of minority-group membership to the minority-group member. Factors such as the following are examined: Values members attached to membership in the group; their goals with respect to intergroup relations; the relationship between group membership values and such factors as personal adjustment, socio-economic level, etc.

MARION RADKE, *Group Belonging of Jewish Children in Relation to Their Age*. Mimeographed, 1951. 21 pp. This study deals with boys and girls between the ages of seven and seventeen who were members of two Jewish Community Centers. The report examines changes with age in the acceptance and rejection of things Jewish.

MARION RADKE, HADASSAH DAVIS, JACOB I. HURWITZ, and PEARL POLLACK, *Group Belonging among Various Subgroups of Jewish Children*. Mimeographed, 1951. 35 pp. Examines the effect of diverse subcultures within the Jewish group on Jewish children's perceptions of themselves as Jews, the problems they confront, and the values they derive from their Jewish group membership.

KURT LEWIN, *Research on Minority Problems*. Reprint from *The Technology Review*, *48*, No. 3, January 1946. 4 pp. Discusses and illustrates the application of scientific research to minority problems.

ISIDOR CHEIN, STUART W. COOK, and JOHN HARDING, *The Field of Action Research*. Reprint from *The American Psychologist*, *3*, No. 2, February 1948. 8 pp. Describes the general characteristics of action research and four specific varieties: diagnostic, participant, empirical, and experimental.

C.C.I. REPORT #2. *An Evaluation of the IAD Car Card Program*. Mimeographed, 1954.

MAX DEUTSCHER and ISIDOR CHEIN, *The Psychological Effects of Enforced Segregation: A Survey of Social Science Opinion*. Reprint from *The Journal of Psychology*, *61*, No. 2, Spring 1948. 28 pp. Reports the results of a nation-wide survey of opinion of social scientists on the psychological effects of enforced segregation of both segregator and segregated.

ISIDOR CHEIN, *What Are the Psychological Effects of Segregation under Conditions of Equal Facilities?* Mimeographed. This article appeared in the *International Journal of Opinion and Attitude Research*, *3*, No. 2, Summer 1949. 6 pp. Discusses a poll of social scientists on the psychological effects of enforced segregation and methods for a further study of this problem.

GERHART SAENGER and NORMA S. GORDON, *The Influence of Discrimination on Minority-Group Members in Its Relation to Attempts to Combat Discrimination*. Mimeographed and reprinted from *Journal of Social Psychology*, *31*, February 1950. Mimeographed. 29 pp. A survey and analysis of reasons for failure of minority-group members to make full use of a fair employment practices law.

GORDON W. ALLPORT and BERNARD M. KRAMER, *Some Roots of Prejudice*. Reprint from the *Journal of Psychology*, *22*, Fall 1946. 30 pp. Studies prejudice through responses to a questionnaire given to undergraduates at Dartmouth, Harvard, and Radcliffe.

B. BELLOW, M. BLUM, K. CLARK, M. HAAS, E. HAYDON, R. HOGREFE, J. HOLZBERG, P. LATCH, L. KAY, R. LOWENSTEIN, M. McDUFF, and I. SCHREIBER, *Prejudice in Seaside*. Reprint from *Human Relations*, *1*, No. 1, Spring 1947. 23 pp. Reports a study of relations between racial and religious groups in a section of a large urban community.

GERHART SAENGER and EMILY GILBERT, *Customer Reactions to the Integration of Negro Sales Personnel.* Mimeographed and reprinted from *International Journal of Opinion and Attitude Research, 4,* No. 1, Spring 1950. Mimeographed. 16 pp. This study of white department-store customers shows the absence of relationship between attitudes toward Negroes and the subjects' actual practice of buying or not buying from Negro sales clerks.

ISIDOR CHEIN, *Securing Our Children Against Prejudice.* Mimeographed. Paper read at National Association of Jewish Center Workers at the Fifty-third Annual Meeting of the National Conference of Jewish Communal Service, Chicago, June 1952.

APPENDIX

F

RESEARCH CENTER
FOR GROUP DYNAMICS
PUBLICATIONS—1945-1950

METHODOLOGY, BASIC RESEARCH AND THEORY IN GROUP DYNAMICS

KURT BACK, "The Exertion of Influence Through Social Communication," *Journal of Abnormal and Social Psychology*, 1951, *46*.

——— et al., "A Method of Rumor Transmission," *Human Relations*, 1950, *3*, 307–312.

ALEX BAVELAS, "A Mathematical Model for Group Structures," *Applied Anthropology*, 7, 3, 16–30.

DORWIN CARTWRIGHT, "Emotional Dimensions of Group Life." (A chapter in *Feelings and Emotions*, New York: McGraw-Hill, 1950, pp. 439–456.)

———, "Some Principles of Mass Persuasion: Selected Findings of Research on the Sale of United States War Bonds," *Human Relations*, 1949, *2*, 253–267.

———, "Survey Research: Psychological Economics." (A chapter in *Experiments in Social Process*, New York: McGraw-Hill, 1950, pp. 47–64.)

———, "Surveys of the War Finance Program," *Proceedings of the Conference on Consumers' Interests*, Philadelphia: University of Pennsylvania Press, 1947.

MORTON DEUTSCH, "A Theory of Cooperation and Competition," *Human Relations*, 1949, *2*, 129–152.

———, "An Experimental Study of the Effects of Cooperation and

Competition upon Group Process," *Human Relations*, 1949, *2*, 99–231.

Leon Festinger, "The Analysis of Sociograms Using Matrix Algebra," *Human Relations*, 1949, *2*, 153–158.

———, "The Significance of Difference Between Means Without Reference to the Frequency Distribution Function," *Psychometrika*, 1946, *11*, 97–105.

———, "Treatment of Qualitative Data by 'Scale Analysis,' " *Psychological Bulletin*, 1947, *44*, 149–161.

———, "Laboratory Experiments: The Role of Group Belongingness." (A chapter in *Experiments in Social Process*, New York: McGraw-Hill, 1950, pp. 31–46.)

———, "The Role of Group Belongingness in a Voting Situation," *Human Relations*, 1947, *1*, 154–181.

———, Stanley Schachter, and Kurt Back, *Social Pressures in Informal Groups; A Study of a Housing Project*, New York: Harper's, 1950.

———, Dorwin Cartwright, et al., "A Study of a Rumor: Its Origin and Spread," *Human Relations*, 1948, *1*, 464–486.

——— et al., "Theory and Experiment in Social Communication: Collected Papers," Ann Arbor: Institute for Social Research, 1950.

———, "Informal Social Communication," *Psychological Review*, 1950, *57*, 271–282.

——— and John Thibaut, "Interpersonal Communication in Small Groups," *Journal of Abnormal and Social Psychology*, 1951, *46*.

John R. P. French Jr., and Alfred J. Marrow, "Changing a Stereotype in Industry," *Journal of Social Issues*, 1945, *1*, 3, 33–37.

———, "Field Experiments: Changing Group Productivity." (A chapter in *Experiments in Social Process*, New York: McGraw-Hill Company, 1950, pp. 79–96.)

——— and Lester Coch, "Overcoming Resistance to Change," *Human Relations*, 1948, *1*, 512–532.

Murray Horwitz and Dorwin Cartwright, "A Projective Test for the Diagnosis of Groups," *Human Relations*, 1951, *4*.

David Jenkins and Ronald Lippitt, "The Interpersonal Perceptions of Teachers, Students and Parents," National Education Association Monograph.

Harold H. Kelley, "The Warm-Cold Variable in First Impressions of Persons," *Journal of Personality*, 1950, *18*, 431–439.

———, "Communication in Experimentally Created Hierarchies," *Human Relations*, 1951, *4*, 1.

KURT LEWIN, "Behavior and Development as a Function of the Total Situation." (A chapter in L. Carmichael [ed.], *Manual of Child Psychology*, New York: John Wiley & Sons, 1946, pp. 791–844.)

————, "Frontiers in Group Dynamics: Concept, Method and Reality in Social Science: Social Equilibria and Social Change," *Human Relations*, 1947, *1*, 5–41.

————, "Frontiers in Group Dynamics: II. Channels of Group Life: Social Planning and Action Research," *Human Relations*, 1947, *1*, 143–153.

————, "Group Decision and Social Change." (A chapter in *Readings in Social Psychology*, New York: Henry Holt and Company, 1947, pp. 330–344.)

————, *Resolving Social Conflicts*, New York: Harper's, 1948.

RONALD LIPPITT and R. K. WHITE, "An Experimental Study of Leadership and Group Life." (A chapter in *Readings in Social Psychology*, New York: Henry Holt and Company, 1947, pp. 315–330.)

———— and M. RADKE, "New Trends in the Investigation of Prejudice," *The Annals of the American Academy of Political and Social Science*, 1946, *244*, 167–176.

————, "A Program of Experimentation on Group Functioning and Group Productivity." (Chapter 1 in *Current Trends in Social Psychology*, Pittsburgh: University of Pittsburgh Press, 1949, pp. 14–49.)

———— and JOHN R. P. FRENCH, JR., "Research and Training: The Research Program on Training and Group Life at Bethel," *The Group*, 1948, *10*, *2*, 11–15.

————, *Training in Community Relations*, New York: Harper's, 1949.

R. DUNCAN LUCE and ALBERT D. PERRY, "A Method of Matrix Analysis of Group Structure," *Psychometrika*, 1949, *14*, 95–116.

ALBERT PEPITONE, "Motivational Effects in Social Perception," *Human Relations*, 1950, *3*, 57–76.

NORMAN POLANSKY, RONALD LIPPITT, and FRITZ REDL, "An Investigation of Behavioral Contagion in Groups," *Human Relations*, 1950, *3*, 319–348.

————, ————, and ————, "The Use of Sociometric Data in Research in Group Treatment Processes," *Sociometry*, 1950, *13*, 39–61.

M. RADKE and D. KLISURICH, "Experiments in Changing Food Habits," *Journal of the American Dietetics Association*, 1947, *23*, 403–409.

STANLEY SCHACHTER, "Deviation, Rejection and Communication," *Journal of Abnormal and Social Psychology*, 1951, *46*.

JOHN W. THIBAUT, "An Experimental Study of the Cohesiveness of Underprivileged Groups," *Human Relations*, 1950, *3*, 251–278.

JEANNE WATSON, "Some Social and Psychological Situations Related to Change in Attitude," *Human Relations*, 1950, *3*, 15–56.

ALVIN F. ZANDER, "Resistance to Change: Its Analysis and Prevention," *Advanced Management*, 1950, *15*, 1, 9–11.

———, "The W.P. Club: An Objective Case Study of a Group," *Human Relations*, 1948, *1*, 321–332.

THE ORGANIZATION OF SOCIAL RESEARCH AND THE RELATION OF RESEARCH TO ACTION

DORWIN CARTWRIGHT, "American Social Psychology and the War," *Journal of Consulting Psychology*, 1945, *9*, 67–72.

———, "Basic and Applied Social Psychology," *Philosophy of Science*, 1949, *16*, 198–208.

———, "Kurt Lewin, 1890–1947," *International Journal of Public Opinion and Attitude Research*, 1947, *1*, 96–99.

———, "Public Opinion Polls and Democratic Leadership," *Journal of Social Issues*, 1946, *2*, 2, 23–32.

———, G. MURPHY, and J. S. BRUNER, "Resources for World-wide Research in Human Science," *Journal of Social Issues*, 1947, *3*, 1, 54–66.

———, "Social Psychology in the United States during the Second World War," *Human Relations*, 1948, *1*, 333–352.

LEON FESTINGER, "Current Developments in Group Dynamics," *Social Work and the Current Scene*, Volume II, Proceedings of 77th Annual Convention of National Conference of Social Work, Atlantic City, 1950.

JOHN R. P. FRENCH, JR., and ALVIN F. ZANDER, "The Group Dynamics Approach," *Psychology of Labor-Management Relations*. Volume published by Industrial Relations Research Association based on a symposium of the American Psychological Association, Denver, 1949, pp. 71–80.

KURT LEWIN, "Action Research and Minority Problems," *Journal of Social Issues*, 1946, *2*, 4, 34–46.

———, "The Research Center for Group Dynamics," *Sociometry*, 1945, *8*, 126–136.

RONALD LIPPITT, LELAND BRADFORD, and KENNETH D. BENNÉ, *Group Dynamics and Social Action*, New York: Anti-Defamation League, Freedom Pamphlet Series, 1950.

———, "Kurt Lewin, 1890–1947, Adventures in the Exploration of Interdependence," *Sociometry*, 1947, *10*, 87–97.

———, "Social Psychology as Science and as Profession. (Paper read as the presidential address at the annual meeting of the Society for the Psychological Study of Social Issues, Denver, Colorado, 1949.)

—————, "The Strategy of Socio-Psychological Research in Group Life." (A chapter in *Experiments in Social Process*, New York: McGraw-Hill, 1950, pp. 17–30.)

—————, "Techniques for Research in Group Living," *Journal of Social Issues*, 1946, *2*, 4, 55–61.

—————, *Training in Community Relations*, New York: Harper's, 1949.

ALVIN F. ZANDER, "Psychological Research in the Community Mental Health Service Field," *Journal of Clinical Psychology*, 1950, *6*, 2, 123–127.

CONCRETE APPLICATIONS OF GROUP DYNAMICS PRINCIPLES AND TECHNIQUES

DORWIN CARTWRIGHT, "Public Relations and Opinion Measurement," *Public Relations, A Symposium*, Massachusetts Institute of Technology, 1949, 62–73.

JOHN R. P. FRENCH, JR., ARTHUR KORNHAUSER, and ALFRED MARROW, "Conflict and Cooperation in Industry," *Journal of Social Issues*, 1946, *2*, 1, 2–55.

————— and LELAND BRADFORD (eds.), "The Dynamics of the Discussion Group," *Journal of Social Issues*, 1948, *4*, 2.

—————, "Role Playing as a Method of Training Foremen," *Sociometry*, 1945, *8*, 410–425.

DAVID H. JENKINS, "Counseling Through Group Activities," *The Clearing House*, 1949, *23*, 8, 488–493.

—————, "Research in Group Dynamics," *Social Education*, 1948, *12*, 8, 347–351.

—————, "Social Engineering in Educational Change: An Outline of Method," *Progressive Education*, 1949, *26*, 193–197.

—————, "Training in Being an Effective Group Member," *University of Michigan School of Education Bulletin*, 1949, *21*, 2, 25–27.

—————, "What Is Group Dynamics?" *Adult Education Journal*, 1950, *9*, 2, 54–60.

KURT LEWIN, RONALD LIPPITT, CHARLES HENDRY, JOHN R. P. FRENCH, JR., ALVIN ZANDER, et al., "The Practicality of Democracy." (A chapter in Gardner Murphy [ed.], *Human Nature and Enduring Peace*, Boston: Houghton-Mifflin Company, 1945, pp. 295–347.)

RONALD LIPPITT, "Administrator Perception and Administrative Approval: A Communication Problem," *Sociatry*, 1947, *1*, 209–219.

—————, "Better Human Relations," *The School Executive*, 1948, *67*, 47–49.

———— and LELAND BRADFORD, "Building a Democratic Work Group," *Personnel*, 1945, *22*, 3, 1–12.

————, "Employee Success in Work Groups," *Personnel Administrator*, 1945, *8*, 4, 6–10.

————, "Group Self-Analysis of Productivity in the Work Conference," *Adult Education Bulletin*, 1948, *12*, 3, 74–79.

————, "Personnel Directors' Conference on Training. II. FSA's Approach to Supervisory Training," *Personnel Administration*, 1946, *8*, 6, 9–12.

————, KENNETH D. BENNÉ, and LELAND BRADFORD. "The Promise of Group Dynamics for Education," *Journal of the National Education Association*, 1948, *37*, 350–352.

————, LELAND BRADFORD, and KENNETH D. BENNÉ, "Role-Playing in Group Discussion Method," Monograph of the National Training Laboratory in Group Development.

———— and LELAND BRADFORD, "Role-Playing in Supervisory Training," *Personnel*, 1946, *22*, 6, 3–14.

————, "Social Psychological Research and Group Work." (A chapter in Charles Hendry [ed.], *A Decade of Group Work*, New York: Association Press, 1948, pp. 166–177.)

————, LELAND BRADFORD, and KENNETH D. BENNÉ, "Sociodramatic Clarification of Leader and Group Roles, as a Starting Point for Effective Group Functioning," *Sociatry*, 1947, *1*, 82–91.

———— and LELAND BRADFORD, "The Teacher Growth Program," *Journal of the National Education Association*, 1949, *38*, 204–206.

————, KENNETH D. BENNÉ, and LELAND BRADFORD, "Toward Improved Skill in Group Living: A Discussion," *Educational Leadership*, 1948, *5*, 286–294.

———— and HOWARD PALMER, "Training Community Leadership Toward More Effective Group Living," *Adult Education Bulletin*, 1946, *10*, 168–174.

————, *Training in Community Relations*, New York: Harper's, 1949.

ALVIN F. ZANDER, W. CLARK TROW, W. C. MORSE, and DAVID H. JENKINS, "Psychology of Group Behavior: The Class as a Group," *Journal of Educational Psychology*, 1950, *41*, 6, 322–338.

————, "Current Research in Group Work," *A.A.G.W. Yearbook, Toward Professional Standards*, 1946.

————, "Group Education for Mental Health," *Applied Psychology Monographs*, April 1947, No. 12, 221–229.

————, "Group Work with YMCA Boys," *Work with Y Youth*, 1946, 3.

—————, "The Influence of the Summer Camp on Personality Development," *The Nervous Child*, 1947, *6*, 161–165.

————— and KENNETH D. BENNÉ, "More Effective School-Community Projects," *National Education Association Journal*, 1949, *38*, 364–365.

—————, "On the Symptoms and Survival of Senile Groups," *Educational Leadership*, 1948, *5*, 319–322.

————— and J. MARMOR, "Psychological Problems in Training 16 Year Olds in the United States Maritime Training Station," *Journal of Orthopsychiatry*, 1945, *15*, 571–583.

—————, "Role Playing: A Technique for Training the Necessarily Dominating Leader," *Sociatry*, 1947, *1*, 225–235.

—————, "A Social Psychologist Looks at the Group Work Process," *Association Boy's Work Journal*, 1947, *20*, 17–20.

————— and DAVID JENKINS, "Some Skills for Improving Group Dynamics," *National Education Association Journal*, 1949, *38*, 102.

—————, "Within the Bonds of Freedom," *Childhood Education*, 1947, *24*, 23–26.

—————, "The Wise Use of Consultants," *University of Michigan, School of Education Bulletin*, 1949, *20*, 33–35.

DOCTORAL DISSERTATIONS

ALEX BAVELAS, *Some Mathematical Properties of Psychological Space*, Massachusetts Institute of Technology, 1948.

MORTON DEUTSCH, *The Effects of Cooperation and Competition upon Group Process*, Massachusetts Institute of Technology, 1948.

DAVID A. EMERY, *Industrial Role and Social Perception*, Massachusetts Institute of Technology, 1948.

GORDON HEARN, *The Training of Discussion Groups: An Experimental Study*, Massachusetts Institute of Technology, 1948.

SIMON NATHAN HERMAN, *A Social Psychological Study of Chalutziut (Palestine Pioneering) in America*, University of the Witwatersrand, 1947.

MURRAY HORWITZ, *The Effects of Group Goal Setting and Locomotion on Motivational Processes in the Individual*, University of Michigan, 1950.

HAROLD H. KELLEY, *First Impressions in Interpersonal Relations*, Massachusetts Institute of Technology, 1948.

MARGARET BARRON LUSZKI, *Empathic Ability and Social Perception*, University of Michigan, 1950.

ALBERT PEPITONE, *Motivational Effects in the Perception of Social "Gatekeepers,"* University of Michigan, 1949.

JOHN W. THIBAUT, *The Relationship of Group Cohesiveness to Inter-group Status Differences*, Massachusetts Institute of Technology, 1949.

BENJAMIN WILLERMAN, *Group Identification in Industry*, Massachusetts Institute of Technology, 1949.

Index

285